IN EXCITED REVERIE

W. B. YEATS

IN EXCITED REVERIE

*A Centenary Tribute to
William Butler Yeats
1865 – 1939*

EDITED BY

A. NORMAN JEFFARES

AND

K. G. W. CROSS

NEW YORK
THE MACMILLAN COMPANY
1965

PRINTED IN GREAT BRITAIN
BY R. & R. CLARK, LTD., EDINBURGH

CONTENTS

In Excited Reverie

FOREWORD

For this collection of centenary studies we have commissioned work by critics and scholars from Africa, America, Australia, England, India, Ireland and Scotland. We have included an essay which the late Lennox Robinson had intended should form part of the book he was writing on Yeats, as well as part of the famous B.B.C. programme by W. R. Rodgers.

The range of response to Yeats's work throughout the continents offers a fresh reminder of the power of his writings to stimulate and move an audience, to crystallize, through the hard work of stitching and unstitching words, through the articulation of sound, an apparent moment's thought.

These essays explore aspects of the thoughts and ideas, the background, the reading and the writing, the activity and personality of the poet as well as the reactions of others to his life and work. They are offered as a tribute to the achievement of that life and work.

A. N. J.

K. G. W. C.

ACKNOWLEDGEMENTS

The editors and publishers wish to acknowledge their indebtedness to the following : Mrs. W. B. Yeats, Miss Anne Yeats and Mr. Michael Butler Yeats, for permission to quote all the material by W. B. Yeats ; Mrs. Dorothy Robinson, for permission to include the essay by her late husband; Professor D. J. Gordon, of the Department of English, Reading University, for supplying the photograph for the frontispiece; Mr. Sidney Nolan, C.B.E., for his painting on the theme of W. B. Yeats's 'Why should not Old Men be Mad ?' for the jacket-design; and the National Library of Ireland, for supplying and permitting us to reproduce the autograph of that poem on the back of the jacket.

'William Butler Yeats' is taken from *Poems* by A. D. Hope. Copyright © 1960 by A. D. Hope. All rights reserved. Reprinted by permission of the Viking Press Inc. and Hamish Hamilton Ltd.

The book's title is taken from W. B. Yeats's 'A Prayer for my Daughter'.

W. B. YEATS: A DUBLIN PORTRAIT

*

W. R. RODGERS

'THERE WAS A PECULIAR sort of innocence about the man,' declared O'Connor firmly, as if he had often been contradicted on the point; 'an extraordinary innocence.'

'I never warmed to him, Frank,' said O'Faoláin, 'because I thought there was an absence of innocence and simplicity about his nature, at any rate as he presented it when one met him. Whether that was part of a pose or of a mask that he put on I don't know, but you would sometimes wish that he'd drop it and that he'd say "Hello," or talk in a natural way.'

'But I think he did, Sean. He only posed when he was shy or embarrassed. I kept on telling people, "Now for God's sake don't call him *sir*, because if you call him *sir* he'll start posing."'

'Why should he pose?'

'Simply because he was shy,' hammered back O'Connor; 'and all Irishmen when they are shy instantly fling out into some sort of pose. They keep on talking instead of shutting up.'

'Oh, I know all that sort of thing,' said O'Faoláin, in a downhill rush of words that was meant to carry him up the farther slope. 'Edward Garnett, I think it was, told me when he was very young and they were both poor, in the days when W. B. used to have to black-up his heels so as to cover up the holes in his stockings, saying how they'd walk from his digs to Edward's digs and back again, all night long, absolutely forgetting everything in the most natural way. And once Edward invited him down for a week-end to his country cottage, and he arrived with nothing but a toothbrush and a bit of soap. He said he was absolutely innocent. Although he had seen the same man in a box when a play of his was on, standing up as he used to do in the Abbey Theatre at the head of the stairs, looking around. Clearly an actor.'

'But, Sean,' said O'Connor, 'I remember when I was in Dublin first, going to a party, and being very shy, Mrs. Yeats signalled me to come and sit beside her. She said, "I knew you were shy because you did exactly as Willie does when he's shy — you ran your hand through your hair." And after that, I just looked to see what he did with his hands, and I saw that the man was often shy.'

'Let's try,' said O'Faoláin impatiently, 'to get an example of this pose which I say he had. What about this — was it a habit or was it sincere? The way he had of not recognizing people, who felt that he must really know them perfectly well. A way of saying "Hello, Tierney" when it was really Binchy — that sort of thing.'

'Yes, it was a toss-up whether he would say "Hello, Binchy," trying to pretend that he knew him or, as he often did with me, just hold out his hand and say, "Who have I?" That was the admission that he was blind, which he didn't like to make normally.'

There was an awkward silence. Brinsley Macnamara stepped into the breach.

'I remember,' said he, 'one such meeting with him myself. He brought me walking round Stephen's Green, and he finished up by saying something which may have some bearing on what we're trying to work out now about whether it was a pose or not with him. He said, "A man, an author, should always try to keep the company of his superiors, never of his inferiors."'

'But Yeats,' said dignified Mr. Best, in a gentle voice that somehow had gestures in it, 'Yeats was always very dignified. When he said something humorous he bent his head in — and clasped his hands together as if he were washing them in invisible soap and laughed slightly, but always most dignified. Yeats, so far as I can remember him, was always in full dress. But to tell you the truth, I never felt quite at my ease with Yeats, as I did with George Moore, say, because he was always on a plane, as it were, above me.'

'You know,' said Macnamara — suddenly setting down his glass — 'the only thing he never really got used to was the fact that poets and writers might be found sometimes in the public-houses in the town, and that he never ventured into one of them. There's a story, Higgins it was, who's dead, and Yeats must have approached him, and he said : "Higgins, do you know I have never been in a pub in my life and I'd like to go into a pub." So Higgins came to me and he asked me what was the most likely pub now to which we might bring Yeats without horrifying him too much with what he'd see there in the shape of literature and other things, and we decided on one pub, and Higgins went along with him there, and they called for a mild drink and Yeats looked around and said : "Higgins, I don't like it. Lead me out again."'

A burst of laughter greeted this story, but O'Faoláin jumped on its back.

'There's no trouble,' said he, 'about meeting O'Casey or O'Flaherty in a pub, or talking to him as man to man and calling him Sean or calling him Liam, which you could never do with Yeats.'

'You see, the real problem, Sean,' said O'Connor, 'is in assuming all through that it's necessary that poets should sit in pubs and call one another, as we do, Sean, Frank, and so on.'

'I don't think it's necessary, Frank. I think it occasionally happens, and that if it never happens — I personally very rarely go into pubs — a poet is liable to be thrown into an extraordinary kind of isolation, and will develop a sort of fake Brahminism, the kind that infected Yeats's own work.'

'Well, I think, Sean, that "infected" is the wrong word,

and that poetry *is* Brahminism — it's the soul of a man alone with himself——'

'That is a romantic conception of it,' said O'Faoláin bitingly.

'Very well, it *is* a romantic conception of poetry.'

'And it takes you back to Oscar Wilde, and to Dowson, and to Dobson and to——'

'And to Dante ?'

'But didn't Yeats,' suggested Macnamara — 'the bulk of Yeats's poetry come out of that romantic conception of poetry ?'

'That's true, that's true,' quick-fired O'Faoláin; 'and I have no doubt that probably Yeats, sitting at his desk and writing his poetry, was perfectly natural and innocent within himself as long as he didn't let that thing infect him — and it *did* infect him. And that is the thing that we were talking about a moment ago, his manner of dress, his cane, the lovely — what was it ? — always in grey suits, the carefully chosen colours, the long hair, all that sort of thing stood between him and his natural self.'

'Bless my soul !' burst in O'Connor. 'That a man's taste in shirts stands between him and his own natural self — where is that getting to ?'

'It's getting down the drain of romanticism,' said O'Faoláin.

'Well, the other thing is just getting down the drain of sloppy democratic feeling — I mean you must be dirty because everybody else is dirty.'

'There's no need to go to that extreme,' said O'Faoláin heatedly. 'T. S. Eliot wrote his poetry absolutely personally, absolutely originally, in a rolled umbrella and a bowler hat, coming out of a bank.'

'Well, don't you feel that *that* poetry had been infected — in your own word — by the umbrella ?'

'No, I do *not*. I think it was necessary for Eliot to live

among people as people, mix with people in order that he should get down to the reality of his own time.'

The dry voice of Austin Clarke, the poet, broke in gently, like a wolf in sheep's clothing.

'I think,' said he, 'that it is a great pity that the poet, like the soldier and the clergyman and many others, hasn't got some specific dress, or at least part of a dress, to distinguish him, say, from the business man. As a young poet I wore an enormous bow tie — it was of shimmering gold and green, and I was very proud of it. Well, the reason I wore that bow tie was because in Dublin all the poets wore a bow tie. Yeats from the Abbey Theatre, appearing there frequently, had a magnificent black tie, which we could copy in other colours. When I got to London, I found that poets no longer wore any specific sign or symbol of their art. They were all dressed in hard stiff white collars, like business men. It was the time of the Georgian school, and I think it would have been better for the Georgian poets if they had worn flowing ties. It might have saved them from the terrible rush and pressure of the modern world. It might have protected their art. Look what happened to the Georgian school. I attribute that solely to the fact that they did not wear flowing ties, like the Irish poets !'

'You must remember,' said O'Connor, 'that when *I* met Yeats first he was an old and very authoritative figure, an Olympian figure. He was tall, very very dignified, all his gestures were sweeping, his voice had a soft oratorical cadence which comes back into my ears even at this moment.'

'Well, Frank,' said Lennox Robinson, picking his words daintily like a cat picking its footsteps, 'my first impression of Yeats is of course about twenty years or more earlier than yours——'

'Twenty years humbler,' said O'Connor. 'There must have been another and very different Yeats when he was younger, because I remember A. E. describing him with a sort of longing in his voice, the boy with a beard, as A. E. used to

say, who used to come into his bedroom at two o'clock in the
morning to recite some new poem which he'd written :

> Beautiful lofty things : O'Leary's noble head ;
> . . . Maud Gonne at Howth station waiting a train,
> Pallas Athene in that straight back and arrogant head :
> All the Olympians ; a thing never known again.

At the mention of her name Maud Gonne looked up. Her
face, despite eighty winters, had still that fine bone of beauty
which Yeats had loved — and lost.

'Yes,' she said, 'I was twenty and Willie was twenty-one
when we first met, and it was through John O'Leary. Willie
and I had the deepest admiration for him. Willie was then
twenty-one and I was twenty, and he was extremely proud of
that one year's seniority. He looked much younger than I
did, because he was rather a dishevelled art student — he
intended to be a painter like his father. John O'Leary used to
say, "Your vocation is to be a poet. You have that in you,"
and then he would make him read some of his early poems.
"Don't you understand in the spiritual world, in the faerie
world," Willie would say to me, "everything is the reverse.
Therefore these poems are children, and I'm the father and
you're the mother." But my real use to Willie was, I kept him
in close touch with the people. Willie and I fought very hard
in the struggle for Ireland : he went on all those committees
really to help me more than anything else ; he was wonderful
at a committee meeting and used to be able to carry things
very often. He could be very much on the spot.'

'Yes, indeed,' remarked Iseult Stuart. 'I have known him
to be wonderfully on the spot when he absolutely had to be,
when there was nobody, no grown-up, extrovert grown-up,
to take the burden ; but when there were tiresome things like
seeing to luggage, or getting a cab or anything like that, then
Willie would fall into a great abstraction and he wasn't there,
from which I learnt a great lesson myself, not to be there on
these occasions.'

'But look at his connection with the B.B.C.,' said Lennox Robinson ; 'they wanted to give him the best wireless set they could to his home in Rathfarnham, and they said, "Have you got electric light in the home ?" He had to wire back to his wife to find out whether they *had* electric light — he found they hadn't.'

'Why, yes,' said Anne Yeats, 'we acquired a wireless. For a long time Father wouldn't have one, he didn't like them and — well — I think the first evening it was turned on, he was listening to it, and he couldn't hear very well, so he put his hand to his ear, and said "I beg your pardon !"'

'Yes,' laughed O'Connor, 'I can well believe he was impractical.'

'He wasn't impractical !' said Robinson. 'He could do — he could do a balance sheet better than anybody I knew.'

'But he was an extraordinary man in that way, meeting with the company,' said Dossy Wright of the Abbey. 'He would be talking of the Greek gods or something, and then he'd suddenly say : "Well, we've heard all these figures, but what I want to know is what we have lost and what we have gained in pure simple words."'

'I think,' said Smyllie indulgently, 'I was the first person — certainly the first person in this country — to know that Yeats had won the Nobel Prize. I was on duty at the *Irish Times* office that night, when the message came over the Creed machine to say that for the first time an Irish poet had won the prize, which amounted to quite a considerable sum, I believe between seven and eight thousand pounds. So — I was rather friendly with Yeats at the time, and it was fairly late in the evening, getting on to eleven o'clock I suppose, and I rang him up at his house, hoping that he didn't know the news. He came to the phone himself — he *didn't* know the news. I said, "Mr. Yeats," I said, "I've got very good news for you, a very great honour has been conferred upon you," and I was rather enthusiastic and — oh, I don't know what the word is — rather *gushing* at the time, and I said, "This is a great honour, not only for you, but for the country," and I could see that he was getting slightly impatient to know what it was all about, so I said, "You've been awarded the Nobel Prize, a very great honour to you and a very great honour to Ireland," and to my amazement the first question — the only question he asked was, "How much, Smyllie, how much is it?"'

'Well, I say he was tough,' cried Robinson, 'I say that, from the moment I met him, he was tough, and he was tougher as years went on; and when he was a Senator and when he had this position and when he defended divorce and when he attacked censorship he said, "Nobody can touch me, because I'm so important." Again, in this question of censorship, he said, "I want to read all the dirty English Sunday papers, because I will read the last words of every murderer. Whereas, if I buy the *Observer*, I will read the last words — alas! not the *last* words — of St. John Ervine on the theatre."'

'Talking about words,' said Iseult Stuart, 'I remember . . . Yeats telling me that the greatest lines that were ever written, which had their own particular prose-rhythm which was as great as verse-rhythm, were in Emerson — "The stars, the stars everlasting are fugitives also."'

'Well, I can remember a quite different Yeats,' said Arthur Hanna. 'He came into our shop quite a lot. As a matter of fact, all he bought from us were really detective novels. On one occasion he came in to me, reprimanded me, said I had sold him a detective novel in which there was far too much detection. Well, I sold him an Edgar Wallace, and he went out very happy.'

'I suppose,' said Anne Yeats, 'detective stories and Wild West mightn't seem to come under the category of what was called guided reading, but Father read a great many of them. But Mother always had to vet them to make quite sure that they had happy endings. But about the Wild West, too, when

8

he was ailing in Majorca — he was very ill at the time, and he was delirious — I remember him shouting, "George, George, call the sheriff !"'

'But he began to be altogether more natural in later life,' said Macnamara thoughtfully. 'He played golf and went around.'

'Well, of course,' said Smyllie, 'the idea of W. B. taking up golf was rather amusing to us who knew him, and he came to me and suggested that possibly I might help him, so I did. I was a member of a Club called Carrickmines, and of course the Great Man left everything in my hands ; there was another young man called Duncan, and we had to provide all the clubs, we had to do everything, and the day we were going, I'd a small car, a mad car, and the first day we were going up, I handed W. B. his bag, and he said, "Smyllie, this is my quiver." However, we started off, we played several times, and his idea was, he'd make a wild swipe at the ball, let the club fall on the ground, and walk off with his hands behind his back in the characteristic Yeatsian fashion, leaving myself and Duncan to pick up the quiver and the club and look for the ball. He used to drive the ball into a clump of furze bushes or into a ditch or anywhere, about ten yards, say, from the tee, and we lost several balls this way, but the rather characteristic thing about W. B. was that the next game we went out to play, he noticed we had been losing all these balls and we had been providing him with new ones — not new ones, actually we knew too much about it for that — but the next day he came out, and every time he hit the ball and lost it, he used to produce a half-crown from his pocket, and hand the half-crown either to myself or to Duncan in compensation for the ball that had been lost.'

'But, Anne,' said O'Connor, 'tell us something about what it's like to be the child of a famous man.'

'Well, almost the first thing I remember was — at least I was told it — calling him Willie when I was still in my pram, and a voice coming out of the window, firmly saying, "You

B

are not to call your father Willie !" and then sort of replying "Willie Dada, Willie Dada," which didn't go down very well, either.'

'But good gracious,' said Miss Macnie, 'he was a splendid father. It seemed to me, meeting him as I sometimes did at tea-time, when he came in, he was perfectly delightful with his children. And really one very amusing thing was to watch W. B. coming in with his head well up and with his hands clasped behind his back followed by Michael who, at that time, was about two feet high — he used to walk in after his father in the most sedate manner possible, with his hands clasped behind his back and keeping pace with his father. Anne was very amusing too. She was wiser than Michael was, and when her father would come in, after he had played bears or elephants with Michael, he used to lie down flat on a sofa between the two windows, and this was part of the game apparently, because Anne would always go outside the door, shut it, and then bang it open and rush across the room and jump flat on her father's prostrate belly on the sofa. And yet once I said to Anne, "Anne, were you afraid of your father?" And she said, "I was terrified of him." And I said, "Well, what an extraordinary thing, so was I. Why was it?" "I don't know," said Anne; "there's no explanation as far as I'm concerned, because he never laid a finger on us — he didn't believe in corporal punishment and he never touched either Michael or me — or punished us in any way — and yet I was afraid of him."'

'But the — well, you know, we had to be frightfully quiet really, about the house generally,' said Anne, embarrassed a little. 'I remember, once, Mike and I were fighting, rather more than usual, and Mother couldn't cope with us, so she sent Father in. He just sat down in the chair and intoned in full voice, "Let dogs delight to bark and bite," and then got up and went out of the room.'

'Indeed, yes,' said Mrs. Yeats. 'Of course he had to be

absolutely alone, so completely alone that even when an infant was in the room and silent, he had still to be alone, because no personality must be there at all. It wasn't a matter of merely being spoken to or interrupted or anything else, but he had to be in absolute isolation in a room wherever he was writing.'

O'Connor nodded his head. 'He was,' said he, 'one of the hardest workers that I ever came across, and I know George Moore jeers at this business about his writing four lines in a day and his reaching his record of seven lines. But if you'd seen exactly how much labour those four or seven lines had cost him, you wouldn't think it was anything like a bad day's work ; because he would recite a single line hundreds and hundreds of times in succession ; even in the middle of a conversation with you he would be talking politics perhaps, and quite suddenly he would lift the right hand and would begin to beat time and you would hear him recite a line a couple of times, and then the hand would drop again and he'd go on with the conversation just as though nothing had happened.

> Everything he wrote was read,
> After certain years he won
> Sufficient money for his need,
> Friends that have been friends indeed ;
> '*What then ?*' sang Plato's ghost. '*What then ?*'

They listened impatiently while O'Connor recited the lines.

'Well, I never believed,' said Smyllie, 'that W. B. knew anything about philosophy, though he talked a great deal about it, but he invented a philosophy of his own. There was one very interesting and amusing thing occurred, one night up at the Arts Club. Among those present was a little man called Cruise O'Brien — a very brilliant journalist, and one of the very few who could be rude to W. B. with impunity. W. B. gave him, as he very often gave me, a fool's pardon. This night, at any rate, W. B. was expounding this philosophy of his which was connected in some queer way with the phases of the moon ; and he was telling us all about the twenty-eight phases of the moon, and he equated every phase against some historical figure. He started off by saying, "Well, you know," he said, "number one — the highest phase — is perfect beauty." With a respectful silence for a few seconds we all listened, and then he said, "Number two was Helen of Troy — the nearest approximation to perfect beauty." And he went right round the twenty-seven phases and finally came to the last, and then he said that "the lowest of all, the lowest form is Thomas Carlyle and all Scotsmen." This shook us a little bit, and Cruise O'Brien spoke up at once, then — "W. B.," he said — he'd a very mincing voice, Cruise — "W. B.," he said, "have you ever read a word of Carlyle? You say Carlyle is the lowest form — oh, come — have you ever read a word of Carlyle?" "Carlyle, Cruise, was a dolt," said W. B. "But I insist, W. B., did you ever read one single word of Carlyle?" "Carlyle, I tell you, was a dolt." "Yes, but you haven't read him." "No, even though I have not read him, my wife George has read him, and she tells me he's a dolt." That was the end of the philosophical treatise for the night.'

'There was a young man,' said Miss Macnie reminiscently, 'who came across here from England, and he came uninvited to one of W. B.'s evenings. W. B. saw him, I think, but he took no notice whatever. The young man walked across the room, stood beside W. B. and George Russell for a moment or two, and then went across and sat down in a chair beside a friend in the corner. W. B. paused for a moment or two, looked across at the corner, and then, very slowly and very erect, walked forward to the corner and said very politely to him, "Sir, you have not been invited. You are not welcome. Will you please go." And he walked across the room and opened the door and closed it after this young man.'

There was a silence after this story. Then Austin Clarke spoke.

'As far as the younger generation of poets are concerned here in Ireland, Yeats was rather like an enormous oak tree which, of course, kept us in the shade, but did exclude a great number of the rays of, say, friendly sun; we always hoped that in the end we would reach the sun, but the shadow of that great oak tree is still there.'

'But he had,' said O'Connor, 'this interior thing, living a deep interior life and all the outside things going for nothing — unless he concentrated on remembering them. I remember his once quoting me a lovely poem of Eleanor Wylie's, and he quoted it with an intensity of passion such as I never heard him give any other poem. "Live with the velvet mole : go burrow underground." And he burrowed underground quite a lot. I got the impression that right up to the end he remained a very shy, gentle creature.'

'Well, now, that is rather curious,' said Austin Clarke dryly. 'I had gone down to the Seven Woods at Coole, in a kind of — as a very young enthusiast in a romantic way, and I crossed the wall into the demesne, and came into a dark wood which was surely the Wicked Wood of the poem, in which there was a witch, and then I saw another bright wood ahead, and I moved towards that, and suddenly through the leaves I saw a vision, and for a moment, being very young, well, I almost felt here was an elemental spirit; and then I said no, if this is the great demesne, it's a peacock. I crept forward, I looked through the leaves, and there, crossing the grass towards a Georgian house, I saw a tall figure in a marvellous sky-blue watered-silk raincoat holding fishing rods and lines and all that fierce tackle of the country gentleman, and I said to myself, "I'm in the wrong demesne, this cannot be the Seven Woods." Then I looked again, and I recognized dimly from those frontispieces of the books that it was the poet himself disguised as a great country gentleman and sportsman; as the young romantic poet of the Irish movement, I was shocked and disappointed.'

WILLIAM BUTLER YEATS : PERSONALITY

*

LENNOX ROBINSON

THE SCENE IS WALLA-WALLA, a small town in the extreme north-west of the United States. I arrived there early after travelling all night. I had to lecture to its college in the morning, then there was an official lunch, another lecture in the afternoon (I was advance publicity man for the Abbey Theatre Company), there was to be an evening reception and then a midnight train to Denver. I snatched an hour in the late afternoon and rested on my hotel bed. The inevitable telephone rang ; a young man from the college wanted to see me. He appeared, the editor of the college magazine. He wrote poetry and he left with me a few good poems. But he said : 'Have you ever met Mr. Yeats ?'

'Yes, he has been my best friend for twenty years or more.'

'You have spoken to him ?'

'Of course.'

The young man was speechless, captured by an emotion. How obviously the Browning poem springs to mind :

> Ah, did you once see Shelley plain,
> And did he stop and speak to you
> And did you speak to him again ?
> How strange it seems, and new !

I, too, have 'seen Shelley plain'.

I met Yeats first when I was twenty-two and he was just twice my age. I suppose it was only a young man's impression (I was very inexperienced for my age), but he seemed to me then to be a middle-aged, if not almost an old man. This is

14

strange, for he kept his appearance as a young man well into middle-age — perhaps he had suddenly put on maturity. At any rate by the time I met him he had an air of great authority and dignity, a poise, not a pose. He was often, all through his life, accused of being a *poseur*. It was not the case. He had mannerisms of movement and speech as every person of great individuality is bound to have ; *his* pose would have been to try and pass himself off as an ordinary person. He was extraordinarily striking in appearance, tall, slim, and his hair quite black — the beard of earlier years had disappeared. His eyes were strangely placed, one of them was always weak and by the end of his life its sight had gone. This fact made it forgivable in him to pass a friend in the street without recognition or to fail to identify an acquaintance in a crowded room. He has talked to me for an hour about the Abbey Theatre calling me by the name of a previous Manager — as unlike in appearance from me as it is possible to imagine — then he suddenly stopped and looked at me as if he had only just realized my identity and appearance. There followed an apology which did away with any feeling of hurt on my part, for he was always gentle and courteous save when roused to vehemence — and no one could be more vehement — on some matter which he thought of vital importance.

I have written that when I met him first he was slim ; that was not always the case. He could vary, and very rapidly, from leanness to stoutness. I used to tell him he was like the moon, waxing and waning. He was a very moderate eater and drinker (the most rapid eater I have ever known) and took pains about his figure, doing exercises of some sort to keep himself trim. Up to a few years before his death he could look, on occasion, extraordinarily young, look like that lovely Sargent drawing done just about the time I met him first, and his appearance at the end of his life can only be described by the one word — noble.

In some obituary notice — St. John Ervine's I think — he

is described as unapproachable, and the notice said that no one outside his family ever called him by his Christian name. This is not the case. To his intimate friends he was 'Willie', to his acquaintances 'W. B.' In his early days in the Theatre he was known (but I am sure only behind his back) to players and staff as 'school-boy Yeats', perhaps because of his big black tie knotted in a drooping bow which might suggest some school-boy's uniform. Certainly for the last twenty years he was always 'Willie' to his face, in speaking of him to his friends one used his initials, to strangers he was 'Mr. Yeats'.

In his early years he affected the big black tie, loosely knotted, the correct wear of the poet of the 'nineties. Then he became more orthodox. He liked clothes and he liked them to be correct. He took me aside once in the early days of our acquaintance and gently told me that a gentleman did not wear a 'made-up' evening tie. I protested that mine was home-made, but a year later he warned me again and I again protested my innocence, but from that time forward was always careful that my tie should be slightly awry. Cats he loved and birds, the wild ones that would be fed at his window or the canaries in their cages, and he would write quite undisturbed by their flood of song, but it distressed him that they would use their bath-water for drinking purposes and sought vainly from a bird-fancier for a cure for this deplorable habit.

He was never a rich man, for most of his life he was a very poor one, so he had to be careful of his money. He loved beautiful things and a beautiful way of living but he had to deny himself. He was never mean but he was never extrava-gant, he dared not be. After all, most of his friends were as poor as himself so it was not difficult to live simply. Did not Hugh Lane as a young man, travelling the picture galleries of Europe, spend but a shilling or two a day on food and even, years later, when he was in his fine Chelsea house (it might have been just about the time when he sold his Titian for eighty thousand pounds) cry out in horror when his aunt, Lady

Gregory, expressed the hope that at last he had a fire in his bedroom, the extravagance of a fire in his bedroom being unpardonable. And have I not seen Lady Gregory herself smuggling from an hotel dining-table in Philadelphia a roll and a slice of ham which she meant to use for her supper that night.

In reading his poetry, at any rate when he was reading it to two or three of his friends, his voice was very musical and without affectation. He did not boom his voice as did A. E., nor chant and croon as others do. When he was speaking in a large lecture-hall or over the wireless he became a little affected and too deliberate in his speech, and a record which the B.B.C. possess of his reading of 'The Lake Isle of Innisfree' is not characteristic of him at his best, yet there are tones and cadences in it which are entirely his own and I cannot listen to it without feeling a deep emotion and a sense of irreparable loss.

An 'unbuttoned' Beethoven is often spoken of; there was no unbuttoned Yeats either in his work or in himself, and that is why I deny that he was guilty of pose. He was fastidious in his person and in his choice of friends; he loathed pretentiousness in others and so had none himself.

The only art to which he was almost wholly insensitive was music. He wrote once, 'I am not musical, I have the poet's exact time sense, only the vaguest sense of pitch, yet I get the greatest pleasure from certain combinations of singing, acting, speaking, drum, gong, flute, string, provided that some or all of the words keep their natural passionate rhythm'. He told me once that he composed all his poetry to either of two airs and he hummed them to me. I could make nothing out of them, not even a rhythm. But in later years he seemed to be developing a musical sense and, probably influenced by his friend F. R. Higgins's knowledge and love of Irish folk tunes, some of his latest poems seem to show that he was writing with a definite tune in his head. He rejoiced in George

Antheil's music for 'Fighting the Waves' and described it as 'most strange, most dramatic music' though it committed the crime he so often denounced, the giving of many notes to the same word. He admits, 'I have gone over to the enemy'.

He was the most brilliant conversationalist I have ever known, at once witty and profound. At his lightest his talk was full of anecdote and reminiscence, but if he could fail at times to recognize a friend or a face he had a meticulous, accurate, memory of facts. His sisters have told me how time and time again, turning up some old letter (Lily Yeats kept every letter) they have verified some tiny fact, some insignificant incident which had taken place many years before and which he had written or spoken of with perfect accuracy as to date and occurrence. It was dangerous to argue with him on a question of fact, he was certain to be right. You might hear him tell the same story over a number of years, the story never varied, each detail was the same, the language in which it was narrated remained unaltered. He could rejoice in telling a Rabelaisian story but, ten to one, if you tried to cap it he grew disgusted.

He thought he was born in Sandymount Castle, but he was really born in a 'small house, two storeys high, whitish or greyish' in the castle grounds. That house has since disappeared. It would have been no great thing to have been born in that castle, for it is only a castle in the sense that a large early-Victorian house has been castellated, a touch of our Irish pretentiousness. Near where I am writing there is such a house. It was a plain, decent house, but its owner visited Italy and there fell in with an Italian nobleman and stayed in his medieval castle. Not to be outdone, the Irishman boasted of *his* castle but, to his consternation, a few years later the Italian announced himself for a visit. In a frenzy of haste builders were summoned and battlements erected just in time for the Italian nobleman's visit. And Lady Longford has told

me how, turning over some old family papers, she came on
builders' bills dating from the early nineteenth century when
Pakenham Hall, the Earl of Longford's house in County
Westmeath, was being built, or rebuilt, an item of one bill
read 'To supplying second-class battlements'.

The battlements of Sandymount Castle are certainly second
class. The house stands on a green in the middle of what must
have been a pleasant village long ago, a few miles from the
middle of Dublin, and it still keeps a great deal of its late
eighteenth-century or early nineteenth-century charm. James
Stephens, the Fenian, lived there, so did Padraic Pearse and
Eamonn de Valera. It is a placid village with commodious
houses and ample gardens. Edward Dowden, visiting John
Butler Yeats (the poet's father) when both were under-
graduates at Trinity College, must have found Sandymount
Castle a pleasant spot, for he wrote a lovely series of sonnets
called 'In the Garden' of which I shall only quote the first :

> Past the town's clamour is a garden full
> Of loneness and old greenery ; at noon
> When birds are hushed, save one dim cushat's croon,
> A ripen'd silence hangs beneath the cool
> Great branches ; basking roses dream and drop
> A petal, and dream still ; and summer's boon
> Of mellow grasses, to be levelled soon
> By a dew-drenchèd scythe, will hardly stop
> At the uprunning mounds of chestnut trees.
> Still let me muse in this rich haunt by day,
> And know all night in dusky placidness.
> It lies beneath the summer, while great ease
> Broods in the leaves, and every light wind's stress
> Lifts a faint odour down the verdurous ways.

It was John Butler Yeats's uncle, Robert Corbet, who
made that garden. About him, John Butler Yeats recalls, 'of
business he knew little or nothing and probably neglected it,
but he did not neglect his gardens. Every morning he rose
early and would wander all over the grounds, sometimes with

a small saw and hatchet, making among the trees what he called "vistas". He employed four or five gardeners, and as long as I knew Sandymount Castle none of these men ever left him and no one ever interfered with them. So treated, they were gentle, pleasant and diligent, and the gardens were lovely. There was a piece of water called the "pond" on which we boys did much boating, and there were plenty of wild ducks and swans, and there was also an island on which was a one-roomed cottage in which was a collection of souvenirs and relics brought back from India and the Colonies by my uncle's brothers who had been soldiers. Outside the cottage were two chained eagles.'

But of these things, gardens and chained eagles and Edward Dowden, Yeats has no memory, for he left Sandymount when he was only a year old. Yet who can tell? If there are pre-natal influences, if the things a mother gazes on when she is carrying her child can affect that child, surely what the baby looks on with apparently unseeing eyes cannot be without their effect?

There followed, after a brief period in London, a sojourn with his maternal grandparents, the Pollexfens, in Sligo, and from this dates the first important influence in his life, an influence which got dulled in middle-age but which returned, intensified, in old age. His first living in County Sligo ceased when he was eight years old, but from his grandparents, from his uncles and aunts and cousins came recollections of people of vivid character, the characters that in country or country-town were more deeply incised than they are now. The Pollexfens and the Yeats and the Middletons had been settled in Sligo for generations. They were in trade, in the Church, they were smugglers and sailors and soldiers — one of the latter a General in Marlborough's army.

In truth, these forebears were very much the same sort of people whom any Anglo-Irish family settled in the country can claim as their own. Most of us who belong to that class have forgotten the circumstances of their existence and think of them as a shadowy background the details of which have been forgotten. But to the Yeats, to W. B. and his sisters, the background takes on an importance, one almost thinks an undue importance. There was an old, obscure connection with the great house of Ormonde (their family name was Butler) and therefore Butler must appear in every son's name. I think it always irked Yeats that there was no Yeats 'place', that his father wandered all his life from one house in London or Dublin and finally died in New York. He himself, until 1923 when he bought an ancient 'keep' in the West of Ireland near Lady Gregory's home, had spent his life in rooms in London or Oxford or Dublin. At last, in 1932, he was able to buy a pleasant house for himself on the outskirts of Dublin — exactly the opposite side of the city from Sandymount — it had spacious grounds and gardens and a croquet-lawn, and till the last summer he delighted in playing croquet to the tune of rules of his own invention, invented on the spur of the moment in his favour.

He was proud of at last being a possessor of landed property. Eating roast beef I remember him leaning across the table to his wife and gravely enquiring, '*Our* horse-radish, George?' to which she would as gravely reply, '*Our* horse-radish, Willie.' He had craved all his life for that mode of living. He was no snob, but he was no bohemian. One of the Rhymer's Club, a poet of the Cheshire Cheese, he could but lament back over his companions in later years, lament that 'wine or women or some curse' had driven them to their untimely ends. For him there were no such curses. He loved order, old-established houses, old families, everything which linked the present with the past.

The Sligo background coloured all his early work, prose as well as poetry, and he was to return to that country in his last poems. In a poem published a year before his death he calls on his ancestors to 'judge what I have done'.

He that in Sligo at Drumcliff
Set up the old stone Cross,
That red-headed rector in County Down,
A good man on a horse,
Sandymount Corbets, that notable man
Old William Pollexfen,
The smuggler Middleton, Butlers far back,
Half legendary men.

Those influences were to come to their fruition towards the end of his life. What came at the beginning was his intimacy with country things. I think that the things a boy or girl lives with from the ages of six to sixteen remain with them all through their lives. And those first years in Sligo and the subsequent visits when he was a growing boy colour all those lovely first poems. All the beauty in 'The Stolen Child' derives from Sligo, not only the place-names but the 'brown mice that bob/ Round and round the oatmeal-chest'. And the 'kettle on the hob', and the 'calves on the warm hillside'. Often and often in conversation he was to astonish one by his knowledge of homely, country things. Thus when he said that the disputed Lane pictures had proved a 'nest-egg' for the modern pictures at the Tate Gallery and, now that the hen had started to lay, the nest-egg should be given back. As a boy, he collected butterflies and insects, and when I was making an anthology of Irish poetry and submitted my selection to him for approval one poem was cast out because he declared, almost with passion, 'Bees *don't do* those things.'

He knew that 'cormorants shiver on the rocks', how long the grass grows on the weirs, how a heavy creel of fish makes the wheels of a cart to creak and how the nets are laid out to dry or to be mended on the pebbly shore. He knew what a shoneen is and a slieveen and how the little straws turn round and round in the frosty air. These phrases, apart from the diminutive purely Irish words the reader will say, might be used by any English poet who was observant of country life, but to read that early volume *Crossways* (1889) is to find that every poem, save the Indian ones, bears the stamp of Irish country character and Irish country scene.

Alas, my memory is not like his and it maddens me to think of all the fine talk I heard and how little remains in my mind. His mind worked very rapidly, and having him and George Moore to supper one night in London after the theatre — they were not the best of friends then — it was amusing to watch Moore fumbling for the retort which was to annihilate the poet, but before the right words could be found Yeats had presented a new facet of the subject and Moore was left lumbering up the course, at least one jump behind.

Such trivial recollections, but perhaps they help to paint a personality, the greatest I have ever known.

JOHN BUTLER YEATS

*

A. NORMAN JEFFARES

JOHN BUTLER YEATS, barrister, artist, essayist, letter-writer
and conversationalist, was representative of the best of
Victorian life. He belonged to the heyday of a great civilization and yet was detached from it : as artist, as thinker, as
Anglo-Irishman. Yet his virtues were its virtues : his
capacity for work, his refusal to specialize, his fundamentally
serious-minded approach to poetry and painting, his devotion
to his family and his friends, and his firm belief in the gentler
qualities of life.

He was born in 1839 at Tullylish, Co. Down, where his
father, 'an Irish gentleman of the old school and not at all
thrifty', was Rector. From him he inherited a spacious dis-
regard of time and finance, and a certain optimism and gaiety.
Though as a child he was lonely (for he was older than his
brothers) yet he was perfectly happy. He was taught to read
by a village schoolmaster, after which he read *Robinson Crusoe*
diligently :

> In the evening after dinner my father would sit beside his candle
> reading, and my mother would sit by her candle sewing, and I would
> nestle beside her reading Robinson Crusoe, and I can remember
> that at certain critical passages in this history I would tremble with
> anxiety, and that I was most careful lest my elders should discover
> my excitement and laugh at me.[1]

He was sent to a school at Liverpool, after education by his
impatient father seemed unlikely to succeed. This school was
kept by three maiden ladies :

[1] John Butler Yeats, *Early Memories ; Some Chapters of Autobiography*, Dublin, 1923, p. 4.

My father was evangelical as was then fashionable in the best intellectual circles. He must have said something about hell in my hearing, yet I did not make any real acquaintance with that dismal and absurd doctrine till I went to Miss Davenport's school. The school was managed upon the highest principles of duty, no prizes were ever given for all must work from sake of duty, and we slept with our Bibles under our pillows with directions to read them as soon as we awoke in the morning; but hell was the driving force. Miss Emma Davenport, who was the chief of the school, often spoke of it.[1]

At twelve he went to a school in the Isle of Man. Here the terrors imposed by a flogging headmaster were alleviated in part by the presence of George Pollexfen, a boy from Sligo, very unlike the English boys in the school, whom Yeats disliked, and yet unlike Yeats himself. Indeed there was an attraction of opposites: George Pollexfen was melancholy, John Butler Yeats cheerful and perennially hopeful. Their families were very different. The Pollexfens were well-to-do merchants; the Yeats family intellectual and not much concerned about money. In later years Yeats regarded his friend as tied up in puritanism. Though he himself distrusted and disliked puritanism, he said he didn't think he would like it 'to be entirely removed from the world, unless it be the Belfast variety, which like the East wind is good for neither man nor beast'.[2] Like Dr. Johnson, J. B. Yeats took good care that the Whig dogs should not get the best of the argument. Remarking once that there were more things in heaven and earth than were dreamed of in George Russell's philosophy, he added, 'I used to tell him he was still a *Portadown* boy'.[3]

Owing to the difficulties and expense of travel, Yeats and his brothers stayed at the school in the Isle of Man all the year except for a precious six weeks in summer. It was during these holidays that he learned to appreciate his father, who

[1] *Ibid.*, p. 6.   [2] *Ibid.*, p. 15.
[3] J. B. Yeats, *Letters to His Son W. B. Yeats and Others, 1869–1922* (ed. Joseph Hone), London 1944, p. 232. This book is henceforth referred to as *Letters*.

constantly read Shelley and Charles Lamb, was an enthralling conversationalist and had within him an artist who

incessantly arranged and rearranged life, so that he lived in fairy-land. Sometimes my father's and another man's account of the same incident would widely differ; but I always preferred what my father said. William Morris told my son that Kipling when a boy would come home from a day's walk with stories of the day's adventures which were all fiction. I wonder if Shakespeare would always cleave to the truth in the common matters of every day. At no time did I lose respect for my father, I knew with him it was only the gentle sport of 'make believe' without which life would be intolerable to men who live by their affections. Saints and lovers and men governed by affection, poets and artists, all live in phantasy, its falsehood truer than any reality. By such falsehood we got nearer to truth. His charm to me was his veracious intellect. He would lie neither to please the sentimentalists nor the moralists. What talent I have for honest thinking I learned from him.[1]

Fear of the cane forced Latin and Greek into John Butler Yeats at his school, so that when he arrived, like his father and grandfather before him, at Trinity College, Dublin, the ordinary college examinations gave him no trouble. An attack of rheumatic fever, however, laid him low in his final year just as he was to sit an Honours examination in Metaphysics and Logic.

He spent most of his college years at Sandymount Castle, which belonged to his uncle, Robert Corbet. He took life easily there, toyed with the idea of the Church, and walked frequently to Lough Dan to admire its beauties and fish in its dark waters:

All through my College days I lived the Sandymount Castle life. It was my Capua and only too welcome after my school life. I had been braced too tight, now I was braced too lightly: self-abandoned to a complete relaxation. I left that school, weakened morally by its constant discipline and vigilance, to live all my College days in that pleasant Capua. I did not think, I did not

[1] John Butler Yeats, *Early Memories; Some Chapters of Autobiography*, p. 38.

work, I had no ambition, I dreamed. Week after week went by, and no one criticised. As far as the demands of that sympathetic circle went, I satisfied everybody, and was well-behaved. The only thing that ever troubled my uncle was my habit of going long walks in the mountains, all by myself. His old-fashioned, eighteenth century gregarious worldliness was shocked that I should walk all by myself, it seemed to him abnormal and he distrusted the abnormal.[1]

After taking his degree John Butler Yeats began to study law. He read Butler's *Analogy* and lost his orthodoxy :

. . . I suddenly amazed myself by coming to the conclusion that revealed religion was myth and fable. My father had himself pushed me into the way of thinking for myself; and my Scotch school-master, who had lived on his own resources since he was twelve years old, acquiring thereby a bold and independent spirit, had un-consciously assisted in the process. Thus it came about that I had the courage to reject the Bishop's teachings, drawing an entirely different conclusion from the premises he placed before his reader, and with it went also my worldly-minded uncle's hope that some day I should be a respectable, Episcopalian clergyman. Everything now was gone, my mind a contented negation. At school my ethics had been based on fear of the school-master and now was gone fear of God and God's justice. I went to Church when I couldn't help it, that is once every Sunday. I do not know how it is now-a-days, but at that time Churches were so crowded that young men, unable to find a seat, remained the whole service through standing in the aisle. This exactly suited my inclinations, especially in one of the Kingstown churches down by the sea, for there I could stand all the two hours at the front door, half within and half without, so that while listening to the clergyman I could at the same time comfort my eye and soothe my spirit by looking toward the sea and sky. The Reverend Hugh Hamilton, Dean of Dromore, reckoned the most learned man in the Diocese, had determined that my father should, on presenting himself for ordi-nation, be rejected because of his love for hunting, shooting and fishing and I may add, dancing, but was so impressed by his pro-found knowledge and understanding of Butler's Analogy that he became and continued from that hour on his constant friend. Yet this book that made my father a proudly orthodox man had

[1] *Ibid.*, p. 56.

shattered all my orthodoxy, so that I preferred sea & sky and float-ing clouds to the finest pulpit oratory of the Reverend Richard Brooke, father of the brilliantly successful Stopford. Yet I dared not say so, poetic and artistic intuitions not having reached at that time the dignity of any sort of opinion, theory, or doctrine. The finest feelings are nothing if you cannot bulwark them with opinions about which men wrangle and fight.[1]

When John Butler Yeats won a ten-pound prize for political economy he spent it on a holiday in Sligo with the Pollexfens. This was a significant visit, recorded with warm memory in his autobiographical fragment. It sharpened a dialogue which was to run continuously through his mind for the rest of his life :

At Sligo, I was the social man where it was the individual man that counted. It is a curious fact that entering this sombre house of stern preoccupation with business I for the first time in my life felt myself to be a free man, and that I was invited by the example of everyone around me to be my very self, thereby receiving the most important lesson in my life.[2]

To live among his people, he wrote, was pleasanter, but to live among the Pollexfens was good training. His preoccupa-tion with the Pollexfens ran deep. When his father died suddenly in 1862, he inherited the family property in Co. Kildare. This brought in a few hundreds a year : enough to marry on ; and he had already fallen in love with George's sister, Susan Pollexfen. They married, took a house in Sandymount, and there in 1865 William Butler Yeats was born. By marriage with a Pollexfen, said John Butler Yeats, '. . . I have given a tongue to the sea-cliffs'.[3]

The next year Yeats was called to the Irish Bar : he never

[1] John Butler Yeats, *Early Memories ; Some Chapters of Autobio-graphy*, p. 72. [2] *Ibid.*, p. 89.
[3] *Ibid.*, p. 20. See also p. 92 : 'Inarticulate as the sea-cliffs were the Pollexfen heart and brain, lying buried under mountains of silence. They were released from bondage by contact with the joyous amiability of my family, and of my bringing up, and so all my four children are articulate, and yet with the Pollexfen force.'

practised but devilled for Isaac Butt whom he greatly admired and of whom he made an admirable portrait. (There is a superb copy in chalks in the Irish National Portrait Gallery.) Yeats's views of Trinity varied. He was to regret that his son did not enter college, even though he wrote in his auto-biographical fragment :

Trinity College Dublin did very little for me, which is entirely my own fault, neither did Trinity College Dublin inspire me with affection, and that was the fault of Trinity College Dublin. One night, in the College park, walking under the stars with that brilliant scientist George Fitzgerald, I saw him look round at some new buildings just erected and with a snap of satisfaction he said, 'No ornament, that is one good thing.' I made the obvious retort 'How is Trinity College Dublin to inspire affection, if it is not made beautiful in its buildings, its quadrangle, its trees and its park.' He gave a grunting assent. Had he not been in a contro-versial mood, and ascetic for severe science, he would have responded generously ; for he was a true scientist, that is, a poet as well. Trinity College inspires no love ; outside what it has done for learning and mathematics and things purely intellectual it has a lean history. Still youth is youth, and the time of youth is pleasant to look back upon.[1]

His own youth appeared to have ended when in 1867 he took the decisive step of giving up the law for art. He moved to London and attended Heatherley's School.

It was five years before he received a commission — a long apprenticeship when there were five children to support: W. B., Robert who died of croup in 1873, John Butler (Jack, the artist), Elizabeth Corbet (known as Lolly) and Susan Mary (known as Lily). During these years Mrs. Yeats and the children lived in Sligo with the Pollexfens who disapproved of Yeats's impracticability : his preoccupation with the matter of how to live rather than that of how to make a living, his belief that a gentleman was not concerned with getting on in the world. It seemed to Yeats, however, that he had cut his

[1] *Ibid.*, p. 68.

apprenticeship short, too short, in order to please the Pollexfens.

There were two changes of residence in London before
Yeats moved to Bedford Park in 1876. His chief friends were
J. T. Nettleship, a Pre-Raphaelite water-colourist (whose
daughter Augustus John married) who had begun to turn his
attention to symbolic paintings in the 'sixties, and thence to
realistic studies of animals ; George Wilson, a Scot who died
in 1890; and Edwin J. Ellis, a poet and painter, who later
collaborated with W. B. Yeats in an edition of Blake which
contains an elaborate commentary on Blake's symbolism.
These four friends formed the 'Brotherhood' : they were
befriended by John Todhunter (a fellow undergraduate of
Yeats at Trinity) then practising medicine in London, writing
plays and acting as patron of these artists. They shared views
on the union of the arts and were admirers of Blake and
Rossetti : indeed Rossetti himself admired a drawing by Yeats
so much that he invited him to Cheyne Walk. But during this
period Yeats was so filled with indecision and doubt that he did
not accept the invitation. In *Reveries over Childhood and Youth*
W. B. Yeats remembers his father at work on a painting of a
pond — he began this in spring and continued to work on it
throughout the year, abandoning it when he found himself
painting snow on its banks.

The Land War meant the disappearance of rents from the
unmortgaged part of the Kildare lands, and so at the beginning
of the 'eighties Yeats took his family back to Ireland where
living was cheaper. They lived at Howth — first at Balscadden
Cottage, then at Island View — and then, in 1884, at Ashfield
Terrace, Rathgar. Yeats had a studio in York Street and later
one in St. Stephen's Green.

During this period in Dublin Yeats educated his eldest
son. They travelled to Dublin by train from Howth in the
mornings ; they breakfasted in the painter's studio before
W. B. went on to the High School, and the father read aloud

Shakespeare, Balzac and Blake. He spoke often of the idea of
the solitary man. He was radical in his views, a Home-Ruler,
a questioner of accepted values. He enjoyed discussion; he
encouraged his son to write poetry; he introduced him to
his old friends, among them Edward Dowden, then the first
Professor of English Literature at Trinity College. It was a
period of great domestic liveliness which is reflected in an
essay:

The typical Irish family is poor, ambitious, and intellectual;
and all have the national habit, once indigenous in 'Merry England',
of much conversation. In modern England they like a dull man
and so they like a dull boy. We like bright men and bright boys.
When there is a dull boy we send him to England and put him into
business where he may sink or swim; but a bright boy is a different story. Quickly he becomes the family confidant, learning all
about the family necessities; with so much frank conversation it
cannot be otherwise. He knows every detail in the school bills
and what it will cost to put him through the university, and how
that cost can be reduced by winning scholarships and prizes. As
he grows older he watches, like an expert, the younger brothers
coming on, and is eager to advise in his young wisdom as to their
prospects. He studies constantly, perhaps overworks himself while
his mother and sisters keep watch; and yet he is too serious, and
they on their side are too anxious for compliments. It is indeed
characteristic of the Irish mother that, unlike the flattering mothers
of England, she loves too anxiously to admire her children; with
her intimate knowledge there goes a cautious judgment. The family
habit of conversation into which he enters with the arrogance of
his tender years gives him the chance of vitalizing his newly acquired
knowledge. Father, Mother, brothers and sisters are all on his
mind; and the family fortunes are a responsibility. He is not
dull-witted, as are those who go into business to exercise the will
in plodding along some prescribed path; on the contrary, his
intellect is in constant exercise. He is full of intellectual curiosity,
so much conversation keeping it alive, and therein is unlike the
English or the American boy. Indeed, he experiences a constant
temptation to spend in varied reading the time that should be given
to restricted study. He is at once sceptical and credulous, but,
provided his opinions are expressed gaily and frankly, no one

minds. With us intellect takes the place which in the English home is occupied by the business faculty. We love the valour of the free intellect; so that, the more audacious his opinion, the higher rise the family hopes. He and all his family approve of amusement — to do so is an Irish tradition unbroken from the days before St. Patrick; but they have none. They are too poor and too busy; or rather they have a great deal, but it is found in boyish friendships and in the bonds of the strongest family affection, inevitable because they are Irish and because they have hopes that make them dependent upon one another. The long family talks over the fire, the long talks between clever boys on country walks — these are not the least exciting amusements — even though they bear no resemblance to what is called 'sport'.[1]

This was also a period of strain. Yeats did not succeed in establishing himself in Dublin as a highly successful painter. He charged too little and perhaps he talked too well and too much. And so in 1887 he returned to London, to Bedford Park. There his wife had two strokes from which she never fully recovered. She died in 1900. During these years he renewed his friendships with Nettleship and Ellis, and he found in York Powell, Professor of Modern History at Oxford, who lived at Bedford Park, and Oliver Elton, who left Bedford Park in 1890 for the Chair of English in Liverpool, the kind of academic minds he valued. These men were more appreciative of his originality than most of the Dublin dons, with the notable exception of Dowden:

The late Dr. Salmon was a great man and a great mathematician but it was well known that tho' he was an infallible judge of every kind of investment he paid no attention to what is called the artistic values being exclusively a man of science and therefore a philistine. Mathematicians are as a rule philistines and are apt to think that there is nothing in life valuable except the utilities, and that what is called efficiency is the chief of human faculties. A friend of mine, a fine classical scholar, told me that in his experience, mathematicians could only talk of the price of things — tell them, he said, what you pay for your boots. I once met Dr. Salmon at

---

[1] John Butler Yeats, *Essays Irish and American* (1918), p. 30.

dinner and was much flattered by his taking me aside and asking me what I paid for my lodgings — I thought that the great man was interested in me. Professor Dowden, his relation and my friend, undeceived me. He said it was only Salmon's way. All his long life Dr. Salmon sought for scientific and practical truth and has left a distinguished name. Yet at that dinner table had he listened to me I could have told him things that would have opened his eyes to a world of which he had never dreamed and perhaps he would have acknowledged that the tangible is valuable only for the sake of the intangible. There are whole streets in London, whole districts where the people inhabiting the houses are prisoners each in his cell and to walk through them is to breathe prison air since their houses have no grace, no architectural charm, no artistic decoration, nothing to remind or to suggest that there is anything in life except this and that utility — houses everywhere but nowhere a home, nowhere an asylum for the affections — amid such surroundings humanity is withered. Artists exist that these places be destroyed — a kind of prison reform much needed in great cities.[1]

After his wife's death John Butler Yeats returned to Dublin in 1900. His sons had established themselves; his daughters took a house in Dundrum and there they conducted the hand-press and embroidery department of the Dun Emer Industries, later conducted under the name Cuala Industries. Yeats walked every day to his studio in Stephen's Green, and during this period painted some of his best-known work: portraits of Synge, Lady Gregory, Miss Horniman, George Moore, Padraic Colum, Standish O'Grady, W. G. Fay. His previous stay in Ireland had seen the beginning of the Irish Literary Movement. This period from 1900 to 1907 covered its flowering and Yeats became a lively figure in Dublin's life. His speech at the famous debate on Synge's *Playboy* in 1907 is immortalized in his son's poem 'Beautiful Lofty Things':

My father upon the Abbey stage, before him a raging crowd:
'This Land of Saints', and then as the applause died out,
'Of plaster Saints'; his beautiful mischievous head thrown back.[2]

[1] John Butler Yeats, *Letters*, p. 200.
[2] W. B. Yeats, *Collected Poems* (1961), p. 348.

His own account of the incident is no less vivid ; he wrote
to a friend :

Of course I did not make a speech in favour of patricide. How
could I ? Here is what I said. I began with some information
about Synge which interested my listeners and then : 'Of course
I know Ireland is an island of Saints, but thank God it is also an
island of sinners — only unfortunately in this Country people
cannot live or die except behind a curtain of deceit'. At this point
the chairman and my son both called out, 'Time's up, Time's up.'
I saw the lifted sign and like the devil in *Paradise Lost* I fled. The
papers next morning said I was howled down. It was worse, I was
pulled down. . . . The sentence about the curtain of deceit flashed
on my mind at the moment, and was a good sentence, but manifestly
a blunder, although I did enjoy it. . . .[1]

In 1908 he went on a visit to New York with his daughter
Lily who was showing her embroidery there. He promised
to return after she had left and, as Hone remarks, would sometimes even fix the date of his sailing. But he stayed in New
York ; he lived in various hotels, then settled in a boarding-
house in West 29th Street. The real reasons[2] for his staying
on were his curiosity about and interest in the variety of
America, and his Micawberish belief that something would
turn up. He would have liked to have escaped from New York,
he wrote, 'and all it stands for except one thing that N. York
always holds with bountiful hands held out towards me — and
that is a chance of work — of employment. Anything may
turn up here — a lecture an article a portrait. It is a high
gaming table where the poorest has a welcome and a chance.'[3]

And so despite his family's hope that he would return, he
stayed and lectured and wrote and painted. His letters are
filled with moving passages, full of hope. 'An old man,' he

[1] John Butler Yeats, *Letters*, p. 214.
[2] He remarked once that he did not care to play the rôle of father to
an illustrious son. He 'wrote to Willie some time ago and said it was as
bad to be a poet's father as the intimate friend of George Moore'. Indeed,
in one mood, in 1904, he wrote that he wished Willie did not sometimes
treat him as if he were a black beetle — though the son was at that time
financing his father.   [3] John Butler Yeats, *Letters*, pp. 272–3.

wrote to his artist son Jack Yeats, 'should think of the past, but I am all interested in the future.'[1]

Eventually, exhausted after a walk in a blizzard, he died in February 1922, nearly eighty-three years of age, telling anecdotes and making gay jests to the end.

What did he achieve in his eighty-three years? He was a painter whose sketches and drawings have more attraction for us than his finished portraits in oils. These portraits convey a likeness well, sometimes the better for Yeats's belief that a portrait should illustrate the flaw or weakness that goes to the making of beauty. But, as Professor Bodkin remarked, 'he was not strikingly accomplished in the mere technique of painting'. What interested him was the essential nature of the sitter: from his penetrating portraits of, say, John O'Leary or Lady Gregory or John Synge there radiates some of the individual quality, the dominating desire and mood, the essential character, of the sitter. His own self-portrait, painted at eighty, conveys the curiosity and vitality, even the speculative and sympathetic interest in others that underpinned his whole life. The eyes, those large bright eyes that Oliver Elton described as changeful and ever-watchful, dominate the rendering of the head, as in most of his portraits, where, indeed, the heads dominate the rest of the painting. This is what we might expect; it is explained in Bodkin's remark, 'his bent was intellectual rather than sensuous'.

This bent produced some superb pencil drawings. Yeats used his pencil ceaselessly to capture character. There is a sureness and economy of execution in his drawings which evaded his portraiture, despite his valiant and unceasing hopes that he would achieve success. A few weeks before he died he saw portraits by Laszlo and wrote gaily to John Quinn, his Irish-American patron and friend:

That shining cohort of fashionable horrors was amusing. I got from them one good thing. My self-portrait has been facing me

[1] *Ibid.*, p. 228.

for a long time lying against the wall of my room and filling me with despondency. I now see that it is the making of a masterpiece. To know good you must have seen evil. I have seen Laszlo and now I appreciate Yeats.[1]

In an earlier letter he summed up the same painting with characteristic insight : 'It is an honest portrait'.[2]

This insight and honesty pervaded the work of his pen. He wrote very many letters. Selections from some of them were made by Ezra Pound in 1917, and by Lennox Robinson in 1920, both published by the Cuala Press in limited editions. Joseph Hone edited a larger selection which was published by Faber & Faber in 1944, now, alas, out of print. And there are many unpublished letters which many of us would like to see in print. A small volume of *Essays Irish and American* was published in Dublin and London in 1918, and the Cuala Press issued *Early Memories ; Some Chapters of Autobiography* in 1923. From these brief collections we can discover much of the temper of Yeats's mind ; we can recognize the liveliness and quick, imaginative, paradoxical wit that made a success of what was regarded by many of his contemporaries as his main art, his conversation.

Like many Anglo-Irish writers he had an instinct for finding himself an object of amusement. In part this sprang from what he regarded as an Irish characteristic — 'a perfectly disinterested, an absolutely unselfish love of making mischief, mischief for its own dear sake':[3] in part it was based upon a dislike of self-importance :

Aristocracies and pessimists are malign, and the whole of Nietzsche is malign ; so are college dons and their retinue, but so were not Shakespeare and Shelley. Wordsworth was malign, so was Byron and so is Swinburne. These people could not get away from their self-importance.[4]

[1] John Butler Yeats, *Letters*, p. 287.   [2] *Ibid.*, p. 258.
[3] *Passages from the Letters of John Butler Yeats*, selected by Ezra Pound, Dublin, 1917, p. 60.   [4] *Ibid.*, p. 54.

This dislike of self-importance arose out of the good manners which made him such a good correspondent — *in writing a letter*, he said, *one generally escapes it* [an indulged facility], *because one is so interested in the person who is to receive the letter.* When writing of himself he could, therefore, use irony with casual ease. Here, for instance, is a typical example from a letter in which he is telling Susan Mitchell of his relationship with the *New Republic.* The account builds up from a statement into an ironic contrast before it crystallizes itself into an arrestingly witty generalization :

The *New Republic* is edited by a group of young writers, all supposed to be awfully clever. They are having a fine time, and their magazine is greatly lauded — all the superior people take it in. I might think more highly of it but they without a moment's delay refused some articles and stories I did them the honour to submit. It is reported that the magazine is financed for three years by a rich American woman. I think all American magazine writing far too frightfully clever. It is as if a man had by mistake hired an acrobat for a footman, so that when he asked for a glass of water it was handed to him by a man standing on his head.[1]

His letters are lively because they are able to shift their viewpoint with the ease of a good conversation. He carried serious thoughts with lightness ; his levity was usually exercised in conjunction with a deep sense of the seriousness of art. A letter written to his son in 1917 illustrates this range of tone :

I have always maintained that every man of sense should keep in his library a box of strong cigars, saturate each cigar with some drug soporific, so that if anyone said such a sentence as 'Excuse me, Sir, but what you are saying now is quite inconsistent with what you said earlier in the evening, etc.', you might reply : 'Sir, your views are very interesting. May I offer you a cigar ? It is of a special brand that I only give to my most valued friends.' Ah ! with what pleasure one would watch the gradual lowering of the eyelids and the falling away of the mouth and the paling of the lip as one waited for the blessed silence.[2]

[1] *Letters*, p. 209.
[2] *Ibid.*, p. 241.

Having invented his comic situation he continues the letter on a serious note, defending his own approach to poetry :

> Oriental philosophy is like that cigar. That is why we turn to it. Sir Philip Sidney wrote that poetry cannot lie because it affirms nothing, and if you affirm nothing, what becomes of the fighting intellect ? Either it conceals its instincts, or is converted, like a heathen king listening to the preaching of St. Augustine. — The man with the logical mind does not — for he cannot — read poetry.[1]

The rôle of the poet and the artist were themes which ran through his letters, especially after his stay in New York. He believed that the world of art was a dreamland. The moment a poet meddled with ethics, moral uplift or thinking scientifically he left dreamland, lost his music and ceased to be a poet. He regarded Shakespeare as never quitting this realm :

> . . . We all live when at our best, that is when we are most ourselves, in dreamland. A man with his wife or child and loving them, a man in grief and yielding to it, girls and boys dancing together, children at play — it is all dreams, dreams, dreams. A student over his books, soldiers at the war, friends talking together — it is still dreamland — actual life on a far away horizon which becomes more and more distant. When the essential sap of life is arrested by anger or hatred we suddenly are aware of the actual, and music dies out of our hearts and voices — the *anger subtly present* in ethical thought — as it is also in most kinds of argument ; how many poems has it laid low ? . . .
>
> The poet is a magician — his vocation to incessantly evoke dreams and do his work so well, because of natural gifts and acquired skill, that his dreams shall have a potency to defeat the actual at every point. Yet here is a curious thing, the poet and we his dupes know that they are only dreams — otherwise we lose them. With our eyes open, using our will and powers of selection, we, together in friendship and brotherly love, create this dreamland. Pronounce it to be actual life and you summon logic and mechanical sense and reason and all the other powers of prose to find yourself hailed back to the prison house, and dreamland vanishes — a shrieking ghost.[2]

[1] *Letters*, p. 242.   [2] *Ibid.*, p. 198.

This continued emphasis on the importance of the dream reminds us of his effect on his famous son. Continually he insisted that the real contest was not against material things but between those who want to get on and those who don't want to get on, having more important things to attend to. When York Powell offered to recommend W. B. Yeats for the sub-editorship of a provincial paper, and the young man told his father he could not accept the offer, J. B. Yeats replied, though the family was badly short of funds, 'You have taken a great weight off my mind.' He believed

A gentleman is such, simply because he has not the doctrine of getting on and the habit of it. For this reason a poor peasant and a true artist are gentlemen, but people talk as if the doctrine of getting on was greater than all the law and the prophets.[1]

Here was the idea his son developed after his disillusionment with nationalist politics, the belief stated in his poems praising the virtues of aristocratic life, 'At Galway Races' and 'To a Wealthy Man . . .', and brought to its final assertion in 'The Municipal Gallery Revisited' where he sees the work of John Synge, Augusta Gregory and himself as coming from contact with the soil :

> We three alone in modern times had brought
> Everything down to that sole test again,
> Dream of the noble and the beggar-man.[2]

There are many correspondences between the ideas of father and son. Indeed the first part of W. B. Yeats's *Autobiographies*, *Reveries over Childhood and Youth*, bears ample witness to the early influence of John Butler Yeats on his son's development.[3] Professor Ellmann has, I believe, made far too much out of the arguments between father and son, being,

[1] *Passages from the Letters of John Butler Yeats*, p. 52.
[2] W. B. Yeats, *Collected Poems* (1961), p. 368.
[3] W. B. Yeats wrote to his father (J. B. Yeats, *Letters to His Son W. B. Yeats and Others*, p. 203) : 'Some one to whom I read the book said to me the other day, "If Gosse had not taken the title you should call it 'Father and Son'."'

39

unlike J. B. and W. B. Yeats, over-aware of Freud and his theories. Elizabeth Yeats's diary entry for 9 September 1888, when W. B. Yeats was twenty-three, gives a sensible explanation of the relationship :

I can hear a murmur of talk from the dining-room where Papa and Willie are arguing something or other. Sometimes they raise their voices so high that a stranger might fancy that they were both in a rage, not at all, it is only their way of arguing because they are natives of the Emerald Isle.[1]

It is a commonplace that the painter's influence over his poet son ceased when the latter began to develop his interest in mysticism — a mystic, incidentally, was defined by John Butler Yeats as 'a man who believes what he likes to believe and makes a system of it and plumes himself on doing so'.[2] He thought Blake's mysticism was 'never the *substance of his poetry, only its machinery*',[3] and during the period of the First World War his letters to his son insisted that 'the poet is not primarily a thinker but incidentally he is a thinker and a stern thinker since the source of his magic is his personal sincerity'.[4] Again, he wrote, 'Let poets by all means touch on ideas, but let it only be a "touching" and a tentative groping with the poetical fingers. It is bad poetry which proclaims a definite belief — because it is a sin against sincerity.'[5] These views probably had their effect upon W. B. who wrote to his father describing his own *Anima Hominis* and *Anima Mundi* as philosophical and 'a kind of prose backing' to his poetry.[6]

The question of John Butler Yeats's influence on his son needs fresh exploration. I believe it extended further than the early period of W. B. Yeats's life, though less directly. The printed works of John Butler Yeats, as well as the references to his conversations in W. B. Yeats's prose, show that father and

[1] Cf. J. Hone, 'A Scattered Fair', *The Wind and the Rain*, iii, 3 (Autumn, 1946).
[2] *Passages from the Letters of John Butler Yeats*, p. 16.
[3] *Ibid.*, p. 19.   [4] *Letters*, p. 210.
[5] *Ibid.*, p. 221.   [6] *Ibid.*, p. 238.

son shared very many ideas — for instance, J. B. Yeats writes
to W. B. in 1916 that Stendhal said a novel should be like a
looking-glass dawdling along the road, and W. B. writes in his
Pages from a Diary Written in 1930, 'Because freedom is gone
we have Stendhal's "mirror dawdling down a lane".' This
is but a small echo, like the interest they shared in the hermits
of the desert;[1] the larger, longer echoes are more significant.
The most important idea they shared was probably that of the
rôle of the lonely man. 'The poet is always solitary,'[2] wrote
J. B. Yeats; again he commented:

> The individual man of entire sincerity has to wrestle with him-
> self, unless transported by rage or passion; he has so much mind
> to make up, with none to help him and no guide except his con-
> science; and conscience after all, is but a feeble glimmer in a
> labyrinthine cavern of darkness.[3]

Or again,

> Outside mathematics and science, there is no such thing as
> belief positive; yet there is a certain intensity of feeling whether
> of love, hope or sorrow or fear which we label belief; with the
> solitary man this remains a feeling and is something personal, and
> therefore the very substance of poetry.[4]

These are ideas we find W. B. Yeats carrying on in the poem
'My House' — he describes how 'two men have founded' in
the ancient tower: the original man-at-arms and his score
of horse:

> And I, that after me
> My bodily heirs may find,
> To exalt a lonely mind,
> Befitting emblems of adversity.[5]

[1] See *Letters*, p. 207, and W. B. Yeats's references to the monk of the
Thebaid in 'Demon and Beast', *Collected Poems*, p. 209.
[2] *Early Memories; Some Chapters of Autobiography*, p. 23.
[3] *Ibid.*, p. 90.
[4] He also remarked that 'solitude is food for the intellect but a drain
on the spirits'.   [5] W. B. Yeats, *Collected Poems*, p. 226.

D

On 10 June 1918 John Butler Yeats wrote to his son quite simply, 'The way to be happy is to forget yourself. That is why Robert Gregory was happy....'[1] He distinguished two ways of achieving self-forgetfulness, as in the war, or in a movement for reform, or in games; or again through art and beauty. He saw war as so overwhelmingly gregarious that 'while it lasts it suspends all the movements and the susceptibilities of the solitary man'.[2] The same idea runs through one of W. B.'s poems on Robert Gregory, 'An Irish Airman Foresees his Death', written in 1918:

> Nor law, nor duty bade me fight,
> Nor public men, nor cheering crowds,
> A lonely impulse of delight
> Drove to this tumult in the clouds;
> I balanced all, brought all to mind,
> The years to come seemed waste of breath,
> A waste of breath the years behind
> In balance with this life, this death.[3]

This belief in the necessity of solitude led him to believe also in the detachment needed by a poet. Emotionalism, he thought, was bad because it lacked seriousness — 'Walt Whitman did not believe half what he said' — emotionalism was spectacular. The true poet seemed to him to be like the statesman, and to possess a cold heart, notwithstanding its abiding ecstasy, and therefore to be more serious than any statesman.[4] This emphasis on the cold heart finds echoes in W. B. Yeats's 'Cast a cold eye on death'.[5]

When John Quinn thought J. B. Yeats sentimental about women and marriage he did not fully realize how aware J. B. Yeats was of the dangers of sentimental thinking.[6] It is

---

[1] *Letters*, p. 247.
[2] On 14 June 1918 W. B. Yeats had finished his long poem 'In Memory of Major Robert Gregory'.
[3] W. B. Yeats, *Collected Poems*, p. 152.
[4] John Butler Yeats, *Letters*, p. 237.
[5] W. B. Yeats, *Collected Poems*, p. 401.
[6] See John Butler Yeats, *Letters*, pp. 226–7.

probable that W. B.'s long-frustrated dreams which eventually came true of 'wife, daughter, son' were formed early and upon the example of his father's belief in the virtues of marriage. J. B. Yeats was attractive to women and enjoyed their company, while holding firm, conservative views on marriage :

Marriage is the earliest fruit of civilization and it will be the latest. I think a man and a woman should choose each other for life, for the simple reason that a long life with all its accidents is barely enough for a man and a woman to understand each other ; and in this case to understand is to love. The man who understands one woman is qualified to understand pretty well everything.[1]

The poet must, he thought, have self-control and allow no single feeling to remain single, forcing it into harmony with all the other feelings, an idea shared by his son, who saw that in life courtesy and self-possession and in the arts style arose out of deliberate shaping of all things.[2]

Both men were instinctively aristocratic ('Every day I notice some new analogy between the long-established life of the well-born and the artists' life', wrote W. B. Yeats in 1909) ;[3] both valued manners greatly. 'Damn nervous energy,' wrote the father, 'and damn efficiency. They have killed good manners as they have killed conversation, for the sake of which good manners exist, and they have killed art and literature.'[4] This is a sentiment echoed in W. B. Yeats's 1909 diary where he develops the idea of the mask. Father and son shared a dislike of logic ; they shared a dislike of the English character which arose from their experiences of English schoolboys,

---

[1] *Letters*, p. 236. He could see the difference between his ideal and the reality of some situations, however, remarking, 'I think lots of men die of their wives and thousands of women die of their husbands. But not an American. Here, if there is a little trouble over a hand glass or a tooth brush, they shake hands and part, unless of course, there is a lot of money, when the lawyers take a hand.' (*Letters*, p. 275.)

[2] W. B. Yeats, *Essays and Introductions* (1961), p. 253.

[3] W. B. Yeats, *Autobiographies* (1961), p. 473.

[4] *Passages from the Letters of John Butler Yeats*, p. 1.

from whom they felt essentially different.[1] John Butler Yeats
built up an image of the 'Englishman': Tory, class-conscious,
self-centred, dull, official: 'Someone who enjoys liberty and
believes in it — for himself alone',[2] and in England 'character
always means a man in whom the will power is predominant,
it is in fact the bureaucratic mind, and is as interesting as
Berlin governed by its police'.[3] There were, of course,
exceptions. 'It is a few Englishmen like Paget and York
Powell and Oliver Elton that prevent the Almighty from
destroying England.'[4] He became mellower. In 1917 he
wrote to Oliver Elton that he would do the Englishman full
justice: 'he does not lose his head, even now [in the war] he
ceases neither to love his children nor his wife nor his garden
nor his poetry'. He liked ordinary English people; in 1915
he anticipated a social movement coming after the 1914–1918
war and in this the Irish, he thought, 'must help *their English
brothers* — who certainly won't be the middle class their old
enemies'.[5]

He could generalize about the Irish as easily. Ireland was
accused of a lack of seriousness by England; this, he said,
was because Ireland lacks the collective mind. The Irish have
the charm of being natural; 'the Irish peasant mind is not
common but is stored with rich enjoyment'.[6] He could also
enjoy being epigrammatic about differences: 'The Irish spurn
convention and are called cynical, and the English make of it
a religion and for their pains are called hypocrites'.[7] The

---

[1] John Butler Yeats, *Letters*, p. 108: 'John Bull's pre-eminence is
slipping away so that these airs are becoming a little ridiculous — to me
they always have been so — since I had been at school with so many
English boys'. W. B. Yeats, *Autobiographies*, p. 35: 'I was divided
from all those boys [at a school in Hammersmith] not merely by the
anecdotes that are everywhere perhaps a chief expression of the distrust
of races but because our mental images were different', and p. 33: 'I did
not think English people intelligent or well behaved unless they were
artists'. [2] John Butler Yeats, *Letters*, p. 41.
[3] *Ibid.*, p. 124. [4] *Ibid.*, p. 96.
[5] *Ibid.*, p. 211. [6] *Ibid.*, p. 255.
[7] *Early Memories; Some Chapters of Autobiography*, p. 68.

Americans searched for joy and happiness — talk only fit for athletes and football players — a shallow vulgar paradise, easily come at, he thought, by anyone except the true artist and poet. He mixed up his reflections with anecdotes and gossip : they are often discerning, and always interesting. On democracy he had mixed feelings :

> There are no proud girls in America. Feminine beauty has not that *touch-me-not quality* which is half the charm of the well-bred girl (of other countries). It is the pride of the democracies and the Americans to have no pride, and it does make life pleasant and easy, but it leaves the American girl naked and defenceless against all these false ideas that are so abundant among socialists.[1]

He dwelt long upon the characters of his relatives and friends and found the 'joyous amiability' of the Yeats family a source of comfort, as the orderliness of the Pollexfens was a perpetual challenge. His reflections on dreams and death, on Protestantism, on literature, on women, on art, all have a zest and vitality, which though often lacking polish, have a gnomic quality, a casualness which comes from a consciousness of more to come. '*Genius is personality*,' he remarks and adds, impishly, 'I always say that had Shakespeare had a strong will he would have read for a Fellowship in T.C.D. and there would have been no Shakespeare.'[2]

He was a man of modesty. Many of the letters to his son contained excellent criticism, sometimes of the poet as poet and also as man : always there were phrases — 'I hope I do not weary you', or 'Don't trouble to answer this letter, which is merely a word to the wise'. He thought the only sincerity in a practical world was that of the artist ; he knew when discussing 'real' matters with 'real' people he irritated them by producing phrases or ideas that were expressive, while they sought a practical result.[3] He looked back on his life, lived as a social life on social principles :

[1] *Letters*, p. 274.   [2] *Ibid.*, p. 98.
[3] *Ibid.*, p. 275.

we lived pleasantly, but falsely, and yet we did believe in human nature, at least in *our* human nature, in parental affection & in conjugal faith and loyalty between friends. On this matter we had a trustfulness that was at once romantic and robust. Parents and children and husbands and wives and friends and comrades, at least in our circles, would have stood by each other to the death.[1]

He shared the best virtues of his age, then, and in a remarkable letter to his son showed how his apparent failure was really a magnificent demonstration of the proper defence of art : the distinction of his own enjoyment of life speaks through every sentence :

To find out what was the mind of Shakespeare is valuable, but the real thing is to find out what is my own mind when I read Shakespeare or any other poem. If I know the mind of Shakespeare and in order that I may know it better, am made acquainted with the period in which he lived, it is good because thereby I may come more quickly to know my own mind — for I study him and all other poets exclusively that I may find myself. It is the same with nature itself. As artist, as man, seeking what I have called dreamland I am concerned still to find myself and my own mind, and only incidentally am I concerned with the intentions of Nature and her mind. Herein I am the reverse of the historical and the scientific student. They are concerned with what is other than themselves, whereas the artist in us and in all men seeks to find himself. Science exists that man may discover and control nature and build up for himself habitations in which to live in ease and comfort. Art exists that man cutting himself away from nature may build in his free consciousness buildings vaster and more sumptuous than these, furnished too with all manner of winding passages and closets and boudoirs and encircled with gardens well shaded and with everything that he can desire — and we build all out of our spiritual pain — for if the bricks be not cemented and mortised by actual suffering, they will not hold together. Those others live on another plane where if there is less joy there is much less pain. Like day labourers they work, with honest sweat to earn their wages, and mother nature smiles on them and calls them her good children who study her wishes and seek always to please her and rewards them with many gifts. The artist has not the gift for this assiduity, these

[1] *Early Memories ; Some Chapters of Autobiography*, p. 88.

servile labours — so falling out of favour with his great mother he withdraws himself and lives in disgrace, and then out of his pain and humiliations constructs for himself habitations, and if she sweeps them away with a blow of her hand he only builds them afresh, and as his joy is chiefly in the act of building he does not mind how often he has to do it. The men of science hate us and revile us, being angry with impotent rage because we seem to them to live in profitless idleness, and though we have sad faces we are yet of such invincible obstinacy that nothing can induce us to join their ranks. There are other things about us which perplex and offend them. They always work in gangs, many minds engaged on one task, whereas we live and work singly, each man building for himself accepting no fellowship — for we say it is only thus we can build our habitations. So it follows that they charge us with selfish egotism and insolence and pride, and it is vain for us to say that we work in the spirit of the utmost humility, not being strong enough for their tasks, and suffering many pains because of the anger of our offended and beloved mother. They are mighty men with strong wills. We are weak as water, our weakness is our raison d'être, and now and again when the strong man is broken he comes to us that we may comfort him. We even may make merry together, for we love our fellow men more than we do ourselves.[1]

[1] *Letters*, pp. 199–200.

THE EARLIER POEMS: SOME THEMES AND PATTERNS

*

DAVID DAICHES

THE GREATNESS AND ORIGINALITY of Yeats's middle and later poems have led to the dismissal of his earlier poetry by most critics as of merely biographical interest, illustrating the morass of late nineteenth-century romanticism from which the poet's developing genius eventually rescued him. There is of course some justification for this. The moaning self-indulgence of such a poem as 'The Sad Shepherd', the meretricious Orientalism of 'Anashuya and Vijaya', and what he himself later called 'all that overcharged colour inherited from the romantic movement' found in so many of the poems in his first three collections, are not really worth serious critical attention. Nevertheless, there is much of interest in these early poems, some of which at least are of value in their own right. It is true that when we find ourselves arrested by a particular early poem it will generally turn out to be a drastically revised version that we are looking at, and if we turn to the original version in an early volume or in *Poems and Ballads of Young Ireland* or in the indispensable Allt-Alspach variorum edition we may well find something much vaguer in expression and much less striking in imagery. Even so, the original version sometimes achieves a sufficiently arresting presentation of a theme to make clear that a real poet is at work here. And even where it does not, there may be in the nature of the theme itself or in the occasional line or phrase something that stirs the reader to attention. I do not want to make too great a claim for the quality and interest of Yeats's earlier

48

poetry; but I believe that a fair amount of it is of real interest, not simply to the pedant interested in charting a map of development or a researcher trying to classify themes and techniques, but to the reader and critic concerned with the kinds of imagination and the uses of language out of which poetry develops and indeed to (dare I use such an old-fashioned phrase?) the lover of poetry.

As I have already suggested, we are not very interested in the 'inarticulate moan' of 'The Sad Shepherd', which when originally published in the *Dublin University Review* in October 1886 bore the unpromising title 'Miserrimus'. Nevertheless, the theme of the poem is worth some attention. The sad shepherd tries in vain to arouse the sympathy of nature, but the natural world is unconcerned with him and makes no response:

> Then cried the man whom Sorrow named his friend :
> 'Oh sea, old sea, hear thou my piteous story';
> The sea swept on and cried her old cry still,
> Rolling along in dreams from hill to hill;
> And from the persecution of her glory
> He fled . . .
>
> (Original version)

The poet here is not employing the conventional romantic device of allowing nature to become a sounding-board for human feeling. Man fools himself if he thinks that nature exists to respond to his emotional needs. The poet, said Wordsworth, 'considers man and nature as essentially adapted to each other, and the mind of man as naturally the mirror of the fairest and most interesting properties of nature'. So for Wordsworth the key word is *relationship*. But for Yeats, even in his early romantic phase, it was a conviction of the essential dichotomy between man and nature that most possessed him. Not relationship but difference was what haunted Yeats. Further, a sense of this difference can become intolerable. The shepherd fled 'from the persecution of her glory'

49

(he tightened the line up in a later version, but kept this phrase unchanged). Now 'persecution' is an interesting and indeed arresting word in this context. Nature persecutes man by giving him the expectations of its sympathy — because of its beauty and its mood-creating rôle — only in order to withhold it. Wordsworth held that 'Nature never did betray the heart that loved her'; but Yeats knew better: for him, at least in his early phase, nature's continual betrayal of man's expectations of it was part of the pattern of reality. And that pattern was built of opposites, to be captured in poems whose structure involves a two-term dialectic.

Nothing is more striking in Yeats's development as a poet than his gradual replacement of a two-term by a three-term dialectic. His early poems are full of simple contrasts between pairs, and such contrasts often provide the basic poetic structure: man versus nature, the domesticated versus the wild, the human versus the faery, the temporal versus the changeless, the modern versus the ancient, the familiar versus the remote, and so on. In his later poetry he resolves these 'antinomies of day and night', achieving a resolution of opposites either in a *tertium quid* or else in a sense of the inter-penetration of opposites —

> 'Fair and foul are near of kin,
> And fair needs foul,' I cried.

But the two-term dialectic has its own poetic possibilities, as the word 'persecution' in 'The Sad Shepherd' suggests.

This is not to claim that Yeats consistently explored these possibilities in his early poetry. Sometimes he was content with the more traditional romantic mood-creating use of a natural background:

> The woods were round them, and the yellow leaves
> Fell like faint meteors in the gloom, and once
> A rabbit old and lame limped down the path;
> Autumn was over him: ...

This is well enough done in its way, which is the Tennysonian elegiac way, but less interesting than what Yeats does in, say, 'The Madness of King Goll', where he elaborates the implications of the 'persecution' of the sad shepherd in a highly original manner. It is a disturbing sense of the essential *otherness* of the natural world that drives King Goll mad, his madness being indicated by the refrain with which each stanza ends :

They will not hush, the leaves a-flutter round me, the beech leaves old.

The poem itself has a narrative base, the king describing what he was before he went mad and the circumstances under which he went mad, with the refrain reminding us that at the time of the telling he actually *is* mad. Man cannot come to terms with nature, which haunts, distracts and finally maddens him. And if you have been brought up to believe that man and nature are one, and that the function of nature is to serve man, then the realization of the falsity of this, the discovery of the uncanny otherness of nature, will make your mind snap. It is interesting that in later revisions — and this is a poem whose final text is much changed from the original form — Yeats altered the imagery in order to bring out this theme, which in the first version was almost lost amid the lushness of the detail, though it was very much present in the underlying structure. In revising, Yeats brought structure and imagery into closer unity, and the result is a genuinely impressive poem. Let us look briefly at the final version.

The poem opens with King Goll before his madness, the successful ruler of his kingdom :

> I sat on cushioned otter-skin :
> My word was law from Ith to Emain,
> And shook at Inver Amergin
> The hearts of the world-troubling seamen,
> And drove tumult and war away
> From girl and boy and man and beast ;
> The fields grew fatter day by day,

The wild fowl of the air increased ;
And every ancient Ollave said,
While he bent down his fading head,
'He drives away the Northern cold.'
They will not hush, the leaves a-flutter round me,
    the beech leaves old.

He sat on cushioned otter-skin, thus using wild nature for his comfort and prestige. His victories gave peace to 'girl and boy and man and beast' — with beasts casually included in the world of men. He had power over men and animals : the fields grew fatter, 'the wild fowl of the air increased'. And the wise men flattered him by telling him that he had dominion even over the weather. Only in the refrain at the end are we shaken into the realization that the king is now mad, and that he realizes that nature, far from being the servant and comforter of man, is something alien and haunting.

It was while he was playing his expected rôle of warrior and military saviour of his country that a sense of the appalling alienation of nature from man overcame him. Here is the third stanza :

But slowly, as I shouting slew
And trampled in the bubbling mire,
In my most secret spirit grew
A whirling and a wandering fire :
I stood : keen stars above me shone,
Around me shone keen eyes of men :
I laughed aloud and hurried on
By rocky shore and rushy fen ;
I laughed because birds fluttered by,
And starlight gleamed, and clouds flew high,
And rushes waved and waters rolled.
They will not hush, the leaves a-flutter round me,
    the beech leaves old.

The point is made by a simple juxtaposition of imagery : the 'keen stars' were above him and the 'keen eyes of men' were around him. A sense of the utter difference between the two overcame him, and he broke into mad laughter : 'I laughed *because* birds fluttered by, and starlight gleamed, and clouds flew high'. That 'because' is lunatic logic, and brilliantly establishes the point of the stanza, bringing the imagery into focus (this does not happen in the original version, which is differently worded). As a result of this strange epiphany, King Goll now wanders aimlessly through the countryside, trying to establish contact with that other world of nature. In the process, he becomes alienated from human interests :

> I came upon a little town
> That slumbered in the harvest moon, . . .

He can make no contact with the sleeping town, but finds an 'old tympan' lying 'deserted on a doorway seat' and takes it away with him to the woods, where, to its accompaniment, he sings 'of some inhuman misery'. The tympan — like the Aeolian harp of the earlier romantics — belongs to the world of both man and nature, and King Goll removes it from the former to the latter. His song, which begins as though it might be about the human world ('when day's toil is done') is in fact about the world of nature ; in any case, the suggestion that he might have been using the tympan to bridge the two worlds and to bring himself back into some knowledge of a specifically human emotion destroys the instrument, and he is left at the end with 'the kind wires torn and gone', howling meaninglessly like an animal, condemned to wander through nature but now part of neither man's nor nature's world, only crazily aware of their perpetual difference.

The limitations of a poem of this sort are obvious : the presentation, however hauntingly, of a sense of the dichotomy between the human and the natural world is in itself more of an emotional exercise than a fully realized poem dealing with some genuine centre of human experience. But the poem teases and disturbs and impresses, even if in a somewhat too self-consciously 'poetic' way, and clearly represents — even in its original form — something more than the faded romanticism which is the only quality now ascribed by most critics to the early Yeats.

The poem which follows 'King Goll' in the *Collected Poems*, written about the same time, is 'The Stolen Child', and here too we find that the whole structure and meaning are based on a sense of irreconcilable difference between two worlds. Once again, we have a refrain, but used somewhat differently this time, in order to represent the call of wild nature to the human infant still new enough to the human world to be able to renounce it and move over to the other world, this time not simply the world of nature but the world of faery, which is part of the inhuman world of herons, water-rats, berries, moonlight and 'dim grey sands'. The changes made in later revisions are here much less significant than in 'King Goll' and the poem is in any case simpler in both language and structure. The siren call of the faery world (which significantly changes in rhythmic pattern from the body of the stanza) simply summons the child to come away and join the faery band, leaving a world 'more full of weeping than you can understand'. The first three stanzas of the four-stanza poem build up a picture of the faery world of nature with all the traditional romantic appeal, and it seems that the poem is throwing its weight on the side of the seduction; but when we come to the final stanza the imagery suddenly changes in tone and implication, and the warm, familiar, human world — the 'calves on the warm hillside' (not wild animals but animals bred for human use), the 'kettle on the hob' (presented as an image of peace) and the 'brown mice' which 'bob round and round the oatmeal-chest' (images of domesticity and the friendly humanizing of natural objects) — is presented as something rashly given up in exchange for something cold and inhuman. The point is made very delicately, and the meaning is carried largely by the imagery. As in

'King Goll', there is developed a sense of the mystery and terror of that other world of the natural elements, of beauty untouched by human desire, human need or human familiarity, that derives some of its force from folklore. It is perhaps worth noting that both these poems have a background in Irish myth and legend : it was his use of Irish material that, at a very early stage, redeemed Yeats from the merely picturesque use of exotic detail. The terror of nature has nothing to do with any moral feeling, such as that which led Wordsworth to feel that nature was after him because he had stolen a boat. The moral is a purely human category, a category to which wild nature, in these poems of Yeats, is an utter stranger. One might say that these poems, for all their use of some traditional romantic properties, contain implicit criticisms of the falsity and sentimentality of at least one romantic attitude to nature.

A similar theme can be recognized in such a simple and even trivial-seeming poem as 'To an Isle in the Water', which at first sight seems to be a conventional invitation to the poet's beloved to fly with him 'to an isle in the water'. But the thought of the poem is in fact more interesting than this. The girl is a 'shy one', and shyness is a characteristic of wild creatures ; when the poet sees her in a domestic setting or engaged in domestic duties he feels that she does not belong there, and this feeling prompts him to suggest that he carry her off to where she does belong — the world of wild nature.

> Shy one, shy one,
> Shy one of my heart,
> She moves in the firelight
> Pensively apart.
>
> She carries in the dishes,
> And lays them in a row.
> To an isle in the water
> With her would I go . . .

She moves 'apart' in the firelight — and there can be no doubt that firelight has the same force in the poem as the warm

hillside and the oatmeal-chest have in 'The Stolen Child'. The
domestic precision of the first two lines of the second stanza
keep a careful balance between a suggestion of the comfortable
and familiar on the one hand and the mechanical and boring
on the other. The theme of escape from domesticity to wild
nature is thus given a new dimension : the girl herself because
of her shyness seems to the poet to belong to the wild, and so
to be unfitted for the domestic routine which she carries out,
and that is why he proposes to carry her off to what seems to
him to be her proper element. When 'she carries in the candles,
and lights the curtained room', this may seem at first sight as
though she is being admirably domestic, so much so as to
provoke in the poet a desire to carry her off to a home which
they can share together. But this is not what the poem's true
meaning seems to be. The poet wishes to go off with her to
where she seems really to belong. It is true that the irreconcilable difference between the human and the natural world,
which is suggested in 'King Goll', is here modulated into a gap
across which there can be bridges, so that there can be girls
who, though living in a domestic setting, belong by tempera-
ment to the other side. But the dialectic of the poem remains
a two-term one.

There are many variations on this theme in Yeats's early
poems. 'Who Goes with Fergus?' — quoted by Buck
Mulligan in Joyce's *Ulysses* — suggests that the world of
ancient heroic legend, which Yeats first learned about in the
pages of Standish O'Grady, is divorced from the normal passions of the human world and associated with the impersonal
world of nature :

> Who will go drive with Fergus now,
> And pierce the deep wood's woven shade,
> And dance upon the level shore ?
> Young man, lift up your russet brow,
> And lift your tender eyelids, maid,
> And brood on hopes and fears no more.

> And no more turn aside and brood
> Upon love's bitter mystery ;
> For Fergus rules the brazen cars,
> And rules the shadows of the wood,
> And the white breast of the dim sea
> And all dishevelled wandering stars.

The 'For' which opens the third line of the second stanza is the pivot of the poem, and a rather puzzling one. 'Go with Fergus and don't bother about ordinary human hopes and fears, for Fergus rules both the heroic and the natural world.' It is odd to have the heroic world associated with 'shadows', the 'dim sea' and the 'dishevelled wandering stars', but Yeats's imagination was always liable to do the unexpected, even in the early 1890s (the poem originally appeared in the second act of *The Countess Cathleen*). Further, we must remember who Fergus was. In Yeats's words, 'he was the poet of the Red Branch cycle [who was] once king of all Ireland, but gave up his throne that he might live at peace hunting in the woods'. Yeats made his own uses of Irish heroic story, as he did of Irish popular folklore ; from both he extracted ways of playing variations on the two-term pattern that he was so fond of in his early phases.

A more interesting example than either of the preceding two of Yeats's working with pairs of contraries is 'The Man Who Dreamed of Faeryland', a poem of considerable power and originality in spite of a title calculated to scare off most modern readers. A man involved in ordinary human emotions and ordinary human affairs is made aware, on suddenly confronting objects from the natural world like fishes and worms, of the strange otherness of that world, and after that he can know no peace. Though Yeats made a number of verbal changes in later editions, the poem as it now appears in the *Collected Poems* is not significantly different from the original version which appeared in *The National Observer* in February 1891 and one is not in any way distorting its nature

E

and meaning if one uses the later and more accessible text. The first stanza sets the basic pattern :

> He stood among a crowd at Dromahair ;
> His heart hung all upon a silken dress,
> And he had known at last some tenderness,
> Before earth took him to her stony care ;
> But when a man poured fish into a pile,
> It seemed they raised their little silver heads,
> And sang what gold morning or evening sheds
> Upon a woven world-forgotten isle
> Where people love beside the ravelled seas ;
> That Time can never mar a lover's vows
> Under that woven changeless roof of boughs :
> The singing shook him out of his new ease.

In the first stanza it is 'some tenderness' that he had known ; in the second stanza it is 'some prudent years' ; in the third stanza it is 'vengeance' that he 'mused upon' and in the final stanza it is 'unhaunted sleep' that he 'might have known'. Love, money-making, anger, and finally rest, represent the normal human lot. The hero of the poem had known something of the first and second, but was prevented from venting his anger on those that mocked him by a sudden revival of his awareness of the alien world of nature, and that awareness has since prevented him from finding peace in the grave.

The poem pivots on the single conjunction 'but', which opens the fifth line of each stanza except the last, which employs a slightly different construction with the same logical pattern. He was buying a silk dress for his girl, like any other man, but —. He was worrying about money like any other man, but —. He would have revenged himself on those that mocked him, but —. He might have rested in peace in the grave, but —. This seems an odd way in which to build up a poem, but in fact it succeeds remarkably well. The 'but' in each stanza introduces the result of the man's confrontation with nature. The results are disturbing. They do not involve simply the realization that nature is utterly different from the world of human emotions and plans ; rather, they suggest the existence of a world in which Time does not destroy and where all activity is part of the cosmic dance of life. Indeed, there is an anticipation here both of Yeats's later conception of Byzantium and of his later use of the idea of the Plotinian dance of life — though it was to be many years before he would read the books to which modern scholars have attributed his interest in these ideas. Here is the final stanza :

> He slept under the hill of Lugnagall ;
> And might have known at last unhaunted sleep
> Under that cold and vapour-turbaned steep,
> Now that the earth had taken man and all :
> Did not the worms that spired about his bones
> Proclaim with that unwearied, reedy cry
> That God has laid His fingers on the sky,
> That from those fingers glittering summer runs
> Upon the dancer by the dreamless wave.
> Why should those lovers that no lovers miss
> Dream, until God burn Nature with a kiss ?
> The man has found no comfort in the grave.

Yeats is here combining with his earlier recurring idea of the dichotomy between man and nature a view of the destructive consequences of being possessed by a vision. The vision comes through nature, and it is not entirely consistent, nor is it fully apprehended by the hero ; but its partial and confused character is a guarantee of its genuineness. There is nothing simple or comfortable or utopian about the vision man gets from nature : it may contain glimpses of Byzantium, but it does not give the peace and wholeness of Byzantium ; it disturbs and distracts, unfitting man for his place in the normal human world while not fitting him for any other. This is a very Irish poem, and the material comes from Irish folklore, but Yeats is here using Irish folklore for his own uncanny purposes. It is interesting to see how far he can go in this direction without using any of the apparatus he was later to

develop for himself in *A Vision*. There is a curious deadpan
tone in the poem which belies the strangeness of its content
and adds to its power. The movement from the first four lines
of each stanza through the essential 'but' to the distracting
vision is achieved with extraordinary calm ; the rhythms of
the poem are steady and even throughout. And the final line
— 'The man has found no comfort in the grave' — is done
almost with a shrug, an anti-climactic climax. In the second
stanza the disturbing knowledge comes to him from

> A lug-worm with its grey and muddy mouth.

This is not simply the nature imagery of an Irish poet brought
up on the Pre-Raphaelites. There is an anti-romantic use of
romanticism here which with our hindsight we can see was
surely going to lead to something even more interesting.

What one might pedantically call the mutations of the
two-term dialectic thus represent something of real interest in
the early Yeats, and one could follow them much further than
I have done here. I should like now to discuss another theme
or attitude (it is sometimes one and sometimes the other and
sometimes both) that can be traced in the very earliest poems
and which later becomes a distinguishing quality of much of
his greatest poetry. To turn once more to 'The Sad Shepherd'
(not an especially good but nonetheless an interesting poem) :
we find in the second line the phrase 'high comrade' (originally
'high kinsman'), and we may perhaps say to ourselves that
this use of the adjective 'high' comes from Yeats's preoccupation with Irish heroic legend and has something to do
with the sense of lineage, of heroic manners and of exhibitionist
courtesy which belongs to such literature. This is true
enough, but there are other things at work here as well. Here
is the first stanza of 'The Rose of the World' :

> Who dreamed that beauty passes like a dream ?
> For these red lips, with all their mournful pride,
> Mournful that no new wonder may betide,

Troy passed away in one high funeral gleam,
And Usna's children died.

This poem dates from 1891. Some nineteen years later, writing of Maud Gonne in 'No Second Troy', he talked of her beauty as

Being high and solitary and most stern.

In 'Adam's Curse' (1902), also referring to Maud Gonne, he wrote :

I had a thought for no one's but your ears :
That you were beautiful, and that I strove
To love you in the old high way of love ; . . .

These three examples will suffice. I want to draw attention to the early stage at which Yeats began to use the word 'high' to indicate the kind of aristocratic courtesy which he was later to associate with the life of the Great House, with art patrons of the Italian Renaissance, with 'innocence and beauty', with 'traditional sanctity and loveliness', with the tragic gaiety of Hamlet and Lear, and with the horseman who is enjoined to cast a cold eye on life and on death. There are many elements compounded here, but they can all be related, however circuitously, to Yeats's early admiration of the Irish heroic mode. It is difficult to over-estimate the influence on Yeats of Standish O'Grady's *History of Ireland, Heroic Period* (published in 1878). To O'Grady, wrote Yeats in 1914, 'every Irish imaginative writer owed a portion of his soul'. He went on : 'In his imaginative *History of Ireland* he had made the old Irish heroes, Fion, and Oisin, and Cuchullan, alive again, taking them, for I think he knew no Gaelic, from the dry pages of O'Curry and his school, and condensing and arranging, as he thought Homer would have arranged and condensed. Lady Gregory has told the same tales . . . but O'Grady was the first, and we read him in our "teens".'[1] Beside O'Grady's

[1] *The Autobiography of William Butler Yeats*, New York, 1938, pp. 189–90.

History must be set the influence of the character of John O'Leary, about whom Yeats wrote as follows in 1907:

> O'Leary had joined the Fenian movement, with no hope of success, as we know, but because he believed such a movement good for the moral character of the people; and had taken his long imprisonment without complaining. Even to the very end, while often speaking of his prison life, he would have thought it took from his Roman courage to describe its hardship. The worth of a man's acts in the moral memory, a continual height of mind in the doing of them, seemed more to him than their immediate result. . . . A man was not to lie, or even to give up his dignity, on any patriotic plea, and I have heard him say, 'I have but one religion, the old Persian: to bend the bow and tell the truth', and again, 'There are things a man must not do to save a nation', and again, 'A man must not cry in public to save a nation'. . . .[1]

We must bear this passage in mind when we read

> Romantic Ireland's dead and gone,
> It's with O'Leary in the grave,

if we want to be sure that we know what Yeats meant by 'Romantic'.

In the same essay as that in which he described O'Leary's character, Yeats wrote: 'Three types of men have made all beautiful things, Aristocracies have made beautiful manners, because their place in the world puts them above the fear of life, and the countrymen have made beautiful stories and beliefs, because they have nothing to lose and so do not fear, and the artists have made all the rest, because Providence has filled them with recklessness.'[2] Later in this essay he declared that 'in life courtesy and self-possession, and in the arts style, are the sensible impressions of the free mind, for both arise out of a deliberate shaping of all things, and from never being swept away, whatever the emotion, into confusion or dullness'.[3] And one could quote again and again from Yeats's prose writings to show his admiration for traditional courtesy,

---

[1] *Essays and Introductions*, London, 1961, p. 247.
[2] *Ibid.*, p. 251.   [3] *Ibid.*, p. 253.

his belief in the *gesture* (both in life and in art), his view that heroism, sternness and joy are related in both art and life. 'We will not forget how to be stern, but we will remember always that the highest life unites, as in one fire, the greatest passion and the greatest courtesy.'

The 'high funeral gleam' with which Troy passed away is thus an expression of heroic tragedy, of tragedy done with *style*, an idea that from a very early stage possessed Yeats's mind and continued to possess it until the end : we can set the line 'Gaiety transfiguring all that dread' from 'Lapis Lazuli' beside this line from 'The Rose of the World' as representing the final version of this idea. In his early poetry it is related to Irish heroic legend and history, and though later it becomes involved with many other sources this should not lead us to ignore the importance of the Irish elements in this characteristic Yeatsian notion. Yeats's admiration of the Great House tradition, which he came to see as standing for a way of life which converted chaos into order by custom and ceremony, is generally ascribed to the influence on him of Coole Park ; but in fact his view of the Irish past had already conditioned him to respond in this way, just as it later helped him to construct his own myth of a great eighteenth-century Anglo-Irish civilization which took in Swift, Berkeley, Sheridan, Goldsmith, Burke and Grattan.

Again and again in Yeats's early poetry we find Irish folklore, Irish heroic story, Irish history and even Irish landscape working in his imagination to mitigate the excesses of a self-indulgent romanticism, of mere dreaminess and decorativeness. Long before he knew Pound or became interested in Japanese Nō plays or came under any of those other influences which strengthened his belief in the importance of stylization in art, he had found Irish reasons for moving in the direction he was to sum up towards the end of his life in the lines beginning

> Irish poets, learn your trade,
> Sing whatever is well made,

Even the association of classical and Celtic myth in 'The Rose of the World'

> Troy passed away in one high funeral gleam,
> And Usna's children died.

helps to prevent the image of Helen of Troy from operating as a vague literary reference, concentrating it into a symbol of doomed heroic passion which stands in sharp contrast to the 'cloudy glamour' of his other early poems. His long-continued hopeless love for Maud Gonne also helped to concentrate his conception of the heroic relationship between beauty, dignity and destruction:

> What could have made her peaceful with a mind
> That nobleness made simple as a fire,
> With beauty like a tightened bow, a kind
> That is not natural in an age like this,
> Being high and solitary and most stern?
> Why, what could she have done, being what she is?
> Was there another Troy for her to burn?

These lines come somewhat later. We can see in the earlier poems more clearly the struggle between the vaguely plangent and the stylized heroic. In 'The Rose of Battle' we find:

> Rose of all Roses, Rose of all the World!
> You, too, have come where the dim tides are hurled
> Upon the wharves of sorrow, and heard ring
> The bell that calls us on; the sweet far thing.
> Beauty grown sad with its eternity
> Made you of us, and of the dim grey sea.

This is the early dream style, and adjectives like 'sweet', 'sad' and 'dim' and phrases such as 'the wharves of sorrow' proclaim very plainly to what literary world *this* poem belongs. Sometimes Yeats went over these early poems to change the romantic melancholy into heroic mourning, and the alteration is instructive. Thus the second stanza of 'The Sorrow of Love' originally read:

64

> And then you came with those red mournful lips,
> And with you came the whole of the world's tears,
> And all the sorrows of her labouring ships,
> And all the burden of her myriad years.

This was later changed to

> A girl arose that had red mournful lips
> And seemed the greatness of the world in tears,
> Doomed like Odysseus and the labouring ships
> And proud as Priam murdered with his peers ; . . .

The association of Homeric with Irish themes seems to have done Yeats nothing but good. The Helen-Deirdre identification provided him with many effective poetic attitudes, and sometimes we find even in his more plangent and melancholy lines something that reminds us of Homer in that mood of his that especially pleased Matthew Arnold — what one might call the more Virgilian Homer. It may be mere personal fancy to see in these lines from 'The Secret Rose' (1896)

> Who met Fand walking among flaming dew
> By a grey shore where the wind never blew,

the same kind of tone achieved by Homer in the twenty-third book of the *Iliad* when he describes the grieving Achilles after the death of Patroclus lying alone

> ἐν καθαρῷ, ὅθι κύματ' ἐπ' ἠϊόνος κλύζεσκον

in a lonely place where the waves plashed upon the shore,

but it is certainly true that Yeats in the 1890s was seeking and finding ways of associating the elegiac and the heroic so as simultaneously to discipline the former and humanize the latter.

The attempts are not of course always successful. Even the revised version of 'He Remembers Forgotten Beauty' (originally written in 1896) moves from sighing and kissing and 'white Beauty' to the high and the lonely in a way that does not really unite them :

> And when you sigh from kiss to kiss
> I hear white Beauty sighing, too,
> For hours when all must fade like dew,
> But flame on flame, and deep on deep,
> Throne over throne where in half sleep,
> Their swords upon their iron knees,
> Brood her high lonely mysteries.

But the association of the high and the lonely is interesting : we think of the line from 'No Second Troy', 'Being high and solitary and most stern' and his description of the Irish genius as 'distinguished and lonely'. And we know where this association will take Yeats eventually.

The dreamy and the disciplined are but two of the pairs of opposites that form the patterns of so many of Yeats's early poems, and it would be inaccurate to suggest that the former came from the 'companions of the Cheshire Cheese' and the latter from Irish heroic story. For one of the companions, Lionel Johnson, who much influenced Yeats, had from the beginning emphasized the importance of ritual and ceremony ; Yeats later talked about the 'austere nobility' of Johnson's verse and recalled his favourite adjective 'marmorean'. Later, the contrast between self-indulgent dream and heroic self-discipline gave way to profounder contrasts and complex resolutions — the contrast between 'the foul rag-and-bone shop of the heart' and the timeless world of art and artifice represented by Byzantium being only one modulation of the later pattern. But much of what is often regarded as uniquely belonging to the later Yeats can be found struggling to find expression in the earlier and occasionally succeeding. And even where this is not so, the simpler two-term dialectic of the earlier poems can yield something impressive and memorable more often than recent critics, with their eyes fixed almost solely on the later poems, are prepared to admit. As for what one might call the 'middle poems' — notably those in *The Green Helmet* and *Responsibilities* — they include 'No Second Troy', 'September 1913' and 'To a Shade', all admirable, as well as one of the most important statements of his heroic aesthetics, 'Upon a House Shaken by the Land Agitation'. Irish politics, too (as his Senate speeches show), stimulated Yeats's imagination to further work on the relation between good art and the good life. From the beginning he differed from most other members of the Rhymers' Club in rejecting the escapist view of art represented by the *fin-de-siècle* ideal. His question

> How should the world be luckier if this house
> Where passion and precision have been one
> Time out of mind, became too ruinous
> To breed the lidless eye that loves the sun ?
> And the sweet laughing eagle thoughts that grow
> Where wings have memory of wings, and all
> That comes of the best knit to the best ?

is a question about life, about civilization, about the relation between tradition and the present, as well as about art. The 'written speech/Wrought of high laughter, loveliness and ease' that he prescribed for citizens as well as writers may sound a utopian prescription in these days of mass media. But it represents something deeply pondered and deeply imagined, something that lay close to the core of Yeats's imagination, something that we can see developing in his poetry from a very early stage.

INGENIUM OMNIA VINCIT

*

HUGH MacDIARMID

'The stream has suddenly pushed the papery leaves !
It digs a rustling channel of clear water
On the scarred flank of Ben Bulben,
The twisted tree is incandescent with flowers.
The swan leaps singing into the cold air . . .'

A. J. M. SMITH

WHAT ARE THE WORDS on that stone ? Pilate's words which are the finest rejoinder in all literature to the captious and disputatious : *What I have written I have written.*

Earth has nowhere any grave so deep
As the power of utter withdrawal
Into yourself you had, and Death
no power to restore to life again
like your power, still and forever, to come back
Full of *brio* as if never away
and laughing like a better Lazarus.
(You who knew if Christ had made even one
Joke about sex what vast good He'd have done !)
What is the secret ? You never breathed her name
But the old woman in Euboea was your Muse
Whose lesson to man is not to abstract himself
From immersion in present experience.
So out of death arises fresh life, even as Kenelm's corpse
Touched off springs where it rested. So you practised her rites
That ward off the menace of death
And ensure that life be strong and vigorous
And no song ever a swan-song.

68

'HE TOO WAS IN ARCADIA': YEATS AND THE PARADOX OF THE FORTUNATE FALL

*

EDWARD ENGELBERG

I . . . believe that there [exists] in Ireland . . . an energy of thought about life itself, a vivid sensitiveness as to the reality of things, powerful enough to overcome all those phantoms of the night. Everything calls up its contrary, unreality calls up reality . . .

W. B. YEATS, 'First Principles' (1904)

' "I WANT TO SEE this Yeats thing . . ." She was awake now, and urgent.' The awake and urgent lady so eager to see 'this Yeats thing' is Carol Kennicott, heroine of Sinclair Lewis's *Main Street*. Place: Gopher Prairie, Minnesota; time: shortly before the first Great War; and the name of the 'Yeats thing': *The Land of Heart's Desire* (1894). Carol persuades her husband and they go to see the play (followed by one of Dunsany's !), but only momentarily is Carol able to enter into the make-believe which she desperately seeks as escape from a dull life. Briefly she is 'transported' to the world of thatched cottages and 'green dimness', 'caressing linden branches', 'twilight women' and 'ancient gods'. How romantic ! How different ! How appropriate to hear her counterpart, Mary, also doomed to the drudgery of the kitchen, saying :

> Come, faeries, take me out of this dull house !
> Let me have all the freedom I have lost ;
> Work when I will and idle when I will !
> Faeries, come take me out of this dull world . . .

Though Edmund Wilson saw 'nothing sinister about the Sidhe in themselves'[1] in Yeats's early work, Mary gets a good

---

[1] Edmund Wilson, *Axel's Castle*, New York, 1931, 1954, p. 30.

deal more than she bargained for in her encounter with the Sidhe : at the end of the play she lies dead on the stage. Against all the advice of those who knew the dangers of tampering with that 'other' world, Mary progressively succumbs to the lure of the faeries — until she pays with her life. Carol could not have salvaged much promise from the end of this play : perhaps that is why she finally decides not to leave Main Street.

Her first attempt to bring Yeats into her life occurs shortly after her marriage : she is sitting on a couch, 'her chin in her hands, a volume of Yeats on her knees', from which she is reading to a pair of unwilling ears. 'Instantly she was released from the homely comfort of a prairie town' : linnets, gulls, Aengus, kings, and a 'woeful incessant chanting' flood her imagination. 'Heh-cha-cha!' coughed Dr. Kennicott : the cough breaks the magic spell and one is naturally sorry for Carol (and for Yeats) ; and the yawning husband deserves to be called the country yokel that he is. Yet the poor doctor's cough had perhaps performed an unintentional service, for was Carol being drawn into that ambiguous twilight world which had claimed the life of Mary ?

I

The Island of Statues is juvenilia, and Yeats's decision to omit it from his canon is perfectly sound. But, mindful of Yeats's warning —

> Accursed who brings to light of day
> The writings I have cast away !

I think this early 'Arcadian Faery Tale', published when Yeats was twenty, is worth the risk even of a Yeatsian curse. Aside from the intrinsic curiosity which all juvenilia of a major poet in time arouse, the play is important for two reasons : it anticipates a view of Arcadia as a fallen Eden, and this carries important implications into the later poetry ; and it presents us with an early insight by a young poet into a crucial distinction — that between a state of 'happiness' and a state of 'peace'. Happiness, Yeats concludes in this play, is a condition of fallen man and of mortality; peace is the absence of conflict, and only those beyond mortality (faeries, gods, enchantresses) can possess it. Finally, *The Island of Statues* makes it very clear that when supernatural creatures intrude into — or are intruded upon by — the mortal world, the result is disastrous — depending, of course, on your point of view. Death comes to both mortals and non-mortals in this play, but for mortals death, he shows, already in this early play, is part of the price that 'living man' must pay for the laughter and joy of life.

There were, it is fair to say, moments when peace seemed possible as a human goal, as an escape from human misery: I am thinking of the late 'eighties when Yeats came to London and certainly found his peace disturbed by that cosmopolitan city as it had not been by the quieter Dublin where he wrote *The Island of Statues* (and surely not by the Sligo of childhood). Such hope seems devoutly wished for at least in 'The Lake Isle of Innisfree' — 'And I shall have some peace there, for peace comes dropping slow'. But a touch of irony colours the anecdote he later told to a B.B.C. audience on the origin of that poem. It seems that while walking down the Strand on a very hot day, he caught sight of a rotating ball on top of a jet of water in a shop window, and that reminded him, he said, of lake water lapping. Apparently it was an advertisement for a cooling drink. Everything calls up its contrary: and, indeed, sometimes reality called up unreality.

But such hope for peace was only passing. Soon Yeats returned to his earlier distinctions: 'happiness' was, by and large, the best a man could achieve in this life, even if all that happiness is paled by the perfection of faery land, as the man who 'dreams' of it discovers. Yeats's realization that happiness was neither peace nor perfection does not at first seem

71

profound : but it was perhaps the most significant insight of his youth. By 1900 he had strengthened his youthful insight with conviction, for by now he had made a choice between two views of life and death, both of which were well known to him — and attractive. One was embodied in Pater's *The Renaissance*, especially in the essay on Winckelmann and in its 'Conclusion'; the other in Symons's 'Conclusion' to *The Symbolist Movement in Literature*. Although Yeats made no unqualified choice, he emerged far closer to Pater than to Symons.

Since both books are often seen as a continuum to which the 'early' Yeats was a climax, it is salutary to see that the two 'Conclusions' are far more interesting for their extraordinary differences than for their similarities. Each book, though both deal with a 'school' of writers, is really an attempt to define the 'modern spirit'. Coming some thirty years after Pater's, Symons's 'Conclusion' points in quite another direction (Pater's 'Conclusion' is dated 1868). Indeed, there is no better way to gauge the striking difference between Pater's modern Hellenism and Symons's 'doctrine of Mysticism' and *fin-de-siècle* than a reading of these two books. Symons, a shrewd and perceptive critic, realized this himself when he introduced the American Modern Library edition of *The Renaissance* : he emphasizes Pater's devotion to 'earthly beauty . . . made by men' but adds, speaking more for himself than for others, 'It is a world into which we can only look, not enter, for none of us have his secret'.

At the risk of simplifying : Pater saw art as the best that life could offer while Symons saw death as the worst that life promised ; Pater saw art as a fulfilment of a life otherwise lacking in richness, while Symons recognized art as the only possible escape from life ; Pater asked us to open our senses as generously as we dared — and to engage in the modern world with fully opened eyes, while Symons pleaded, eloquently, that salvation lay in closing our senses, deadening them to reality. 'Our only chance,' writes Symons in the 'Conclusion' to *The Symbolist Movement*, 'in this world, of a complete happiness, lies in the measure of our success in shutting the eyes of the mind, and deadening its sense of hearing, and dulling the keenness of its apprehension of the unknown.' As for Pater, the present is, for Symons, quick and fleeting; but to become conscious of reality, to its 'blinding light', is to die in terror: 'it is with a kind of terror that we wake up':

> Till human voices wake us and we drown.

The great 'conspiracy' is to 'forget death': consciousness is threatening, and only in dreams can we escape the 'sterile, annihilating reality' of life, the dreams transfixed by art and religion.[1]

For Symons happiness was the safety of a shadowed darkness; for Pater it was the joy of light. The chief image of *The Symbolist Movement* is darkness; the chief image of *The Renaissance* is light, the clarity which Pater celebrated as the greatest achievement of Hellenism and its reincarnation in the Renaissance. It is altogether fitting that light should be the dominant image of a book which closes by extolling the example of Goethe, among whose dying words, it is reported, were: 'Mehr Licht'.

More light is what Pater wants in order to illuminate modern life and thus save us both from the darkness of what he over-anxiously feared as a medieval *contemptus mundi* as well as the darkness he saw lurking in the modern habit of too much 'speculation'. The last essay preceding the 'Conclusion' to *The Renaissance*, 'Winckelmann', is in date the earliest, but the essay is ultimately about Goethe and the modern spirit, bridging past glory and future promise: it is about those soul-searching questions which Pater, with

[1] Arthur Symons, *The Symbolist Movement in Literature*, London, 1899, pp. 171–2.

F

remarkable vision, already saw looming large at the end of the 'sixties. In the 'eighties and 'nineties these same questions tore violently into the lives of many who would end the century with something less than triumph. Pater's last essay thus dovetails neatly into his 'Conclusion', where the spirit of Hellenic light in 'Winckelmann' — its 'sharp edge of light' — kindles into the 'gemlike flame'.

The most obsessive question in 'Winckelmann' is : can the light be passed on to the modern age ? The Hellenic torch, so steadfast in its original clarity and sureness, had already been disturbed : nearly extinguished in the early Middle Ages, it had become a flame all aflutter, nervous and tenuous in Michelangelo, a little too intensely melancholy in Leonardo, in danger of too much shadow in Giorgione, dampened in the eighteenth century. But Goethe had given it new strength, had steadied it and lent it the fire of a modern sensibility. Could we now retain its power and its wisdom, or would an indifferent beak of a modern age drop us into another darkness ?

'Et ego in Arcadia fui' : thus the epigraph to 'Winckelmann', just as a similar epigraph had opened Goethe's *Italiänische Reise*. How does Pater mean us to take this Latin phrase, already a famous shibboleth of the elegiac tradition ? Is this nostalgia for an Arcadia once perfect, now irrecoverable ? The substance of 'Winckelmann' indicates the contrary : Arcadia *is* mortality, and we must not bewail elegiacally an irrecoverable loss but, rather, we must continue to celebrate the liveable — the possible — Arcadia, for all its fallen state.

And so Yeats means us to take his Arcadia in *The Island of Statues*, his 'Arcadian Faery Tale', for both Pater and Yeats refuse to acknowledge Death as a destroyer of a life not worth a *conscious* living. Death, for Yeats, was indeed the 'great enemy' who was often discourteous ; but he was never a *memento mori* from which he shrank in terror. In this he stands on the threshold of the kind of 'modernity' we now

74

associate with the name of Freud, for whom, ultimately, an unchallenged 'death wish' became untenable, and who in later life elevated Eros and the urge to live and set them bravely against all the terrors of the abyss into which no one had looked more deeply than he. Yeats and Pater both emphasized man's instinctual resistance to death and his corresponding urgency to cling to life despite the spectacle of its brevity and its sadness. In all religions, even in Christianity, Pater saw a 'pagan sentiment', which 'measures the sadness' of man when he thinks of death descending upon him from the 'irresistible natural powers'. Yet such fear was also 'the secret ... of his fortune', for it made him cling to life all the more : 'It is with a rush of home-sickness that the thought of death presents itself. [Pagan man] would remain at home for ever on the earth if he could.'[1] Yeats too saw all ancient people possessed by a 'melancholy', a trait which made them 'delight in tales that end in death and parting', not because they wished themselves to die, but because death seemed after all so final : 'Life was so weighed down by the emptiness of the great forests ... by the loneliness of much beauty ; and seemed so little and so fragile and so brief, that nothing could be more sweet in the memory than a tale that ended in death' — of others. As Yeats makes clear, men did not set to mourning for what the Fates had either bestowed or deprived, for 'such mourning believes that life might be happy were it different, and is therefore the less mourning'. Men mourned 'because they had been born and must die with their great thirst unslaked'.[2]

Yeats feared the loss of this 'old simple celebration of life tuned to the highest pitch' with the coming of the 'dangerous' revolution which might 'establish the scientific complement

[1] Walter Pater, *The Renaissance*, London and New York, 1893, pp. 212–13.
[2] 'The Celtic Element in Literature', *Essays and Introductions*, London, 1961, p. 182.

of certain philosophies that in all ancient countries sustained heroic art'.[1] It is only the *un*fulfilled man who can die heroically, the man who would stay on earth forever if he could : hence Yeats's own almost arrogant claim to his 'soldier's right' to 'live it all again', even the 'crime of death and birth'. The pagan yearning for life and earth, the resistance to death with its accompanying melancholy — these Yeats recognized as essential elements of the Celtic temper. And just as Pater knew that the primitive was eventually modified by Doric vigour and ascetic Christian discipline, so Yeats came to see that Celtic sorrow needed to be leavened by Greek 'proportions' and that melancholy must give way to 'tragic joy'.

Pater saw all of Europe balanced by the marriage of Faust and Helena, modern Europe and Hellenic Greece, the 'Romantic spirit' with its 'profound subjectivity of soul' wedded to 'transparency . . . rationality . . . desire of beauty. . . .' The matchmaker was, of course, Goethe : but would the marriage last ? 'Can we bring down that [Hellenic] ideal into the gaudy, perplexed light of modern life ?' asked Pater, and the image remains that of light. As any young man fresh from a reading of Kant and Hegel, and no doubt flushed to the cheeks with 'historical' self-awareness, Pater admitted that the Greeks had an easier world in which to attain unity, blitheness, repose. None the less, more than ever, he urged, we demand 'completeness' and 'centrality', and 'Goethe . . . ready to be lost in the perplexed currents of modern thought . . . defines, in clearest outline, the eternal problem of culture — balance, unity with one's self. . .'.[2]

It was Yeats's Unity of Being, but he knew that man runs his course 'between extremities', that 'vacillation' was the necessary condition of attaining balance. For Pater as for Yeats, Time is the ultimate measure of one side of reality — and of all mortality. Reality is neither a mystical union with God

---

[1] *Introduction* to *Fighting the Waves, Wheels and Butterflies*, London, 1934, p. 65.   [2] *The Renaissance*, pp. 240–2.

nor the terrible confrontation of alienation — it is both. It is for Yeats also the tumult of life under the semblance of order :

> Civilization is hooped together, brought
> Under a rule, under the semblance of peace
> By manifold illusion ; but man's life is thought,
> And he, despite his terror, cannot cease
> Ravening through century after century,
> Ravening, raging, and uprooting that he may come
> Into the desolation of reality: . . . ('Meru')

The numinous, never denied, leads to the phenomenal '[There are] certain abstract thinkers, whose measurements and classifications continually bring me back to concrete reality. . . .' This in Yeats's *Diary* of 1930. And further : 'An abstract thinker when he has this relation to concrete reality passes on both the thought and the passion ; who has not remains in the classroom'. He saw his whole life as a 'drama' in which he struggled 'to exalt and overcome concrete realities perceived not with mind only but as with the roots of my hair'.[1] He would be Sancho Panza to his own Don Quixote, ravening and raging through 'manifold illusion' into the 'desolation of reality' where acceptance became finally possible.

Like Pater, Yeats had to locate meaning in the life of 'perpetual motion', in the drama that both exalts and overcomes reality. Pater's challenge to modern times, voiced at the end of 'Winckelmann', was clear enough : can the artist deal with the 'conditions of modern life' ? Modern art, 'in the service of culture', must 'rearrange the details of modern life, so to reflect it, that it may satisfy the spirit'.[2] Spirit is reached through the sensible world. Here again is Yeats in his *Diary* : 'Through the particular we approach the Divine Ideas'.[3] To withstand modern life, said Pater, the spirit needs a 'sense of

---

[1] 'Pages from a Diary written in Nineteen Hundred and Thirty', *Explorations*, London, 1962, pp. 302–3. (Hereafter cited as *Diary*.)

[2] *The Renaissance*, p. 244.   [3] *Diary*, p. 299.

freedom', but gone forever was the 'naïve' freedom checked by the ultimate power of a superior force. If one looks carefully at Pater there is always a little of Darwin : 'The chief factor in the thoughts of the modern mind concerning itself is the intricacy, the universality of natural law, even in the moral order.' Yeats could never have said that, nor could he have agreed with Pater's philosophical cosmopolitanism : 'For us, necessity is not, as of old, a sort of mythological personage without us' — but he would have assented to what followed, namely that modern man lived in a kind of 'magic web woven through and through us . . . penetrating us with a network . . . bearing in it the central forces of the world'. This being so, 'Can art represent men and women in these bewildering toils so as to give the spirit at least an equivalent for the sense of freedom ?' An audacious question for a young Englishman to be asking in 1867, but Pater was under no illusions about modern life : it was neither to be avoided as ugly nor to be distorted by making it beautiful. It was what is was : 'this entanglement, this network of law . . . the tragic situation, in which certain groups of noble men and women work out for themselves a supreme *dénouement*'. Like Yeats, then, Pater saw life as a drama with its 'tragic situation', for we know Yeats's famous aphorism that we begin to live only when we have conceived of life as tragedy. And Pater's 'tragic situation' is never bemoaned. 'Who,' he asks in the final and eloquent sentence of 'Winckelmann', 'if he saw through all, would fret against the chain of circumstance which endows one at the end with those great experiences ?'[1]

'Experience' : it is the key word of Pater's famous 'Conclusion'. Only by refining experiences can man comprehend their seemingly meaningless, random and ceaseless assaults upon our senses. Death allows Pater to plead for life : 'this sense of the splendour of our experience and . . . its awful brevity' is what makes sense out of the 'one desperate

[1] *The Renaissance*, pp. 244–6.

effort to see and touch. . . .' If, as Pater quotes, from Hugo, '*les hommes sont tous condamnés à mort avec des sursis indéfinis*', we have at least the 'interval' of light, and our 'one chance' is to brighten it, by 'expanding that interval. . . .'[1] It is an echo of Faust's magnificent, hopeless — because all too human — cry to the moment, the *Augenblick*: 'Verweile doch, du bist so schön!' — a cry which he defiantly attempts to resist.

Yeats must have light, for 'the greater the passion the more clear the perception, for the light is perception', as he writes in his *Diary*. Conflict is a price we must pay: 'Passion is conflict, consciousness is conflict'. Like Pater's 'network' and 'tragic situation', it is a consciousness and conflict we dare not refuse. Symons's comfort lies in darkness, and his sense of freedom is neither Pater's nor Yeats's: it is the 'freedom of . . . sweet captivity' in the bosom of Beauty, and that is, warns Symons, a very perilous freedom indeed.[2] To release men from immobile captivity into the freedom of a world of risks is perhaps the major theme of Yeats's early play.

II

Set in Arcadia, *The Island of Statues* has, properly enough, a *dramatis personae* of shepherds and shepherdesses and the appropriate setting of woods and fields. Somehow Yeats also manages to place an island within his Arcadia, which is ruled by an Enchantress who has been busy for centuries turning to stone various individuals who have come to pluck a certain flower of magical properties but have failed to choose the correct one. The play opens as two crude shepherds quarrel over the fair Naschina who, of course, scorns both and is secretly in love with an Adonis named Almintor. In order to test his courage, Naschina eventually sends Almintor to the magic island, but he, as have all others in the past, fails the

---

[1] *Ibid.*, pp. 251–3. [2] *Diary*, p. 331; Symons, p. 175.

crucial test, chooses the wrong flower, and is summarily turned to stone. Only Naschina, we later learn, can save him, for she is fated to have the knowledge of the correct choice — though unconscious of that knowledge herself. Naschina hurries to the island disguised as a page and the Enchantress falls in love with her, a mistake that will cost her the power of rule. However, before plucking the correct flower, Naschina needs a human sacrifice, which she gets; once having over-come that last barrier, she undisguises herself, plucks the right flower, inherits the powers of the Enchantress — who must now die — and liberates all the statues on the island, turning them back into mortals. This, in brief, is the 'plot' of the play.

Yet it is the ending which is intriguing and one may work backwards through the play to glimpse Yeats's intention. As the play closes, the grateful humans, restored from their stony sleep, elect as their royal couple Naschina and Almintor. The final stage direction reads :

The rising moon casts the shadows of Almintor and the Sleepers far across the grass. Close by Almintor's side, Naschina is standing, shadowless.

The shadowless Naschina has replaced the Enchantress — this much we know ; she is no longer purely a mortal and per-haps was never intended to be, since she was 'fated' to rule by the pronouncements of some timeless prophecy or oracle.

Yeats is intent on emphasizing that his Arcadia is not timeless but a place in history : it has experienced Clytem-nestra, the 'fires of Troia', and Dido. A second essential idea, planted early in the play, is that 'Joy's brother, Fear, dwells ever in each breast' : it is Naschina who says this and it is also what prompts her to send Almintor on his dangerous quest for the flower. But, for all his courage, Almintor is a discouraged knight-errant, a melancholy youth for whom 'The whole world's sadly talking to itself'. Though such

Weltschmerz is common to youthful lovers in Arcadian circumstances, the point seems more insistent: Almintor's melancholy is that of a fallen Adam aware that he will disturb the ultimate Paradise. When he is about to arrive on the enchanted island a 'Voice', just before sensing the approach of some 'un-faery thing', tells us that it recalls 'When the tree was o'er-appled / For Mother Eve's winning / [I] was at her sinning'. This Arcadia is as old as Creation: it is a place not only of history but one in which history repeats itself in the obvious parallels of Almintor's and later Naschina's flower-picking and Eve's apple-plucking. A fallen Arcadia is not the conventional land of literature.

In his brilliant essay, 'Poussin and the Elegiac Tradition', Erwin Panofsky tells us that there have been traditionally two views of 'natural man': 'One view, termed "soft" primitivism . . . conceives of primitive life as a golden age of plenty, innocence and happiness . . . civilized life purged of its vices. The other, "hard" . . . conceives of primitive life as an almost subhuman existence full of terrible hardships . . . stripped of its virtues.' Arcadia has traditionally been associated with the 'soft' view — 'golden-age primitivism' — but Yeats's view of 'natural man' is really neither 'soft' nor 'hard'. The best we can safely say about the Arcadia of Almintor and Naschina is that it rather resembles the world itself, and that life here is accordingly also very much more the risky business we would expect outside Arcadia, not within it.

Panofsky's essay traces the origins and meanings, particularly in iconography, of the Latin phrase 'Et in Arcadia ego', a variant, we recall, of Pater's epigraph for 'Winckelmann'. Panofsky explains that the phrase meant both 'I, too, was born, or lived, in Arcady' and 'Even in Arcady, there am I' — the latter 'I' being Death, as in Poussin's two famous paintings. The second version is further divisible: either a 'thinly veiled moralism' which warns of Death's ubiquitousness, or as part of the 'elegiac sentiment', 'quiet, reminiscent meditation'. The later Poussin painting shows the Arcadians coming upon a tomb neither shocked nor surprised at discovering Death (as they were in the earlier painting) but rather 'immersed in mellow meditation on a beautiful past'. It is this latter attitude which Panofsky calls 'elegiac' and which, he claims, held sway, especially in England, where melancholia has been a consistently attractive and indulgent source for the arts. Again Yeats does not clearly fall into either subdivision — *memento mori* or elegiac — though quite possibly he knew of Poussin's paintings or some of their English imitations.[1]

Here is Naschina's speech to Almintor's page, just prior to leaving for her rescue mission to the island of statues :

> Antonio, if I return no more,
> Then bid them raise my statue on the shore . . .
>   . . . and no name gild ;
> A white, dumb thing of tears, here let it stand . . .
> And when the summer's deep, then to this spot
> The Arcadians bring, and bid the stone be raised
> As I am standing now . . .
> And once a-year let the Arcadians come,
> And 'neath it sit, and of the woven sum
> Of human sorrow let them moralize ;
> And let them tell sad histories, till their eyes
> All swim with tears . . .
> And let the tale be mournful each one tells.

Naschina's orders for her tomb are almost a poetic gloss on Poussin's later painting, 'Et in Arcadia ego', where the Arcadians, in melancholy attitudes, gather round the tomb and elegiacally contemplate Death. However, such a tomb will be unnecessary, for Naschina triumphs in a world that operates under something less than elegiacally Arcadian rules : instead of tombs being raised for her she raises the 'dead' to life. Ironically, it is precisely with her magical act of animating the

[1] Erwin Panofsky, '*Et in Arcadia Ego* : Poussin and the Elegiac Tradition', *Meaning in the Visual Arts*, New York, 1955, pp. 295–320.

statues, that the now supra-mortal Naschina violates the last island where reality had not prevailed. It is with magic that she destroys magic : what she will do with her powers henceforth no one knows.

This violation occurs immediately on Naschina's arrival at the island. The Guardians of the flowers, hitherto innocent of 'grief or care', are filled with 'sudden melancholy' : it is they who sit in mournful repose, singing baleful words in anticipation of some vague disaster. While awaiting the human sacrifice which must be made for Naschina before she can successfully choose the right flower, the Enchantress and the disguised Naschina converse about the central issue of the play : what is happiness ?

Still duped by Naschina's disguise, the Enchantress snatches Naschina's laughter, cherishing this as a great conquest, for 'e'en the fay that trips / At morn, and with her feet each cobweb rends, / Laughs not. / It [laughter] dwells alone on mortal lips . . .' Laughter, then, is a human privilege denied even to the 'happiest' of faeries. Or *are* faeries 'happy' ? The Enchantress makes the distinction :

Thou'lt teach me laughing, and I'll teach thee peace . . .
For peace and laughter have been seldom friends.

To the insistent questions put to her by Naschina — is she 'happy' ? — the Enchantress answers only : 'Youth, I am at peace'. And peace, it is clear, is a condition no mortal can know : it is hearing 'Mid bubbling leaves a wandering song-rapt bird / Going the forest through', or seeing 'with visage meek, / A hoary hunter leaning on his bow'. Peace is an experience 'deeper than men know'. Those vignettes of 'peace' which the Enchantress describes are, like the 'Cold Pastoral' of Keats's urn, Attic shapes in 'Fair attitude ! with brede / Of marble men and maidens overwrought' — indeed like the Sleepers on the island, themselves turned from humans into 'attitudes' of stone.

Such peace then is also the source of the Enchantress's power ; and to break the spell of that peace, and with it the power, Naschina must now pluck the magic flower. The results will be no less far-reaching than Eve's plucking of the apple, for Sin and Death now enter the last sanctuary on Arcadia — the island itself. On the verge of death, the Enchantress prophesies a not altogether promising future for Naschina : she shall 'outlive' her own 'amorous happy time' and be witness to the death of her lover ; she shall be committed to 'dream*less* truth', and her soul, 'pitiless and bright', shall, like her beauty, 'fail . . . day and night / Beneath the burthen of the infinite, / In those far years'.

Burdened with immortality, Naschina inherits ceaseless life but a failing soul, no longer human. When Naschina beholds only the traces of a dead green frog where once the powerful Enchantress ruled she exclaims :

> O Arcady, O Arcady, this day
> A deal of evil and of change hath crossed
> Thy peace . . .

Realizing that the 'fall' has truly come to pass, Naschina now prepares to make the best of things : her first act is to awaken the Sleepers on the island. Again we are reminded how old this Arcadia is, for the Sleepers ask about Dido and Troy, Arthur and Pan, and for each the answer is the same : 'He is long dead', or 'Nay, he is gone. Wake ! wake !' And awake they do, not into an immortal world of peace but into a mortal world of happiness — and death. In that state of 'happiness' Almintor and Naschina are chosen as their royal couple 'Until we die' — for they know that die they now must, in the natural course of time. But Naschina must know that she will outlive their happiness, that she will be soon without a husband and without laughter, for the sun fails to throw its light, and hence her shadow, on the grass. The price of happiness and laughter is mortality ; the price of mortality is

Death. The fall of man is therefore — as we have been told
from the perspective of theology — 'fortunate' in the context
of Yeats's Arcadian play.

III

The opening poem to Yeats's *Collected Poems*, 'The Song
of the Happy Shepherd', was originally the Epilogue to *The
Island of Statues* and to another work of his youth, *The Seeker*.
As the Epilogue, it was called 'Song of the Last Arcadian',
and that the 'last Arcadian' should be singing a 'happy' song,
whose opening words are 'The woods of Arcady are dead',
is in itself suggestive. Far from being a lament for a lost
Arcady, the poem is, rather, an attempt to come to terms with
that loss. What the shepherd tells us is that, indeed, Arcady
is dead, the old order is gone, and the world now feeds on
'Grey Truth' in place of 'dreams'. The only remedy appears
to be to tell one's tale to a seashell which, in turn transmuting
that tale into 'melodious guile', will retell it. So in a sense
Yeats at twenty envisions the seashell as his symbol or mediator
between artistic impulse and articulation. Since Arcady is
now dead, the only recourse for the poet is to keep it alive
through poetry: 'Words alone are certain good . . . / The
kings of the old time are dead'. Indeed, the whole world may
be merely a 'sudden flaming word' — a view of a self-
generating and world-creating Imagination which Yeats never
entirely abandoned as at least one half of an antinomy of his
vision of reality. The final injunction of the shepherd is to
dream, for both dreaming and singing are not elegiac requiems
for a dead past but stratagems of art for preserving a once
enviable world. It is true that Yeats would learn, in time, to
rely less on the sovereignty of both words and dreams: in
both, he would discover, begin responsibilities.

Yet the poem is very close to Pater's 'Winckelmann' and
his 'Conclusion', to Pater's recognition that Greek serenity is
gone forever, that the modern world is feverish and disturbing,

but that our only salvation lies in creating an art which at once
celebrates the past while fixing its vision on the future, an art
written *in* the present. The shepherd in the first poem of
Yeats's work is happy in the certainty that art alone is 'good';
Yeats then wrote a parallel poem, 'The Sad Shepherd', in
which a self-pitying creature, a friend to Sorrow, bewails his
state to an audience he can nowhere find. Stars, dew-drops,
and seashell, each in turn, refuse to hear his 'heavy story'.
His only aim is to send sadness through his listeners, and such
simplistic attempts to find a listener in order that one's 'burden
may depart' through a kind of art-as-therapy Yeats does not
allow. Indeed the seashell changes the shepherd's tale of
sorrow — 'Changed all he sang to inarticulate moan / Among
her wildering whirls, forgetting him'. No warning could be
clearer: the poet must not succumb to mere self-pity; he
must not write simply to rid himself of sorrow, lest his tale be
doomed to dissolve into 'inarticulate moan'. In no way does
the happy shepherd advise that we ignore reality; and his
happiness comes in part from confronting the reality of its
loss and finding his defences in 'words': he is dedicated to
self-trust, but not to self-pity, not to a wasteful regret for a
vanished past.

To 'dream' is not to forget: as Richard Ellmann recently
suggested, the word is extraordinarily important and difficult
in Yeats's poetry.[1] We would expect to find the word
'dream' frequently in Yeats's early poetry and so we do.
Though it disappears almost entirely from *Responsibilities*
(1914), it reappears in *The Wild Swans at Coole* (1919) and
thereafter contributes to major lines of major poems: 'I
dream of a Ledaean body', 'there is no deformity / But saves
us from a dream', 'When sleepers wake and yet still dream',
'Man makes a superhuman / Mirror-resembling dream',
'Phidias / Gave women dreams and dreams their looking-

[1] Richard Ellmann, 'Yeats Without Analogue', *Kenyon Review*
(Winter, 1964), pp. 30–47.

glass'. In two poems, especially, the word functions rather dramatically and gives some indication of the subtlety with which Yeats used such words.

In 'The Fisherman' Yeats repudiates the audiences that have scorned him (and Synge) and creates in his imagination 'A man who does not exist, / A man who is but a dream'. To take 'dream' here as wish-fulfilment or escape from realities that are unpleasant to confront is a misreading. For Yeats the dreamer is also the creator : we 'Dream and so *create* / Translunar Paradise'. So in 'The Fisherman' Yeats recognizes that what does not exist must be created, by 'God-appointed Berkeley' or by the poet. As in the later poem, 'The Statues', Yeats envisions the creations of types that, ideally, a culture can emulate : if fishermen do not exist he must 'dream' them — that is, create them. The entire *dramatis personae* of the later poetry function as so many rubrics of the master builder who rearranges with his 'mythy mind' — to borrow a phrase from Wallace Stevens — the fictive world become real.

Why '*Broken* Dreams'? This beautiful love poem in which the poet dreams of his beloved whom he shall meet again in 'the first loveliness of womanhood' is Yeats's clearest poetic embodiment of what was surely one of his main beliefs : that the 'correspondence' of heaven must never distort, through perfection, the realities lived on earth. Though beautiful, the beloved had a flaw : the 'small hands were not beautiful'. The line hurts as it withers into the truth, and the image following is almost surrealistic and grotesque : 'And I am afraid that you will run / And paddle to the wrist / In that mysterious, always brimming lake', where there *are* perfect beings. A plea concludes the poem that she 'Leave unchanged / The hands that [he has] kissed, / For old sake's sake', the possessive 'sake' implying 'cause' or even 'crime' (else the phrase makes no sense). For the sake of preserving the violation of perfection keep your imperfection in Paradise, keep your dream broken.

The insistence in 'The Fisherman' that dreams create a reality and in 'Broken Dreams' that a broken reality must remain broken even in dreams suggests something of the difficulties of the word in Yeats's poetry : we must be always on guard when we call him a 'dreamer'. No doubt that the dream — word and experience — undergoes transformations from youth to age ; but the later poetry is again an attempt to 'create' new dreams, in that special sense in which the dreaming sleepers of *The Island of Statues* are awakened into the dream of reality :

> Resemble forms that are or seem
> When sleepers wake and yet still dream,
> ('Under Ben Bulben')

As dreams became realized, or defeated, Yeats searched anew : though he knew that 'The painter's brush consumes his dreams ' — and so the poet's must consume *his* ? — the heart remains a 'resinous . . . foul rag-and-bone shop'. Like the awakened sleepers in Yeats's juvenile Arcadian fantasy, Yeats's poetry progressively moves towards a certainty : living dreams and dreaming life are part of a single and indivisible process. So the final line of Yeats's opening poem, 'Dream, dream, for this is also sooth', remains consistent. When dreams have gone he must create new ones and re-dedicate his imagination : to escape from the ghetto of a dreamless imagination into an 'acre of green grass' ; to redeem the soul from the pawnshop of exhausted dreams and in exchange purchase something from the heart ; to prove once more that 'He that sings a lasting song / Thinks in a marrow-bone'. Yeats was a consistent economizer : one feels he held many dreams in escrow, and they would have begotten many more still had life granted him not only an old man's frenzy but more time.

Yeats's dreams were, initially, dreams of 'islands'. 'I am haunted by numberless islands . . . / Where Time would surely forget us, and Sorrow come near us no more', cries the lover in 'The White Birds', an early poem. The early Yeats was indeed haunted by islands : besides *The Island of Statues* there was Oisin's odyssey to the three islands and islands in many poems, all traditionally used as places out of Time where Yeats, conventionally, located his faeryland. But just as Yeats needed to sail the seas — literally and meta-phorically — from his own island to other continents, so islands began to disappear from his poetry, and in 'The Circus Animals' Desertion', 'sea-rider Oisin' is recalled as having been 'led by the nose / Through three enchanted islands, allegorical dreams . . .' All the islands were humanly unendurable : 'Vain gaiety, vain battle, vain repose'. Vain because, as also in the *Odyssey*, Time is also Memory which brings men back to what they have abandoned : country, soil, wife, child — joy and sorrow. Eternal peace is for Oisin, as for Odysseus, the promise of uncertain happiness, and it is indeed Sorrow which beckons Oisin to return to the real world, and to abandon the 'dreams of the islands . . .'.

In *The Island of Statues* Yeats, in violating that special refuge within Arcadia with human happiness, and hence with sorrow, had already destroyed his 'islands' though he was not then aware of it. When Pater said that the arts of the future are no longer sculpture and painting but music and poetry, he meant that the former arts had expressed, to perfection, a repose that was no longer suited to the motions of modern life. It is certainly interesting that Yeats should so early have envisioned an island of statues which quite literally comes to life. In 'The Statues' those Grecian forms 'moved or seemed to move / In marble or in bronze' : they are not humans turned to stone but the artifacts that humans may kiss, thus joining life and art, animation and repose, without the aid of an intercessory magician. Perhaps this tells the parable of Yeats's journey from islands, statues, and magicians to art within history, and to 'living man' alone. From that point of view his poetic journey reverses Shakespeare's, and — from a naïver perspective, of course — Prospero and Perdita begin, rather than end, his creative life.

IV

We must not be too harsh with Carol Kennicott for misreading some of Yeats's early poetry in Gopher Prairie, Minnesota. In an essay written more than twenty years ago, Allen Tate was convinced that Yeats's poetry was 'nearer the centre of our main traditions of sensibility of thought than the poetry of Eliot or Pound', but he foresaw — correctly — that there would be some delay in such a valuation of Yeats. He also prophesied, again accurately, that '. . . Yeats's romanticism will be created by his critics'.[1] Of course one must always be cautious with Yeats, and to rid him of all 'romanticism' in his early verse by reshaping him into the suave and sophisticated Villon of thirty that undoubtedly he wished to be at twenty-five is as perverse as to make him purely a poet of the *symboliste* movement or a major figure of the English 'nineties. Clearly we must also not overstress the 'toughness' of the 'point of view' in the early verse as if that were an effective cover for its obvious 'vapour' of language or as if, in re-examining the totality of a great poet, we are now anxious to find aspects of his work admirable which we had hitherto regarded more critically. That way lies bardolatry and we should have none of that now. But Mr. Tate's warnings were real enough : Yeats simply never was the total romantic or aesthete that provides critics with a label for his 'early period'. In a recent phrase by David Daiches Yeats was, from the first, a kind of 'practical visionary'.[2]

[1] Allen Tate, 'Yeats's Romanticism : Notes and Suggestions', reprinted in *The Permanence of Yeats*, ed. James Hall and Martin Steinmann, New York, 1950, p. 105.

[2] David Daiches, 'The Practical Visionary', *Encounter*, xix (September, 1962), p. 71.

The major emphasis here has been to show this by illuminating his earliest distinction between 'happiness' and 'peace', a separation that permanently influenced all the subsequent work. I have already mentioned Freud's increasingly emphatic conclusion that man must cast his lot with life against death, with Eros against the imposing enemies ranged against him. Freud, no more than Yeats, could imagine conscious man at 'peace'; but happiness was not impossible. The possibilities of achieving happiness are the central theme of *Civilization and its Discontents*, as it is of much of Yeats's poetry. Freud and Yeats, each clear-sighted men, put enormous faith in Eros, though neither flinched from the world of violence, death and aggression. Each was in his way an exile; each died away from home in the same year; and both suffered much and endured it with dignity, and with a faith in life.

'Civilized man', said Freud, 'has exchanged a portion of his possibilities of happiness for a portion of security' — the security of becoming, and remaining, a 'community'. Yeats placed a high premium on the proper sort of 'community': it is difficult to imagine that he would have found anything to disagree with in this sentence of Freud's book: 'civilization is a process in the service of Eros, whose purpose is to combine single human individuals, and after that families, then races, peoples and nations, into one great unity, the unity of mankind'.[1] Such an ideal is increasingly made possible, according to Freud, as man rids himself of 'guilt' and 'remorse', acts of self-acceptance and self-forgiveness which allow Eros to take the measure of Death: '. . . Measure the lot; forgive myself the lot ! / When such as I cast out remorse / So great a sweetness flows into the breast / We must laugh and we must sing . . .'[2]

[1] *Civilization and its Discontents*, tr. and ed. James Strachey, New York, 1961, pp. 62, 69.
[2] 'A Dialogue of Self and Soul'.

'Words alone are certain good' and 'We must laugh and we must sing'; still the human laughter which the Enchantress, at peace as she was, so much envied in *The Island of Statues*, and the song which the happy shepherd sings. With that laughing and singing we have come almost full circle, and this is the mature vision of the 'human condition' Yeats offers but a decade or so before he died. It is true that Yeats was often bitter; so was Freud: neither might have believed so much in Eros and in self-forgiveness had they not been spared the horrors of the war that was to come. Yet even now, when hatred and guilt rule over Eros, their vision can still teach. Their acceptance of life was not stoical: it was the plea for 'Mehr Licht' of the dying Goethe, the benediction of sweetness and light of Arnold, the celebration of Hellenic light which Pater expressed so eloquently. Yeats chooses as his 'emblem' of life the day against the night, the shining, razor-keen blade of Sato's sword, 'still like a looking glass / Unspotted by the centuries . . .'.

The recently published *Concordance* of Yeats's poetry confirms his reputation as a man of dualistic vision for, give or take a few variants, 'light' and 'dark', 'life' and 'death' occur with almost equal frequency in his poetry. Certainly Yeats was aware of Death and of the price of mortality as a very young poet, which is not to say that he had not *been* in Arcadia: he was there, as were Goethe and Pater. But Yeats's Arcadia, as a fallen Eden, makes mortality worth its own rewards, and the 'fall' is therefore 'fortunate'. I do not know what his dying words were, but 'Mehr Licht' would have suited him as well as they had Goethe. After all, for all the use Yeats makes of the moon it is the full moon which brightens all into perfection and beauty. Nor would we expect Yeats to forget the light of day, 'solar light, intellectual light; not the lunar light, perception'. Upon that solar light he bestowed the quality of 'changeless purity'.[1]

[1] *A Vision* (1937), p. 220.

YEATS ON SPENSER

*

A. G. STOCK

I

EVEN AS A YOUNG MAN, dedicated to poetry though he was, Yeats could never keep wholly aloof from the world. He was full of convictions and social passion which he could not help taking seriously although his conscience, his father and his companions of the Cheshire Cheese combined to tell him that it was treason to the goddess. Between 1887 and 1902 he formulated to himself most of the leading ideas that were to serve him for the rest of his life. They were kept out of his poetry till much later, because as he said, it took time to distinguish 'truths that belong to us from opinions caught up in casual irritation or momentary fantasy',[1] but they are scattered through the prose writings of those years, and often one can see the process of sifting and integrating at work. It took shape against a background meditation on poetry which, because it was continuous and was the centre of all his thinking, was as much a part of his formative experience as his encounters with the men, women and events of the world around him.

Four poets in particular influenced the course of this meditation. Before he was twenty he read Spenser and Shelley and tried to combine their styles in a poetic drama that he left out of his collected poems. When he was twenty-two he first came under the lasting spell of William Morris's personality (he must have known some of his poetry a good

[1] W. B. Yeats, *Autobiographies*, London, 1955, p. 189.

93

deal earlier).[1]   From 1889 to 1893 he was at work, in partnership with Edwin Ellis, on editing and interpreting William Blake.   Spenser perhaps meant least to him of the four, nevertheless he was a catalyst of many thoughts.

II

His later dislike of *The Island of Statues*[2] is rather like a grown man's embarrassment when the photo of a baby, all too unmistakably himself, is passed round for admiration.   All the same it is a good poem of its own imitative kind.   The colouring, and the singing voice of many lyric passages, come from Shelley.   The Shelleyan ardours are in it too, but disciplined and distanced, partly by a certain formality in the verse that he must have learnt from Spenser, partly by a tinge not so much of satire as of courtly irony that is authentically Spenser's in one of his moods, partly too by a youthful heartlessness of Yeats's own.   At twenty he might have little to say, but he knew how to learn his craft discriminatingly from more than one master.

Spenser perhaps dropped from his thoughts after that, but returned for a passing mention in 1892, when Tennyson died, in a letter to *The Bookman* about the laureateship.[3]   He claims, rather unexpectedly, that it should be 'nationalized', stripped of its traditional obligation to celebrate royalty and bestowed as an honour on the leading poet of the people ;   for kings and nobles are no longer what once they were, a focus for the imagination of common men.   He wants the wreath to go to William Morris, or failing him to Swinburne, but surely neither will touch it while the smell of the court hangs round it.

[1] *The Letters of W. B. Yeats*, London, 1954, p. 46 (To Katharine Tynan, Summer 1887) : 'Morris's chief woman, I suppose, is Gudrun . . . but it is some years since I read the poem'.
[2] *The Variorum Edition*, London, 1957, pp. 644–79.
[3] *The Letters*, p. 219.

We can only just tolerate Spenser's comparison of the Queen of the Fairies to Queen Elizabeth, for even then all such comparisons were growing obsolete ...

and the dedication of *The Idylls of the King* to Queen Victoria was beyond forgiveness.

Yeats was full of Morris at the time, and there is a visible struggle here to fuse his own hierophantic notion of poetry with Morris's zeal for the common people. A touch of the Irish nationalist's mockery of his rulers' antics goes into the picture too, for there is little to show that such comparisons were growing obsolete in Elizabethan English eyes, however inept they were felt to be for Queen Victoria. It is one of his earliest attempts to think sociologically about poetry : the incentive is from Morris, and though it leads up a blind alley it contributes something to his later assessment of Spenser.

Ten years later a publisher offered him £35 for a selection from Spenser's poems with an introductory essay. The money was tempting, the work not too uncongenial. 'I have a good deal to say about Spenser', he wrote to Lady Gregory, 'but tremble at the thought of reading his six books.'[1]

III

Yeats cared too much for poetry to deny it where he found it, but in other ways he had little of the scholar's detachment ; he was too much bent on combining all his understanding of experience into a single inclusive philosophy. When he re-read Spenser there was much in his mind that the young author of *The Island of Statues* had not troubled about. Ireland had absorbed his thoughts for at least fifteen years, and he had both asserted and acted on the conviction that literature and nationality were indispensable to each other. He had identified what he hated in England, and hoped to keep out of Irish life and thought, as the spirit of commercialism

[1] *Ibid.*, p. 365 (20 January 1902).

and the worship of size and power for themselves. His study of Blake, and of his own poetry, had made him think deeply about symbolism and distinguish it from allegory.[1] And quite recently he had been preoccupied with another but related theory, about poetry and tradition.

> I would, if I could, add to that majestic heraldry of the poets, that great and complicated inheritance of images which written literature has substituted for the greater and more complex inheritance of spoken tradition, some new heraldic images, gathered from the lips of the common people.

This is in the preface to the third edition of his poems, dated January 1901.[2] The idea is elaborated in the essay of the same year called *What is Popular Poetry?*[3] All genuine poetry, he claims, belongs to one tradition, 'the unwritten tradition which binds the unlettered, so long as they are masters of themselves, to the beginning of time and the foundation of the world'. It is woven of immemorially old associations of thought and image too subtle for the logical intellect to trace, and is therefore strange and obscure. The common people have always liked it that way, just as they like a craftsman to know technical secrets that can be explained to no one not of his trade, and the literate poetry of 'courts and coteries' is a stylized offshoot from it. The versifiers of straightforward thoughts, in words with the minimum of reference outside their immediate context, are poets only for the raw middle class, cut off by literacy from the unwritten and by imperfect culture from the written tradition.

In the main, this is a way of reconciling Yeats's admiration for the country people of western Ireland with the rather mannered poetry he himself was writing. It also makes room for William Morris and his democratic medievalism, and

[1] See particularly the essays on *Symbolism in Painting* (1898), *The Symbolism of Poetry* (1900) and *Magic* (1901) in *Essays and Introductions*, London, 1961. [2] *The Variorum Edition*, p. 847.
[3] *Essays and Introductions*, pp. 3–7.

isolates, as the enemy of poetry, the hated modern middle class. The talk he listened to in Morris's circle must have made him more aware of social conflict than he was when he wrote 'To Ireland in the Coming Times' : he was constrained now to justify his art against a background of social revolutionary as well as of nationalist politics. But it became one of the durable pillars of his thinking : the essence of it is taken up in his poetry even thirty years later :

> We were the last romantics — chose for theme
> Traditional sanctity and loveliness,
> Whatever's written in what poets name
> The book of the people.[1]

IV

With so much to go into it the essay on Spenser became a problem in construction. All his thinking about generalities could not rob Yeats of his delight in Spenser's art, recaptured from boyhood when his mind was not on the poet or his times but the timeless enchanted world he created. There is a passage of close critical comparison between Spenser's verse and Shelley's that brings out Yeats's indefatigable craftsmanship.[2] Since in *The Island of Statues* he had avoided, deliberately as it seems, the troubled rhythm and vague suggestiveness he notes in Shelley, he may have thought out part of it even at that early age. The delight is now mixed with hatred of the ruthless civil service intelligence that could write the *View of the Present State of Ireland* ; yet even from that horrifying government report Yeats cannot withhold his admiration, commending 'that powerful and subtle language of his which I sometimes think more full of youthful energy than even the language of the great playwrights'[3] — and quoting a substantial passage to show what he means. He makes no attempt to pretend that Spenser's inhumanity spoilt his prose.

[1] 'Coole Park and Ballylee, 1931.'
[2] *Essays and Introductions*, p. 379.   [3] *Ibid.*, p. 373.

He needed a generalization to pick out what he admired in Spenser from what he rejected and make it fit in with the rest of his thought. What he admired was not the too-straight-forward allegory, but the glorification of life that the allegory so often seemed to be fighting down. A sudden illumination came, and he wrote to Lady Gregory :

I had no sooner begun reading in the British Museum after my return when it flashed upon me that the Coming of Allegory co-incided with the rise of the Middle Class. That it was the first effect on literature of the earnest spirit which afterwards created Puritan-ism. I have been hunting through all sorts of books to verify this and am now certain of it.[1]

The suitability of this theory to all that he wants to say is obvious ; its chief drawback is the difficulty of squaring it with the facts of history. How for instance, without being modified out of all meaning, will it cover Dante and Chrétien de Troyes and Chaucer himself ? Yeats soon discovered this, or someone pointed it out, for five days later he had changed a social for a racial hypothesis and told Lady Gregory :

I am basing the whole thing on my conviction that England up to the time of the Parliamentary War was the Anglo-French nation and that the hitherto conquered Saxon elements rose into power with Cromwell. This idea certainly makes my essay very striking, it enables me to say all kinds of interesting things about that time.[2]

This idea, too, appears to have been toned down before the essay went to the publisher some three weeks later. His next report says :

It is much saner than it was and yet quite as original. It is all founded on a single idea — the contrast between Anglo-French England and Anglo-Saxon England.[3]

The shift, in a month's work, in his view of his own theories is interesting. The first 'flashed on him' and became a certainty which he felt he had already verified by research.

[1] *The Letters*, p. 386.   [2] *Ibid.*, p. 387.   [3] *Ibid.*, p. 391.

The second was simply 'my conviction', put forward without objective proof and justified, a shade disingenuously, by the striking things it enabled him to say; finally it was reduced to 'a single idea' to hold the essay together. In much the same way, when the Communicators came years later to set his whole philosophy in order, he saw them first as messengers of a revelation he would gladly spend the rest of his life proclaiming, but quickly learnt that their true mission was to give him 'metaphors for poetry'.[1]

V

The idea, however doubtful, does serve his purpose, which is not to write history but to organize all he has to say about Spenser and his age. 'Anglo-French' does duty for everything in the Elizabethan world that belonged to what he recognized as the tradition of poetry; 'Anglo-Saxon', tendentiously, for 'earnestness and logic and the timidity and reserve of a counting-house'.[2] What he saw in Spenser was an English poet writing for most of his life in Ireland where he had no roots. He could feel the beauty of its woods and waters, but his office in the service of an alien government cut him off from the imaginative life of its people: he never knew that the men he harried through those woods drew on the storehouse of unwritten tradition to fill their verses with the same images of passion and fantasy that were filtered down to himself through the written literature of Europe. For by right of his themes Spenser belonged with the poets of the Red Branch and the Fianna.

And yet not altogether. His glorification of Elizabeth was not, like the older poets' stories of Charlemagne or of the Round Table, the expression of an age-old delight in heroic living so much as a figure of speech for the new religion of the State. Through Gloriana his allegory tried to equate the

---

[1] *A Vision*, London, 1962, p. 8.
[2] *Essays and Introductions*, p. 368.

whole duty of man with the service of the State — and the result was his acceptance of a government policy of genocide and his embodiment of ideal justice in the form of Artegall with his Iron Servant. It is likely that Yeats's reflections on Spenser went some way to clarify, though not to phrase, his distrust of those political abstractions to which 'Too long a sacrifice / Can make a stone of the heart'.[1]

They also occasioned some further thinking about allegory, and by bringing it into the context of politics welded together two sides of his thought. There are moments when Spenser's allegory melts into vision, as in the 'Garden of Adonis' in Book III and the 'Vision of Scudamour' in Book IV of *The Faerie Queene*. Then the images take on a life of their own, take control of the meaning, say what could not be said in any other way. But most of the time it uses concrete images to illustrate some abstract idea, already clearly understood and formulated, so that the visible objects are robbed of all meaning beyond their reference to abstractions ; and then Spenser's anxiety to edify brings him too near the 'popular poetry' that Yeats condemns. He tries too hard to be a man of his age, committed to an ideology that his poetry must expound and inculcate. And against this 'committed' seriousness Yeats sets the dramatists whose irresponsible imagination

put on something of the nature of eternity. Their subject was always the soul, the whimsical, self-awakening, self-exciting, self-appeasing soul. They celebrated its heroical, passionate will going by its own path to invisible and immortal things.[2]

It was his father, when Yeats was still a schoolboy, who taught him to love the dramatists for exalting passionate personality above the moral and intellectual codes that seek to contain it.

There seems to be no reason for Yeats to remember this essay for years. It was a job done to order, completed, despatched and paid for, and once out of his hands was not even

[1] 'Easter 1916'.
[2] *Essays and Introductions*, p. 370.

published till 1906. But passion has a way of overflowing, cooling itself on whatever object comes in its way and making that object memorable by association, and it is possible that some burst of indignation against Maud Gonne was worked off on Spenser. However that may be, seventeen years later when he wrote 'A Prayer for My Daughter', after speaking of the 'intellectual hatred' that had destroyed Maud Gonne, he described its opposite in almost the very phrases of this passage :

> Considering that, all hatred driven hence,
> The soul recovers radical innocence
> And learns at last that it is self-delighting,
> Self-appeasing, self-affrighting,
> And that its own sweet will is Heaven's will ;

There are other points that could be picked out to show how closely this essay on Spenser is linked with all Yeats's thinking, past and to come. I do not want to suggest that his study of Spenser was crucial to his development in any special sense hitherto unrecognized. As a rule he chose his own subjects, because the current of his thoughts seized on them of its own accord. He might not have chosen to think about Spenser if the essay had not been commissioned, and for that reason he may have had to draw more widely on thoughts already in his mind, and assemble them more deliberately. But there is hardly one among his prose writings that could not be studied in the same way, as a focus of much past thinking and a stage in the development of ideas that went into his poetry, sometimes years later. Opinions caught up in momentary fantasy — such as the abortive theory of allegory and the opposition of Anglo-French and Anglo-Saxon — dropped out ; thoughts that belonged to him were retained, to reappear, stripped of excrescences and gaining new facets in different contexts, till they were fused into hard crystal and given that finality of phrasing that sets him among the great poets of the world.

THE RHETORIC OF YEATS

*

T. R. HENN

'I AM PARTICULARLY INDEBTED to you for your essay on Byron. My own verse has more and more adopted — seemingly without any will of mine — the syntax and vocabulary of common passionate speech. The passage you quote that begins "our life is a false nature",[1] down to almost the end of the quotation where it becomes too elaborate to "couch the mind"[2] and a great part of the long passage about Haidée — I got a queer kind of half-dream prevision of the passage the day before your book came out with a repetition of the words "broad moon" — are perfect passionate speech. The over childish or over pretty or feminine element in some good Wordsworth and in much poetry up to our date comes from the lack of natural momentum in the syntax. This momentum underlies almost every Elizabethan or Jacobean lyric and is far more important than simplicity of vocabulary.'[3]

I

I think that Rosamund Tuve was the first to point out how closely Yeats's technique seems to follow the traditional 'devices' to be found in the Renaissance textbooks of rhetoric.[4] To these Yeats had been led by his early work on

---

[1] *Childe Harold's Pilgrimage*, canto iv, stanzas 126-7.

[2] *Ibid.*, 'The beam pours in — for Time and Skill will couch the blind'. Yeats's use of 'mind' is due to a misprint in Grierson.

[3] Yeats to H. J. C. Grierson, 21 February 1926. The book is *The Background of English Literature*, London, 1925 ; the reference is to the essay 'Byron and English Society'.

[4] *Elizabethan and Metaphysical Imagery*, Chicago, 1947.

Spenser, and he knew the two books of Cicero called *De Inventione*, the four books of *De Rhetorica, ad Herennium*, and the Epistle of Horace to Piso. Are these the works that appear in that 'mechanical little song', 'Mad as the Mist and Snow'?

> Horace there by Homer stands,
>   Plato stands below,
> And here is Tully's open page.
>   How many years ago
> Were you and I unlettered lads
>   *Mad as the mist and snow?*

Now we need not impute to any modern writer the conscious exploitation of the traditional formalities of rhetoric, though it is worth while to recall J. M. Manley's words:

Let no one scoff at this method of producing interesting and attractive writing. It has been practised very commonly in all lands and epochs. It is recommended and taught in a widely-used series of text books. It is the method recently revealed by that most charming of stylists, Anatole France, and is perhaps the only method by which he or Lawrence Sterne could have achieved such effects as they achieved.[1]

But in Yeats's work it is possible to trace many elements of the traditional technique, as, for instance, the *descriptio, meditatio, invocatio* in the two Byzantium poems, and in 'All Souls' Night'. It is, after all, only natural that his wide, excited, and somewhat random reading (and the long retention of that reading whenever it fired his imagination) in the Elizabethans, Jacobeans and Romantics, should lead him to the traditional *exampla*, for

> Nor is there singing school but studying
> Monuments of its own magnificence.

He was 'intoxicated' by the 'Nocturnall on S. Lucies Day'; 'I have used the arrangement of the rhymes in the stanza for a poem of my own, just finished'; the Byron passage that

---

[1] 'Chaucer and the Rhetoricians', *Proc. Br. Acad.*, 1926, p. 95.

Grierson had quoted was 'perfect passionate speech'. He lamented the passing of a rhetorical tradition :

> Every generation has more and more loosened the rhythm, more and more broken up and disorganized, for the sake of subtlety or detail, those great rhythms that move in masses of sound.[1]

and when he compared modern writers (with the exception of Balzac) to Dante, Villon, Shakespeare and Cervantes, Yeats found, instead of 'strength and weight' something 'slight and shadowy'. This was partly because the great writers had attained to 'a vision of evil', as Shelley had not.

My concern in this essay is to suggest some aspects of Yeats's 'rhetoric', not in order to engage in the unprofitable business of classifying it under the headings of the manuals (though the poems would furnish abundant instances) but to examine his 'rhetoric' in the older sense. It is perhaps unnecessary to point out that I wish to reject in this context the pejorative overtones of 'rhetorical', as well as Yeats's own statement that 'we make out of the quarrel with others rhetoric, out of the quarrel with ourselves, poetry', as well as the parallel view implied in the lines

> The rhetorician would deceive his neighbours,
> The sentimentalist himself. . . .[2]

I wish to return to the older meaning of rhetoric as a form of persuasion, and to consider a suggestive remark by Miss Tuve :

> The line the earlier period [the Renaissance] ignores is the line nervously drawn by modern poetic practice between a poet himself moved and a poet persuading or convincing.[3]

The point is not without importance in the light of recent questionings of Yeats's 'sincerity'.[4]

[1] Preface to Spenser, p. xliii.
[2] 'Ego Dominus Tuus.'   [3] *Op. cit.*, p. 183.
[4] *E.g.* by Yvor Winters, *The Poetry of W. B. Yeats*, Denver, 1960 : 'a home-made mythology and a loose assortment of untenable social attitudes . . .'. 'Yeats' poems are inflated ; they are bardic in the worst sense.'

II

Yeats is a professional and accomplished poet working in media where a rhetorical bent, partly native and partly traditional, is given full scope. An almost impeccable ear, a laborious method of composition in search of phonetic 'decorum' and exactitude by repeated redrafting and by *sotto voce* declamation until 'words obeyed his call', a method of reading aloud that was close to ritual declamation ; all these show a love of 'those great rhythms that move in masses of sound'. We may quote from 'The Cutting of an Agate' :

Walter Pater says that music is the type of all the Arts, but somebody else, I forget who, that oratory is their type. You will side with one or the other according to the nature of your energy, and I in my present mood am all for the man who, with an average audience before him, uses all means of persuasion — stories, laughter, tears, *and but so much music as he can discover on the wings of words.*[1]

Of this kind of 'discovered' music we may quote from Oliver St. John Gogarty's recent Memoir.[2] When Yeats was ill in Majorca he was attended by a Spanish doctor, who made a report to his Irish colleague. Yeats saw the report : it contained the sentence 'We have here an antique cardio-sclerotic of advanced years'. The Memoir goes on :

Not wishing to impart the import of such a message, I said it was all doctors' Greek to me. He insisted, so I read rather slurringly, for it foreboded little health. 'Read it slowly and distinctly,' he ordered. There was no escape, so I read it slowly and distinctly. He inclined his head. 'Read that again.' He followed the cadence with his finger. At last the sound died away, he exclaimed, utterly ignoring the meaning :

'Do you know that I would rather be called "Cardio-Sclerotic" than "Lord of Lower Egypt" ?'

The tale is at least credible, though it recalls, too clearly

---

[1] *Essays and Introductions*, London, 1961, pp. 267–8.
[2] Edited by Myles Dillon, Dublin, 1962.

perhaps, 'the blessed word Mesopotamia' or the 'carminative' of Aldous Huxley's young poet.

Certain formative influences are clear. In the background are Spenser and the 'brightnesse of braue and glorious words' : Donne, Ben Jonson, Byron and Shelley, Tennyson and Morris. Dramatic resonances are picked up from Browning and Rossetti. In the background there is the comparatively unknown popular nineteenth-century Anglo-Irish tradition, from Moore, Keating, Allingham, Todhunter, Dowden, Davis, Ferguson, Mangan, O'Leary, O'Shaughnessy, Lionel Johnson, Katharine Tynan Hinkson : together with Hyde's translations, and that somewhat neglected poet, Basil Bunting.[1] In the forefront, of course, are the 'nineties and the Tragic Generation. For prose there was Swift who haunted him, Berkeley in his more assertive and less mathematical modes, Burke, Grattan, Mitchel, O'Connell, Parnell ; and for a time the rhythms of Pater to give a certain stilted quality, almost as of parody,[2] to *Per Amica Silentia Lunae*.

Consider first the dramatic nature of traditional Anglo-Irish rhetoric. There is clearly an intense love of the powerful, the resonant ; of strong cadences, of the 'great masses of sound'. A few examples will serve ; from Ferguson's *The Burial of King Cormac* :

> They loosed their curse against the king ;
> They cursed him in his flesh and bones ;
> And daily in their mystic ring
> They turned the maledictive stones . . .

from F. R. Higgins's 'The Ballad of O'Bruadhir' which Yeats included in *The Oxford Book of Modern Verse* :

When first I took to cutlass, blunderbuss and gun,
Rolling glory on the water ;

---

[1] *1930 Diary*, p. 7 n.
[2] 'He wrote of me in that extravagant style
He had learned from Pater.'
('The Phases of the Moon')

With boarding and with broadside we made the Dutchmen run,
  Rolling glory on the water ;
Then down among the Captains in their green skin shoes,
I sought for Hugh O'Bruadhir and got but little news
Till I shook him by the hand in the bay of Santa Cruz,
  Rolling glory on the water.

from George Fox's translation of Lavelle :

  'Tis my grief that Patrick Loughlin is not Earl of Irrul still,
  And that Brian Duff no longer rules as Lord upon the hill :
  And that Colonel Hugh McGrady should be lying dead and low,
  And I sailing, sailing swiftly from the County of Mayo.

or from the poem that Lionel Johnson dedicated to O'Leary,
and that he himself quotes : [1]

        A dream ! a dream ! an ancient dream !
        Yet, ere peace come to Inisfail,
        Some weapons on some field must gleam,
        Some burning glory find the Gael.

        That field may lie beneath the sun,
        Fair for the treading of an host
        That fields in realms of thought be won
        And armed minds do their uttermost.

Essays and *Autobiographies* show us the rhythmic and gnomic
scraps which he treasured ; the passage from Nashe's 'Bright-
ness falls from the air', the 'old hunter talking with gods'
from Browning's 'Pauline', Blake's

  The gay fishes on the wave when the moon sucks up the dew.

He preferred Burns's 'Elegy on Capt. Matthew Hender-
son' to Shelley's 'Adonais', finding in it speed, energy,
naturalness, 'a great voice'. It is worth while to quote two
stanzas from the Elegy that may have appealed specially to
Yeats :

        Mourn, sooty coots, and speckled teals ;
        Ye fisher herons, watching eels ;

[1] *Essays and Introductions*, p. 258. Note the strong cadences of the
second and fourth lines of each stanza ; the whole must be read aloud.

Ye duck and drake, *wi' airy wheels*
    Circling the lake ;
Ye bitterns, till the quagmire reels,
    Rair for his sake.

   .   .   .   .

Go to your sculptured tombs, ye Great,
In a' the tinsel trash o' state !
But by thy honest turf I'll wait,
    Thou man of worth !
And weep the ae best fellow's fate
    E'er lay in earth.[1]

In prose, too, such memorable things are hoarded, tasted : 'There are things a man must not do to save a nation', 'I saw my thoughts going past me like blazing ships', 'When the goddess came to Achilles in the battle . . . she took him by his yellow hair'. 'Where did I pick up that story of the Byzantium bishop and the singer of Antioch, where learn that to anoint your body with the fat of a lion ensured the favour of a king ?' The dramatic, the esoteric, is woven into the cadences, themselves traditional. 'I seek more than idioms, for thoughts become more vivid when I find that they were first thought out in historical circumstances which affect those in which I live, or, which is perhaps the same thing, were thought first by men my ancestors may have known . . . it is as though I most approximate towards that expression when I carry with me the greatest possible amount of hereditary thought and feeling, even national and family hatred and pride.'[2] Such 'charged' words were clearly those in 'The Seven Sages', the names of the heroes of 'Easter 1916', the O'Rahilly, and so forth. The classical 'names' as recommended by 'Longinus'[3] are, one suspects, used as much for their sound-savour as for their evocative effect ; Plato, Plotinus, Parmenides, Homer, Donne, Smaragdine, Cretan,

[1] The italics are mine : the echoes in the poems, and in *The Herne's Egg*, are perhaps suggestive.   [2] *1930 Diary*, p. 6.
[3] *On the Sublime* (e.g.) xvi, 2 ; xxiii, 4.

Salamis, Ledaean, Agamemnon, Callimachus are woven, usually with great skill, into the sound-fabric. A classical example of the desire for rhetorical weight is the conversion of the earlier draft of the second stanza of 'The Sorrow of Love', from

> And then you came with those red mournful lips,
> And with you came the whole of the world's tears,
> And all the sorrows of her labouring ships,
> And all the burden of her myriad years.

into the more grandiose

> A girl arose that had red mournful lips
> And seemed the greatness of the world in tears,
> Doomed like Odysseus and the labouring ships
> And proud as Priam murdered with his peers;

The complicated arguments for and against the two versions are well known;[1] but the simplest and perhaps adequate explanation (for the alteration does little but extend and universalize the alignment between Maud Gonne and Troy) is the sheer resonance that the 'names' give. There are many instances of the typical Yeatsian cadence :

> Troy passed away in one high funeral gleam,
>   And Usna's children died.[2]

> A shudder in the loins engenders there
> The broken wall, the burning roof and tower
> And Agamemnon dead.[3]

> . . . Where seven Ephesian topers[4] slept and never knew
> When Alexander's empire passed, they slept so sound.
> Stretch out your limbs and sleep a long Saturnian sleep . . .[5]

---

[1] See, in particular, the study in J. Stallworthy, *Between the Lines*, London, 1962.   [2] 'The Rose of the World.'

[3] 'Leda and the Swan.'

[4] Again the traditional 'vulgar word which is not vulgar because it is so expressive' ('Longinus') ; and 'In later years, through much knowledge of the stage, through the exfoliation of my own style, I learnt that occasional prosaic words gave the impression of an active man speaking.' *Autobiographies*, p. 263.   [5] 'On a Picture of a Black Centaur.'

> Hector is dead, and there's a light in Troy.
> We that look on but laugh in tragic joy.[1]

There are even times when one suspects that the sound has perhaps submerged the meaning :

> I mock Plotinus' thought
> And cry in Plato's teeth . . .[2]

Virgil's resonances are placed under tribute in the 'Two Songs from a Play' :

> Another Troy shall rise and set,
> Another lineage feed the crow,
> Another Argo's painted prow
> Drives to a flashier bauble yet . . .

and we can see the Yeatsian energy more clearly if we set beside it Dryden's translation :

> Another Tiphys shall new seas explore
> Another Argo land the chiefs upon the Iberian shore ;
> Another Helen other wars create,
> And great Achilles urge the Trojan fate.

The sureness of touch is apparent even in the minute. 'To a Wealthy Man . . .' is a proud and aristocratic poem, whose quick nervous rhythms are integral with its tone. We remember the consummate *ordonnance* behind the rhythms of

> And when they drove out Cosimo,
> Indifferent how that rancour ran,
> He gave the hours they had set free
> To Michelozzo's latest plan
> For the San Marco Library . . .

— so that the poem comes alive and prepares us for the alignments with Lutyens and the Municipal Gallery, which (we are persuaded) have become part of a great processional movement. In the lines

> What cared Duke Ercole that bid
> His mummers to the market place

[1] 'The Gyres'.   [2] 'The Tower', III.

— the keen edge of the rhythm would be blunted if we substituted 'Hercules' for the Italian form that picks up the hard consonants of *Duke*. But indeed the whole attacking mood of the poem, the proud triumphant rhetoric of hatred, is superb. We may think that the alignments between Coole and Urbino, between Michelozzo and Lutyens, are slender enough : but the 'stride' and energy of the poem combine with similar assertions elsewhere to make these alignments convincing. 'It is in the arrangements of events as in the words, and in that touch of extravagance, of irony, of surprise ... that leaves one ... caught up into the freedom of self-delight.'[1] All three terms — extravagance, irony, surprise — would be familiar to a Renaissance rhetorician. But the integration of rhythm with sound is peculiarly a Yeatsian gift :

> What are the tones that verse[2] sets ringing in the mind ? What is the power, in which you are pre-eminent, of summoning to our understanding, with one swift, wrought phrase, a landscape, a sky, a weather and a history ? We do not think about, till we realize that in the words before us there is no logical warrant for that rush of feeling and knowledge. ... It is a precise and definite art ; the cutting of an agate.[3]

We are reminded of

> ... that stern colour and that delicate line

of 'The Elegy', and of Palmer's appraisal of Blake's woodcuts :

> that intense, soul-evidencing attitude and action, and that elastic, nervous spring which belongs to emerged and immortal spirits.[4]

III

It has been argued that the Celtic 'namings' are less successful, and indeed an obstacle to Yeats's communication ; partly because they are difficult to pronounce, partly because their

---

[1] *Essays and Introductions*, p. 254.
[2] He has just quoted a stanza from 'The Mountain Tomb'.
[3] L. A. G. Strong, *A Letter to W. B. Yeats*, London, 1932.
[4] *Life and Letters* (1892), p. 16.

significance can only be ascertained by study. Synge used
them effectively, but then he had Villon's precedent and
Villon's music behind him ; and the admixture of the classical
relieves, as it were, the Celtic :

> Etain, Helen, Maeve and Fand,
> Golden Deirdre with tender hand . . .

There seems to have been a significant change in Yeats's
technique. We may quote from the Morrisian Wanderings
of Oisin with its long stumbling rhythms :

Came Blanid, MacNessa, tall Fergus, who feastward of old
time slunk,
Cook Barach, the traitor ; and warward, the spittle on his
beard never dry,
Dark Balor, as old as a forest, car-borne, his mighty head sunk
Helpless, men lifting the lids of his weary and death-making eye.[1]

At the end, the decorative effect has been abandoned, the
names tightened into the layers of history :

> Are those things that men adore and loathe
> Their sole reality ?
> What stood in the Post Office
> With Pearse and Connolly ?

> What comes out of the mountain
> Where men first shed their blood ?
> Who taught Cuchulain till it seemed
> He stood where they had stood ?[2]

In the early work there is some Marlowe, and Yeats seems to
fall into the snare of Longinus's 'frigidity' or perhaps 'turgi-
dity' ; the imagery fails to support the thought :

> Destroyers of souls, God will destroy you quickly.
> You shall at last dry like dry leaves and hang
> Nailed like dead vermin to the doors of God.[3]

---

[1] iii, 89.
[2] *The Death of Cuchulain* ; see also the last stanza of 'The Statues' for
a successful use of this myth.
[3] *Countess Cathleen*, Sc. I.

or the 'frigid'

> — men yet shall hear
> The archangels rolling Satan's empty skull
> Over the mountain-tops.[1]

Sometimes the rhetoric falls into pseudo-Jacobean not far from that of Beddoes :

> O, look upon the moon that's standing there
> In the blue daylight — take note of the complexion,
> Because it is the white of leprosy
> And the contagion that afflicts mankind
> Falls from the moon . . .[2]

We may assess something of Yeats's development in this mode from 'The Gift of Harun Al-Rashid' (1923). It is the last of the long traditional poems, and shows the 'interior variety' which he had looked for as far back as 1902,[3] as well as the movement between 'passion and reverie', 'turbulence and stillness'. Here is the progression of a paragraph towards the rhetorical cadence, with full mastery of all the resources of blank verse :

> That love
> Must needs be in the life and in what follows
> Unchanging and at peace, and it is right
> Every philosopher should praise that love.
> But I being none can praise its opposite.
> It makes my passion stronger but to think
> Like passion stirs the peacock and his mate,
> The wild stag and the doe ;[4] that mouth to mouth
> Is a man's mockery of the changeless soul.

— so that the final line seems mortised and tenoned by its weight and alliteration. The whole poem rises and falls with

[1] *Ibid.*, Sc. V.
[2] *The King's Threshold.*
[3] *Essays and Introductions*, 'Speaking to the Psaltery'.
[4] See 'A Last Confession'.

its own peculiar rhythms, to embody sound-masses locked home in the rhythmic structure by alliterative subtlety :

> . . . Self-born, high born, and solitary truths,
> Those terrible implacable straight lines
> Drawn through the wandering vegetative dream,
> Even those truths that when my bones are dust
> Must drive the Arabian host.

IV

It is worth considering, as a separate section, what I would wish to call the 'rhetoric of the ghost'. Traditionally the ghost must be called by the proper invocation ; only then will it appear. So the openings of 'All Souls' Night', 'A Prayer for My Son', the second stanza of 'Byzantium'. These poems are for the most part hieratical, measured. They project a pattern of sound and imagery to work as all invocations do ; its own energy gives life, intensity, and some kind of suspension of belief grows steadily ; it returns as it were, to carry the poet himself into a particular *kind* of belief generated by the poem itself. 'The wheels take fire from the mere rapidity of their motion.'[1] The sense of the supernatural in the West of Ireland (of both races and of both religions) is highly ambivalent. The dead walk, or play on the roads at night ; Synge's Bride Dara sees the dead man with the child in his arms. In certain moods and in certain psychological states[2] their acceptance is complete. But it is a delicate thing, dependent for its life on the perfection of the incantation, of which the full force is felt only when the poem is read aloud. I myself am now clear that Yeats wished to believe in the supra-natural, and that the belief was an integral part of his dramatic perception of life and death and the fate of the soul at the Gates of Pluto. He had seen Coleridge achieving this, and he had borrowed a couplet from 'The Ancient Mariner'

[1] Coleridge, *Biographia*, xviii.
[2] As, for example, those which accompany the stimulation, by means of symbols or meditation or ritual, of ultra-rational perceptions.

to strengthen 'Byzantium'. Into the structure of the rhetoric of the supernatural he incorporates freely those aspects of the Christian tradition which are dramatically appealing ; to produce ironies, tensions, ambivalences which are carefully subordinated to the major rhythms that 'move in great masses of sound'. So 'The Cold Heaven' :

> Ah, when the ghost begins to quicken,
> Confusion of the death-bed over . . .

We remember the account in *A Vision* of the events that follow closely on death, and what anthropologists tell us of the custom of leaving the spirit in peace to find its bearings like a homing bird. And on the roads the spirit becomes a wanderer, seeking to relive fragments of its past, as Crazy Jane knew.

In the fourth stanza of 'Byzantium' — and in its source drafts — the spirits or flames arrive on the Emperor's pavement. In the second stanza Yeats has invoked the traditional Guide to the Underworld to watch their coming. Behind them is a mass of converging imagery, carried excitedly on an accelerated rhythm that culminates on the rhetoric of

> The golden smithies of the Emperor.

Plotinus, Moore, Cudworth, Milton, Blake, the Noh play — the fire-imagery is common form ; with it, perhaps, Pentecost, Isaiah, and the text 'Who maketh his angels spirits, and his ministers a flame of fire'.

This 'rhetoric of the ghost' seems to me to demand for its communication those massive strong rhythms, which 'trade with the living and with the dead' to enrich it, to generate the excitement by which its assertions are supported. So the processional Presences, so the tightly-laminated 'And must we part, von Hügel ?', that moves towards the orotundities of sound which he loves

> Homer is my example, and his unchristened heart . . .
> Though mounted in that saddle Homer rose . . .

A woman Homer sung . . .
What theme had Homer but original sin ?

Something of the peculiar Yeatsian quality may be seen if
we consider a poem by Oliver St. John Gogarty, which he
included in *The Oxford Book of Modern Verse* :

> Our friends go with us as we go
>   Down the long path where Beauty wends,
> Where all we love foregathers, so
>   Why should we fear to join our friends ?
>
> Who would survive them to outlast
>   His children ; to outwear his frame —
> Left where the Triumph has gone past —
>   To win from Age, not Time, a name ?
>
> Then do not shudder at the knife
>   That Death's indifferent hand drives home,
> But with the Strivers leave the Strife
>   Nor, after Caesar, stalk in Rome.

This is superficially attractive : its rhythm is strong and
definite, its statement agreeably neo-Stoic. Yet it reveals
itself quickly as a 'made' poem, shallow and pretentious ;
using outworn personifications, archaisms ; with a confused
syntactical structure which is an index to its kind of composition. Beside it we may set (though with the usual reservations
about all such comparisons) an example of Yeats's technique
in 'The New Faces' :

> If you, that have grown old, were the first dead,
> Neither catalpa tree nor scented lime
> Should hear my living feet, nor would I tread
> Where we wrought that shall break the teeth of Time.
> Let the new faces play what tricks they will
> In the old rooms ; night can outbalance day,
> Our shadows rove the garden gravel still,
> The living seem more shadowy than they.

Yeats's variations of speed and tone, the economy and symmetry of his statement, make all comparisons invidious. The poem turns as it were on a hinge with the proud

> Where we wrought that shall break the teeth of Time

where the hard t's are picked up on the momentum from the previous line. *Time* is the only abstraction, where Gogarty has seven ; and that is no longer 'abstract' when we remember Ronsard. The rhetorical questions of the first poem are replaced by the strong assertions grafted on the opening conditional. We need not know that the background to Yeats's poem is Lady Gregory's sickness, nor that the catalpa tree was one of the glories of Coole. But we are aware of the triumphant rhythm of that second line, the circumstantiality of the setting : and we remember

> For what but eye and ear silence the mind
> With the minute particulars of mankind ?[1]

It carries over, a little misted (as the syntax demands) to the fourth line. The second half of the poem uses the colloquialism approved by 'Longinus'

> Let the new faces *play what tricks* they will

which throws into relief the arrogant and deliberately indefinite

> *Where we wrought that* . . .

V

There is, I think, something that we might call a 'rhetoric of war' ; and here it seems to me that, in general, Yeats is far less convincing. I have no doubt that in the famous passage from *On the Boiler*, 'Desire some just war . . .', he was sincere, seeing in this at least one possibility of re-integrating the State after its fragmentation at the end of the gyre. But the earlier references to war seem to me strained, and too close

[1] 'The Double Vision of Michael Robartes.'

to Morris; always excepting the magnificently ambivalent 'Who will go drive with Fergus now?' where this excitement comes from other sources than the 'brazen spears'. Yeats, writing to order, as in the *Marching Songs*, and to some extent in the 'patriotic' balladry, seems to me to fail to attain the momentum or the life. In this class I would include (against popular estimation) 'Sixteen Dead Men' and 'The Rose Tree'. I think that the integrity of the rhythm is apparent when the experience has been, as it were, within his own reach; to be meditated on, absorbed in relation to his own position. And that, I believe, falls into two more or less distinct parts: a bardic but abstracted celebration of the Easter Rising, its actors, their epic part, his own imagined responsibility, through play or speech, in the events which led to it. On the other side there is the poetry arising out of the events which he was aware of at first hand. 'The Stare's Nest by My Window', with its polarities that are stated in a letter to Grierson: 'The one enlivening truth that starts out of it all is that we may learn charity after material contempt. There is no longer a virtuous nation and the best of us lives by candle-light.'[1] He could never compass the sense of the brutality and exaltation of remote Celtic war (which is best left in prose) and he recognized his failure in 'The Circus Animals' Desertion':

> . . . vain gaiety, vain battle, vain repose

though in that poem we occasionally get the strong accent —

> Cuchulain fought the ungovernable sea.

But indeed the thought of Cuchulain, with all its heroic and violent connotations, seems to stimulate in the verse a special strength and weightiness. Perhaps the strange incantatory vowel-changes had some auxiliary force. For his personal

[1] 21 October? 1922.

part in the war, it is the incidents round Coole and Kiltartan
that seemed to etch themselves in his memory :

> a drunken soldiery
> Can leave the mother murdered at her door
> To roll in her own blood, and go scot-free.

and, from 'Reprisals' (where the rhetoric of war links with
that of the ghost of Robert Gregory)

> Half-drunk or whole-mad soldiery
> Are murdering your tenants there.[1]

Beside it, the 'popular' poems about the Rising and its actors,
and the Casement poems, seem forced ; the image that they
present appeals more strongly to an English than to an Anglo-
Irish audience.   On the other hand 'The Curse of Cromwell'
lives by reason of its astounding energy, the rhythmical checks
and substitutions, embodied in the violence of popular Balladry
which he has transcended.   We touch the edges of rant in a
favourite thought, that he had used before in *The Countess
Cathleen* but which is now given a peculiar proud energy :

> And there is an old beggar wandering in his pride
> His fathers served their fathers before Christ was crucified.
> *O what of that, O what of that,*
> *What is there left to say ?*

VI

There is, too, a 'rhetoric of love'.   That long-enduring
imposthume in the heart and brain could be in some sense
eased by perpetual alignment and realignment with the heroic
or aristocratic ideal.   If (as I think) he was at times 'in love
with love for its own sake', it was natural that Helen should be
the chosen archetype, as he had seen her in an early essay on
Morris[2], contrasting her with Morris's vision of his own gentle

---

[1] *The Variorum Edition*, London, 1957, p. 791.
[2] *The Happiest of the Poets.*

and abundant women, as he knew them in the pastoral worlds of Calvert and Palmer. Troy is linked to Emain, and the story of Deirdre ; perhaps to the burning house that had impressed him so deeply, and the burnings during the Troubles. So the image-clusters turn and fuse :

> Why, what could she have done, being what she is ?
> Was there another Troy for her to burn ? [1]

'The verses may make his mistress famous as Helen or give a victory for his cause, not because he has been either's servant, but because men delight to honour and to remember all that has served contemplation.'[2] Both Yeats and Synge are much concerned with Queens ; in 'Long Legged Fly' the rhetoric of Troy is picked up and reinforced from Marlowe and Shakespeare with a memory of Antony and Cleopatra :

> That the topless towers be burnt
>> And men recall that face,
> Move most gently if move you must
>> In this lonely place.
> She thinks, part woman, three parts a child,
>> That nobody looks ; her feet
> Practise a tinker's shuffle
>> Picked up on a street.[3]

Women are exalted ceremoniously, in the tradition — itself moving between extremities — that he had learnt in the 'nineties. Again and again there is this attempt at self-conviction, the alignment with aristocracy, the verse giving at times forced tone. The word *common* — which may carry overtones in Anglo-Irish speech of a peculiar intensity — occurs often in this context. So, of Mabel Beardsley, and superbly done :

> She knows herself a woman
> No red and white of a face

[1] 'No Second Troy.'
[2] *Essays and Introductions*, p. 255.
[3] *v. A. & C.* II.2.234.

> Or rank, raised from a common
> Unreckonable race . . .[1]

Less successfully 'To Dorothy Wellesley', which seems to me
an architected poem, a little tumid and pretentious :

> What climbs the stair ?
> Nothing that common women ponder on
> If you are worth my hope ! Neither content
> Nor satisfied conscience, but that great family
> Some ancient famous authors misrepresent,
> The Proud Furies each with her torch on high.

VII

It would be possible to give many instances of these traditional rhetorical devices. The traditional Yeatsian 'attack' is
often the *exclamatio* :

> What shall I do with this absurdity . . .
>
> That is no country for old men . . .
>
> O but there is wisdom
> In what the sages said . . .

There is the *quaestio*, often gnomic, of which he is fond :

> What's water but the generated soul ?

(with its reference to Porphyry) —

> What theme had Homer but original sin ?
>
> Was there another Troy for her to burn ?

But for a last example we may consider some passages from
Purgatory, a play which shows an astonishing variety and
control ; as well as the tact with which the rhythm is adjusted
precisely to the speaking voice :

> Great people lived and died in this house —

(we remember the remark of the old countryman when he had
seen the pictures at Coole)

> Magistrates, Colonels, members of Parliament,

[1] 'Upon a Dying Lady'.

(the rhythm gathers itself for the momentum of the 'heroic-myth' names)

> Men that had fought at Aughrim and the Boyne

or

> Had loved the house, had loved all
> The intricate passages of the house,
> But he killed the house ; to kill a house

(the repetitions, I think on a rising tone, lengthen the rhythm to prepare for the climax)

> Where great men grew up, married, died

then the rhetorical hieratical condemnation

> I here declare a capital offence.

But the whole ebb and flow of the dramatic rhythm of the play repays detailed study. Beside it the *ordonnance* of *The Death of Cuchulain* is relatively crude.

It would be easy to develop examples of Yeats's achievement under the traditional divisions : his use of the tropes and figures, the *preparation* for the culmination of the poem (as in the third movement of 'Easter 1916') ; the *sprezzatura* or pride that Professor Tuve has noted ; [1] above all, his adherence to the 'high', 'middle' and 'low' styles. But this 'eminence and excellence of language' is in all respects in the main current of Renaissance poetic theory. Its similarities with the basic techniques of Spenser, King, Donne, can be shown. But above all it is the product of this traditional reading and training :

No new man has ever plucked that rose, or found that trysting place, for he could but come to the understanding of himself, to the mastery of unlocking words, after long frequenting of the great Masters, hardly without ancestral memory of the like. [2]

[1] *Op. cit.*, p. 279.
[2] *Essays and Introductions*, pp. 255–6.

'AMONG SCHOOL CHILDREN' AND THE EDUCATION OF THE IRISH SPIRIT

*

DONALD T. TORCHIANA

I

ONE MONDAY MORNING in February 1926, a present member of the Convent of Mercy, Waterford, at that time a thirteen-year-old student, watched from a window as Senator W. B. Yeats, in soft hat and with magisterial presence, took his distinguished way up the driveway of St. Otteran's School. His famed turkey strut — a gait combining short, jerky steps with body erect, head thrown back and hands clasped behind his back — was unforgettable. He had already visited the school, often known as the Phillip Street National Schools, the previous day with his wife. They had been regaled with the kind of overflowing dinner that Ireland does so well and spent the afternoon visiting the empty classrooms prior to an equally extraordinary tea. The visit had been private and unheralded, but St. Otteran's as a model school was important to Yeats, for he was on a government committee pledged to investigate the conditions of schools in Ireland.

There may also have been another reason for Yeats's enthusiasm and curiosity in accepting the invitation from the Superior, the Rev. Mother de Sales. Trained by a sister of the Abbot Marmion (a noted Belgian educator), she inaugurated in St. Otteran's, on St. Patrick's Eve 1920, the Montessori method for teaching four- to seven-year-olds,[1] in which Yeats was particularly interested. Hence on Sunday, he had seen

[1] Eleanor Gibbon, *Ireland, Freedom and the Child*, Waterford, undated, pp. 9, 18.

123

the characteristic long Montessori classroom with its chosen emblem, Raphael's 'Madonna della Seggiola'. He had also learned that children from eight on were offered the system named for the Parents National Education Union. Here, in addition to the Montessori emphasis on spontaneity and a training of the senses to prepare for and reinforce a child's first intellectual ventures, each child was encouraged to read his own choice in books, then allowed to narrate his reading, to write about it — or even to make a poem from his impressions. Senator Yeats, without his wife this Monday morning, now visited the school full of children.

After seeing the primary grades, Yeats entered the school-room of the thirteen-year-old watcher, now a teacher in the school. She was one of those asked to recite a poem before the great man. Yet even more fortunate was her class neighbour who had chosen *Gulliver's Travels* for her reading book and poem. Yeats commended her verses on the little people, read her poem aloud himself, and remarked enigmatically that her performance reminded him of one of his friends. He could hardly believe, as he told his wife later, that the children's recitations had not been specially got up for him. But they had not. As he proceeded from classroom to classroom — the children standing as he entered each room — the Rev. Mother Philomena, Mistress of Schools, answered his questions, as did the Rev. Mother de Sales before and after his tour. The Montessori children had been particularly occupied with their sums and singing, while the P.N.E.U. children had also been rendering an account of their reading and history lessons. All, from seven years on, had been taught to cut and sew their own school bags and even more difficult articles. Neatness was, of course, a watchword in the school. Moreover, according to the present member of the Mercy community, Yeats asked repeated questions on the children's preparations in art. Later in the day he paid a visit to the Ursuline convent in the same city, where again the primary

school was run on Montessori lines. Yeats left Waterford
without so much as a brief notice in the *Waterford Star* or in
the *Munster Express* to mark his stay. But for the observant
thirteen-year-old, all are gone today from that religious community and school who might have remembered him. Yeats's
visit, however, is fixed indelibly in the opening stanzas of one
of his greatest poems, 'Among School Children'.[1] Hence,
with this visit in mind, along with Yeats's speeches, essays and
reading on education at the time, I would like to take one more
look at the poem, despite the previous dazzling glances by
Cleanth Brooks, John Wain and Frank Kermode.[2]

II

Beyond his consuming desire after the Treaty to help to
educate the new Ireland artistically, and aside from his equally
powerful Shandean preoccupation with his own growing
children, Yeats on this trip — one of many in Ireland — was
also marking his official concern with Irish education.

Yeats made three important Senate speeches on the Irish
schools during March and late April of 1926. They came
close to his Waterford trip and close also to the time when the
idea of the poem first struck him. The last two, on the
30th of March and the 28th of April, were desperate pleas for
a national loan to ensure that schools would be in good repair,
clean and habitable — worthy to be centres of culture, and
cheerful ones at that. But Yeats's most important speech on
education had come on 24 March. Remarking on the primitive
condition of many Irish schools, he contrasted a shabby

1 The information in this section was gathered from conversations
with Mrs. W. B. Yeats or with members of the Convent of Mercy,
Waterford. The member of this community who witnessed Yeats's visit
must remain, by rules of the Order, anonymous. See also Joseph Hone,
W. B. Yeats, *1865–1939*, London, 2nd ed., 1962, pp. 373–4.
2 See *The Well Wrought Urn*, New York, 1947, pp. 163–75 ; *Inter-
pretations*, London, 1955, pp. 194–210 ; and *Romantic Image*, London,
1961, pp. 83–91, 163–4.

Dublin school with St. Otteran's in these words: 'I have seen a school lately in a South of Ireland town managed by the Sisters of Mercy, and it is a model to all schools'.[1] Then, after objecting to the out-of-date system of education that imposed the usual harsh strain on both teacher and child, Yeats bluntly questioned the whole scheme of education. These remarks, especially, compel our attention. The first looks at a child, like the young Maud Gonne of Stanza II, under a harsh system:

> Whether it [schooling] is good for the children or not depends not only on the building but on the nature of the system under which they are taught. I am sure for a child to spend all day in school with a stupid, ill-trained man under an ill-planned system, is less good for that child than that the child should be running through the fields and learning nothing.[2]

A second passage asks Ireland to consider the Italian system, which included the Montessori ideal, so ably established by Gentile, the Italian Minister of Education:

> I should like to draw the attention of the Government to one nation which has reformed its educational system in the most suggestive and profound way; that is Italy . . . now teaching a system of education adapted to an agricultural nation like this or Italy, a system of education that will not turn out clerks only, but will turn out efficient men and women who can manage to do all the work of the nation. This system has been tried in Ireland. There are some schools carrying it out. There is one large primary school managed by nuns in the South of Ireland which has adopted practically the entire Italian system and which is carrying it out with great effect. . . .[3]

Finally, there is Yeats's closing thought, to my mind extremely important in understanding his poem:

> I would like to suggest another principle, that the child itself must be the end in education. It is a curious thing how many times

[1] *The Senate Speeches of W. B. Yeats*, ed. Donald R. Pearce, Bloomington, 1960, p. 108.   [2] *Ibid.*, p. 110.
[3] *Ibid.*, pp. 110–11.

the education of Europe has drifted into error. For two or three centuries people thought that their various religious systems were more important than the child. In the modern world the tendency is to think of the nation ; that it is more important than the child. . . . There is a tendency to subordinate the child to the idea of the nation . . . we should always see that the child is the object and not any of our special purposes.[1]

The aim is the development of national excellence by the best modern education available. Yet with equal insistence Yeats asks that the growing child be guided towards self-fulfilment without being sacrificed to the codes of any particular religious or patriotic abstraction.

III

Behind the faint light of these Senate speeches, three essays of these years also throw distant beams on 'Among School Children'. 'Compulsory Gaelic', appearing in the *Irish Statesman* on 2 August 1924, remains to this day a seldom-read symposium of Yeats's own conflicting thoughts on the Irish language. Cast in the form of a dialogue, it asks that Ireland avoid the usual school-book apathy associated with compulsory study and that it not become 'a little potato-digging Republic' cut off from Europe. The most provocative statements on education are put into the mouth of Timothy, described as 'an elderly student', who, in his convictions about the uncertainty of life, seems the speaker most like the real Yeats. On the last page of the essay he declares his faith :

I have no practical experience, but perhaps it might be possible to choose a schoolmaster as we choose a painter or sculptor. 'There is so-and-so,' we would say, 'who thinks that Ireland should be Gaelic-speaking, and because he is a very able, cultivated, and learned man, we will give him a school and let him teach. . . .' I am not sure that I like the idea of a State with a definite purpose, and there are moments, unpractical moments, perhaps, when I think

[1] *Ibid.*, pp. 111–12.

that the State should leave the mind free to create. I think Aristotle
defined the soul as that which moves itself, and how can it move
itself if everything is arranged beforehand ? [1]

Such a teacher, like a pleasant guest, would neither bore nor
tyrannize.[2]

Yeats's third and last essay on education appeared in the
Dial for February 1926. At its centre lies an angry protest
against the ignorance of a clergy, specifically the Christian
Brothers, who had condemned as blasphemous an old carol,
to be found in Irish and English, that celebrated the Incarnation. Yeats's condemnation of their condemnation is focused
in this passage :

There is the whole mystery — God, in the indignity of human
birth, all that seemed impossible, blasphemous even, to many early
heretical sects, and all set forth in an old 'sing-song' that has yet a
mathematical logic. I have thought it out again and again and can
see no reason for the anger of the Christian Brothers, except that
they do not believe in the Incarnation.[3]

To these notions of the child as a guest of a creative education, of the 'sing-song' logic of a verse that presents the
Incarnation through a child, or of education as a matter of
gracious cultivation before an uncertain future, I should like
to add some considerations from Yeats's second and most
important essay on education, 'The Child and the State',
delivered first as a lecture to the Irish Literary Society in
London on 30 November 1925.

Yeats makes several recommendations here that are near
a good many of his thoughts in 'Among School Children'.
In the first place, he asks again that educational practice be
revised according to methods already used in Italy and,
incidentally, long advocated in the teaching of art :

The tendency of the most modern education, that in Italy, let
us say, is to begin geography with your native fields, arithmetic by

[1] 'Compulsory Gaelic', *Irish Statesman*, 2 August 1924, p. 652.
[2] *Ibid.*
[3] 'The Need for Audacity of Thought', *Dial* (February, 1926), p. 116.

128

counting the school chairs and measuring the walls, history with local monuments, religion with the local saints, and then to pass on from that to the nation itself. That is but carrying into education principles a group of artists, my father among them, advocated in art teaching. These artists have said : 'Do not put scholars to draw from Greek or Roman casts until they have first drawn from life ; only when they have drawn from life can they understand the cast.' That which the child sees — the school — the district — and to a lesser degree the nation — is like the living body : distant countries and everything the child can only read of is like the cold Roman or Greek cast. If your education therefore is efficient in the modern sense, it will be more national than the dreams of politicians.[1]

Striking here are the possible analogues between the capture of the living body in art — as music might hold a dancer — and the tactile progression of the child from the immediate to the distant in time and space — after the manner of a tree's growth. Nor is the mention of inert casts, Greek, Roman or otherwise, completely irrelevant.

The conclusion is extremely provocative, if we keep in mind the last two stanzas of the poem :

The proper remedy is to teach religion, civic duty and history as all but inseparable. Indeed, the whole curriculum of a school should be as it were one lesson and not a mass of unrelated topics. I recommend Irish teachers to study the attempt now being made in Italy, under the influence of their Minister of Education, the philosopher Gentile, the most profound disciple of our own

[1] *Senate Speeches*, pp. 170–1. As early as 1906 Yeats had held something of the same beliefs. In a newspaper interview on the proposal to hand over the Hibernian Academy to the Agricultural and Technical Department, he could say : '"It does not matter to the Dublin student whether he gets his art teaching in the Academy or from a Professor of Painting at an Art School. What does matter is that he shall not be put under any sort of official system, and that there is a living model for him to draw from daily. No doubt a powerful personality will teach after some system, but it will be a personal one. Anything like the South Kensington routine, which bores a student out of his wits with drawing from the flat, drawing from the round, drawing from the antique for several years before it lets him get to Nature, destroys the student. . . .'" Unidentified clipping, December–January, 1906–7 ; in possession of Mrs. W. B. Yeats.

Berkeley, to so correlate all subjects of study. I would have each religion, Catholic or Protestant, so taught that it permeate the whole school life . . . that it may not be abstract, and that it may be part of history and of life itself, a part, as it were, of the foliage of Burke's tree.

·   ·   ·   ·

Every child in growing from infancy to maturity should pass in imagination through the history of its own race and through something of the history of the world, and the most powerful part in that history is played by religion. Let the child go its own way when maturity comes, but it is our business that it has something of that whole inheritance, and not as a mere thought, an abstract thing like those Graeco-Roman casts upon the shelves in the art schools, but as part of its emotional life.[1]

After this insistence on unity in education, and after the equally direct references to Gentile and the Italian system of education, it will be worth while to briefly sketch Yeats's reading in these matters. It may also do no harm to conclude this briefest of surveys with but a glance at another spirit, presence or memory that hovers over the poem, that of Maud Gonne.

IV

Although Yeats may not have read any of Dr. Maria Montessori's own work, he had, according to his wife, made himself thoroughly familiar with literature on the Montessori method in education. From his remarks, speeches and essays on education, one would expect Yeats to observe to his wife that Dublin boys might well learn arithmetic by counting Guinness barrels, and he did. Hence, though his exact reading in the literature remains unknown, he doubtless agreed to most of the major points of Dr. Montessori's book, *The Montessori Method.*

The counting of Guinness barrels would be part and parcel of the Montessori emphasis on reality brought to the child

[1] *Senate Speeches*, pp. 173–4.

through sense training and spontaneous work, those ultimately self-disciplining activities. Freedom and discipline, exactness and spontaneity, reality and spiritual growth go hand in hand in the Montessori system. The appeal, as Eleanor Gibbon, Montessori representative in Ireland during Yeats's time, put it, is to a 'sense of symmetry — an Ancient Irish trait'.[1] Yeats would have seconded Miss Gibbon's statement in her speech in Waterford in 1919 when she summed up the system by calling it 'a training for life as it is actually lived in the workaday world'.[2] The children worked as might the poet or artist himself — with easy confidence and a naturally motivated inner force.

Liberty likewise becomes a matter of 'form, what we universally consider good breeding'.[3] Nor does the educator confuse the good child with the passive, inert child, the bad with the active. Further, the hope is not for an intellect that separates man from the world but for one that through work and liberty will bring the whole being into biological and social acquaintance with the world. The hallmark of the Montessori-trained child should be 'a special grace of action which makes his gestures more correct and attractive, and which beautifies his hands and indeed his entire body now so balanced and so sure of itself; a grace which refines the expression of his face and of his serenely brilliant eyes, and which shows us that the flame of spiritual life has been lighted in another human being'.[4] If this description recalls Yeats's dancer and 'brightening glance' at the end of the poem, how truly relevant is this one:

I have seen here [at the 'Children's House'], men of affairs, great politicians preoccupied with problems of trade and of state, cast off like an uncomfortable garment the burden of the world, and fall into a simple forgetfulness of self. They are affected by this vision of the human soul growing in its true nature, and I

[1] *Ireland, Freedom and the Child*, p. 19.　　　　[2] *Ibid.*, p. 20.
[3] *The Montessori Method*, translated by Anne E. George with an Introduction by Professor Henry W. Holmes, London, 1912, p. 87.
[4] *Ibid.*, p. 353.

believe that this is what they mean when they call our little ones, wonderful children, happy children — the infancy of humanity in a higher stage of evolution than our own. I understand how the great English poet Wordsworth, enamoured as he was of nature, demanded the secret of all her peace and beauty. It was at last revealed to him — the secret of all nature lies in the soul of a little child.

· · · ·

Truly our social life is too often only the darkening and the death of the natural life that is in us. These methods tend to guard that spiritual fire within man, to keep his real nature unspoiled and to set it free from the oppressive and degrading yoke of society. It is a pedagogical method informed by the high concept of Immanuel Kant : 'Perfect art returns to nature.'[1]

I have reserved for an all too brief discussion Yeats's reading of Gentile. Mrs. Yeats had extracted and translated for her husband a good many bits and pieces from the work of this writer and other Italian writings on education. Thus, for instance, Yeats had also some knowledge of Gentile's work on secondary education. But the book he had sought after most, according to Joseph Hone, during his stay in Italy in 1924, was Gentile's *The Reformation of Education*.[2] This he found and read in Dino Bigongiari's translation, with an 'Introduction' by Benedetto Croce. A total reading of the book strikes me as the best preparation for re-reading the poem, for it offers not only much of the matter that Yeats came to use, but, in one chapter, it virtually furnishes his poem's organization.

Although this book is the key to the philosophic background of the poem, its treatment of education is much like that of Dr. Montessori, though more profoundly idealistic.

[1] *The Montessori Method*, translated by Anne E. George with an Introduction by Professor Henry W. Holmes, London, 1912, p. 377.

[2] Joseph Hone, *W. B. Yeats*, p. 368. Yeats's enthusiasm for Gentile's theory of unified education is, of course, part of the poet's enduring preoccupation with unity of being, voiced as recent to this narrative as 1919 in his essay 'If I Were Four-and-Twenty'. See *If I Were Four-and-Twenty*, Dublin, 1940, pp. 1–21.

To start with, the chapter on 'The Spirituality of Culture' takes us into the real drift of Gentile's subject, for it demonstrates that only our thought can give material reality any true unity. Otherwise matter as multiple is merely an abstraction. Here then Gentile can conclude — and I have already oversimplified his argument — that

> The world then is in us; it is our world, and it lives in the spirit. It lives the very life of that person which we strive to realise, sometimes satisfied with our work, but oftener unsatisfied and restless. And there is the life of culture.[1]

This idea of culture as activity or a constant becoming, the life of the spirit, is described like Yeats's dancer at the end of the poem : 'in no manner comparable to a moving body in which the body itself could be distinguished from motion' (p. 126). In the chapter, 'The Attributes of Culture', culture is equated with the whole body of education, and yet is not considered a *thing* to be located in schoolrooms or libraries but only existing in so far as it continues to form, develop, become, and thus to live. At one point, having called this dance of the spirit 'motion without mass', Gentile goes on to refine his argument by terming 'the spirit a gazing motion' (p. 132). Constant becoming would presumably brighten that gaze or glance. This gaze is also one of joy, for the life of the spirit, culture, is a drama of self-awareness, our work is our own blossoming, and like music it is *ours*. Culture, according to Gentile, 'is not simply effort and uneasy toil, it is not a tormenting restlessness which we may sometimes shake off, from which we would gladly be rescued. Nor is it a feverish excitement that consumes our life-blood and tosses us restlessly on a sick-bed' (p. 133). It is rather a kind of beatification. In this process of constant realization of self, culture aspires to a truth which is good, answers a call to duty shared by all men. So education, at least by this argument, is both ethical and divine.

[1] *The Reformation of Education*, London, 1923, p. 108.

In his chapter on 'Character and Physical Education', Gentile offers this central example of the soul's preponderance in the body. The picture is very close, again, to another central image in Yeats's poem :

The mother who tenderly nurses her sick child is indeed anxious for the health of the body over which she worries, and she would like to see it vigorous and strong. But that body is so endeared to her, because by means of it the child is enabled to live happily with her ; through it his fond soul can requite maternal love by filial devotion ; or in it he may develop a powerful and beautiful personality worthy to be adored as the ideal creature of maternal affection. If in the bloom of physical health he were to reveal himself stupid and insensate, endowed with mere instinctive sensuality and bestial appetites, this son would cease to be the object of his mother's fondness, nay, he would arouse in her a feeling of loathing and revulsion. It is this sense of loathing ... that we ... feel for the human corpse from which life has departed ; for life is the basis of every psychological relation, and therefore of every possible sympathy.[1]

To repeat, then, 'the spirit is the root and possibility of every unification' (p. 195). This idea is Greek in the best sense : The soul and body are one, with 'gymnastics ... the essential complement of music, including in music all forms of spiritual cultivation' (p. 195). Moreover, Gentile conceives of physical activity as Christian, especially after the Italian Renaissance ; consequently, the emphasis is on the spirit, the body by his argument being itself spirit.

The central chapter is that entitled 'The Ideal of Education', subtitled 'Art and Religion'. It is primarily a defence of education as a becoming of the spirit before the objections of so-called realistic educators and the more old-fashioned pedants of sheer multiplicity. Gentile's ideal education, where 'the spirit *is* in that it *becomes*, that it becomes in so far as it acquires self-consciousness, that its being therefore is consciousness in the act of being acquired' (p. 226), identifies the

[1] *The Reformation of Education*, London, 1923, p. 194.

subject with the object, the spirit with its culture, the pupil with his education. Here, too, we come to an important idea, which Yeats seems to have made full use of in the last enigmatic line of his poem :

The spirit's being is its alteration. The more it *is*,— that is, the more it becomes, the more it lives,— the more difficult it is for it to recognise itself in the object. It might therefore be said that he who increases his knowledge also increases his ignorance, if he is unable to trace this knowledge back to its origin, and if the spirit's rally does not induce him to rediscover himself at the bottom of the object, which has been allowed to alter and alienate itself more and more from the secret source of its own becoming. Thus it happens, as was said of old, that 'He that increaseth knowledge increaseth sorrow.' All human sorrow proceeds from our incapacity to recognise ourselves in the object, and consequently to feel our own infinite liberty.[1]

Gentile goes on to say, almost immediately, that 'the reality of the spirit is not in the subject as opposed to the object, but in the subject that has in itself the object as its actuality' (p. 229). There then follows what I take to be an elaboration of this reality and, even more important, an explanation of what came to be the organizing principle of 'Among School Children'. This long passage can be said to lie at the heart of the poem :

This dialectic in which the spiritual becoming unfolds itself (subject, object, and unity of subject and object), this self-objectifying or self-estrangement aiming at self-attainment,— this is the eternal life of the spirit, which creates its immortal forms, and determines the ideal contents of culture and education. The spirit's self-realisation is the realisation of the subject, of the object, and of their relationship. If of these three terms (the third being the synthesis of the first and second) any one should fail, the spiritual reality would cease to be.
This threefold realisation admits empirically of a separation that makes it possible to have one without the others. On the strength

[1] *Ibid.*, pp. 228–9.

of this triple division we speak of art, of religion, and of philosophy, as though each of them could subsist by itself.

     •   •   •   •

But in reality they are so indissolubly conjoined, that separation would destroy their spiritual character, and put in its place mechanism, which is the property of all that is not spirit.

Art is the self-realisation of the spirit as subject. Man becomes enfolded in his subjectivity, and hears but the voice of love or other inward summons. . . . He simply spreads out over his own abstract interior world, and dreams ; and as he dreams, he escapes from the outer bustle into the seclusion of his enchanted realm, which is true in itself until he issues from it and discovers it to be a figment of his phantasy. This man is the artist, who, we might say, neither cognises nor acts, but sings.

     •   •   •   •

This lyrical bent, peculiar to the artist who enhances himself by exalting his own abstract individuality, is in direct contrast with the tendency of the Saint, who crushes and annihilates this same individuality in the face of his God,— that God who infinitely occupies his consciousness as the 'other' in absolute alterity to him, so that the subject is hurled into the object in a total self-abstraction. . . . So he deifies this other self, places it on the altar, and kneels before it. Thus the saint's personality is nullified ; or rather, it is actualised and realised in this self-annulment, which is the theoretical and practical characteristic of mysticism and the specific act of religion.

     •   •   •   •

The nature then both of art and of religion implies a flagrant contradiction which comes to this, — that the subject to be subject is object, and the object to be object is subject. Hence the torments of the poet and the spasms of the mystic.

     •   •   •   •

The concrete spirit is neither subject nor object. It is a self-objectifying subject, and an object which becomes the subject in virtue of the subjectivity that alights on it as it realises it. The spirit is therefore a becoming. It is the synthesis, the unity of these two opposites, ever in conflict and yet always intimately joined. And the spirit, as this unity, is the concreteness both of art (reality of the abstract subject) and of religion (reality of the abstract object). It is philosophy.[1]

The gist of Gentile's discourse is clear. The first of the triad, art, allows the spirit to realize itself as subject ; but to avoid the mere retreat into dream, with the consequent pain of return to reality, the subject must objectify itself. The religious man, on the other hand, banishes the subject by completely identifying it with the object, God. In both cases, the images of the artist and the saint are literally self-born. The unifier of these two poles, subject and object, is the concrete spirit which can be neither one nor the other but is a synthesis, a becoming, in short both. It goes by names of the third member of the triad — philosophy. Religion and art, unless they inform each other, become abstractions that leave the self in a despair of egotism or a sacrifice to an ascetic illusion. Nor is the philosophy which brings them together the arcane profession of the specialist. Yet something of a paradox remains. For this ideal philosophy 'is never finished, never completed, for it is his [man's] own spirit, his very self, which to live must grow, and which must constitute itself as it develops. And therefore this philosophy cannot help being man's ideal, which is always being realized and which is never fulfilled' (p. 239). But it is those fragments, those incomplete men — 'the aesthete, or the superstitious worshipper, or the star gazer, always unaware of the pit under his feet' — who are most to be pitied. Gentile labels them nuisances to be contrasted in 'strength, agility, balance' with the rounded spirits (p. 244). The aim of Gentile's education would seem to be an exalted, superhuman, cosmic dancer attuned to the infinite vibrations of life at every moment of its becoming.

V

Maud Gonne herself tells us in *A Servant of the Queen* that by her mother's wish she had no formal schooling but was

[1] *Ibid.*, pp. 230–6.

taught privately by a slow-witted English governess in Ireland
and later by a more witty lady in France. Her early memories
are those of virtually running wild over the hills and heather
of Howth with the native Irish. Her childhood there had been
like that depicted in those other dancing girls — Iseult Gonne
and Margot Collis — that Yeats celebrated. Her beauty was
girlish, combining the symmetry of Greek statuary, the pride
of a Pallas Athene, and what Yeats called a 'classical impersonation of the Spring'.[1] Like 'A Woman Homer Sung', Maud
is inevitably described in Yeats's verse as 'half lion, half
child', or as possessed with 'the simplicity of a child', or as an
Irish Helen learning her tinker's dance, 'part woman, three
parts a child'. Not only did he associate her with light and
blossoms, but according to Mrs. Yeats, he held in memory the
beauty of the flowering chestnut trees in the Paris springtime
as a remembrance of her beauty then. Moreover, her love
of birds — including a Donegal hawk — was shared with
an equally powerful love of children. She had organized
the Daughters of Ireland. Though she cannot be called the
wisest of mothers, she once said to Yeats after a trip to
Italy that she loved the cascades of Italian children, the large
families so much like those in Ireland.[2] During the 1913
Strike her special concern was the feeding of the workers'
children.[3]

There is even something childlike in her relationship with
Yeats: she had once believed that they had been sister and
brother; they once acknowledged themselves spiritually
married.[4] Between the two a remarkable harmony remained,
despite periodic exasperations on both sides. Yeats could say,

[1] *Autobiographies*, p. 123.
[2] Information from Mrs. W. B. Yeats.
[3] 'Meals for School Children', *Irish Times*, 29 October 1913, p. 8.
Maud once 'drafted a parliamentary bill for meals for school children',
Hone, *W. B. Yeats*, p. 151 n.
[4] Unpublished draft of Yeats's *Autobiographies*. All unpublished
material in this essay is copyright © Michael Butler Yeats and Anne Yeats
1965.

for instance, in an early unpublished draft of his *Autobiographies* :

> My outer nature was passive but for her I should never perhaps have left my desk, but I knew my spiritual nature was passionate even violent. In her all this was reversed, for it was her spirit only that was gentle and passive, & full of charming fantasy as though it touched the world only with the point of its fingers.

.   .   .   .

> I who could not influence her actions, could dominate her inner being. I could then have use [of] her clairvoyance to produce forms that would arise from both minds. . . . There would be, as it were, a spiritual birth from the soul of a man & a woman.[1]

And, curiously enough, their relationship sometimes reminds one of the two elder children of Lir, once described thus : 'Fionnuala was the eldest and she was as beautiful as sunshine in blossomed branches ; Aodh was like a young eagle in the blue of the sky'.[2] Not only does their love, their transformation to swans, their tragedy, and their reunion in the Tir-na-nOg vaguely relate to the poem, but this description also recalls Yeats's own memory of Maud in 1889, published in 1921 : 'Her complexion was luminous, like that of apple-blossom through which the light falls'.[3] His own self-identification with the eagle is well enough known. I have, moreover, purposely taken this description of Fionnuala and Aodh from Ella Young's *Celtic Wonder-Tales* because there among Maud Gonne's decorations and illustrations is one recurring motif, original with her so far as I can tell, of a sphere containing two swans intertwined, ultimately blent as one, an obvious symbol of kindred souls. This, but one more of Maud's gifts for children, Yeats knew and may have consciously remembered. Perhaps then, a child's 'colour upon cheek or hair' and 'Plato's

---

[1] *Ibid.*
[2] Ella Young, *Celtic Wonder-Tales*, illustrated and decorated by Maud Gonne, Dublin, 1910, p. 145.
[3] *Autobiographies*, p. 123.

parable' in the poem are even more widely suggestive than we had thought.

Hence as perennial subject for Yeats's verse, as lover of children, spiritual counterpart, classic living beauty (even in sibylline old age), epitome of blossoms, dancing, light and flowering chestnut, perhaps even as imagist for children, Maud Gonne belongs to the poem. She loved best Yeats's poem about her, 'The Two Trees'. Did she see that both trees lived on in 'Among School Children'?

VI

It is best to introduce the poem itself with a caveat Yeats made at the beginning of his essay on Berkeley. There he admitted the utility of various abstractions — among them the educational notion that those who could not read might be called degraded. Such abstractions, he declared, helped maintain community life. They were useful if not final. But truth itself, Yeats warns us, 'is always mothlike and fluttering and yet can terrify'.[1] Thus in turning to 'Among School Children' we must face not only Yeats's hopes for education in Ireland but also his ultimate feelings about generation and becoming. Something of this truth appears in a passage in a white vellum notebook begun 7 April 1921. The passage seems to have been written in March 1926, some time close to the 14th. Here it is:

> Topic for poem — School children &
> the thought that live [*sic*] will waste them
> perhaps that no possible life can fulfill
> our dreams or even their teacher's
> hope. Bring in the old thought that
> life prepares for what never happens.[2]

---

[1] 'Bishop Berkeley', *Essays and Introductions*, p. 400.

[2] Unpublished journal. See *Letters* (ed. Allan Wade), p. 719; for a thoughtful discussion of this note and early versions of the poem, see also Thomas Parkinson, 'Vestiges of Creation', *Sewanee Review*, lxix (Winter, 1961), pp. 92–111. A journal begun in December 1908, from which the passages in *Estrangement* are taken, contains this unpublished entry dated

The whole poem resolves the praise of a practical ideal of education as shown in Stanza I and the reservations about this revealed in Yeats's journal.

The first stanza of 'Among School Children' strikes me initially as not at all ironical in its context. With thinly veiled references to place and time, it presents us with an occasion — an Irish Senator visiting a model school. Both the long room and the children's co-ordinated activities suggest the Montessori and P.N.E.U. systems. The standing children stare for a moment, but the assumption is that they have been preoccupied and presumably happy at work. The 'kind old nun' rounds out the religious and divine coif, hinted in her white hood, that seems to crown their labours. Nor do I find any immediate mockery in 'the best modern way'. We are ushered into an excellence on the corporate and communal level. The questions, the kindly replies, and the public smile among the happy children are a prosy homage to an ideal that at least tries to face life's uncertainties, if not the truth that is 'mothlike' or terrible. Perhaps such mixed thoughts, along with mention of Yeats's age, also suggest the beginning of the faint poetic ache which is elaborated time and again in the succeeding stanzas. Yet it must be insisted upon that these children would not be better off running wild in the fields. Most important, however, they with their singing, ciphering, reading, history, home-making and religious instructions have silently provided the poet in this first stanza with all the strands of his three themes — art, religion and philosophy, as they

6 September [1909]: 'I thought of this house [Coole] slowly perpetuating itself & the life within it, in ever increasing intensity of labour, & then of its probably sinking away through courteous incompetence or rather sheer weakness of will for ability has not failed in young Gregory, and I said to myself "Why is life a perpetual preparation for something that never happens ?" Even as Odysseus only seems a preparation to think of ruin or remembrance. Is it not always the tragedy of the great and the strong, that they see before the end the small & the weak, in friendship or in enmity, pushing them from their place, & marring what they have built, & doing one or the other in mere lightness of mind.'

present themselves alone, and then together united by the divine philosophy of the concrete spirit.

The second stanza offers a contrast with the first. The pain that arises from poor or obsolete education is revealed in the poet-Senator's reverie. In contrast to the children of the first stanza, Maud Gonne is recalled as a young woman confiding in a half-lit scene the educational stupidity that had made a day of her childhood tragic. In this dream or reverie, Yeats also remembers how for that moment their natures *appeared* to be one, as though sympathy had brought their complementary natures together as one soul. Such are the dangers of artistic fantasy, as Gentile warned : the subject fixes on itself, on what might have been when — both young and handsome and of the same mind — Yeats had given reality to a dream of Maud that was not to be.

In an effort to objectify — as Gentile might say — his reveries, the poet looks at the children, only to be made even more wildly and painfully aware of Maud's beauty as a child, for both she and they are birds of a sort, though of different kinds. Then, in his wondering — the children's had been momentary — still in his partial dream, she appears as a child. But this appearance gives way in the fourth stanza to something else. This third and present image is obviously that of Maud in her sixties : 'with her great height and the unchangeable lineaments of her form, she looks the Sibyl', as Yeats wrote in those years.[1] There is a contrast then in images, even in beauties, that is immediate and powerful. A Quattrocento finger might well have fashioned the girlish Maud as well as it had fashioned a Leda, any number of Madonnas, babes and assorted gods and goddesses. A Botticelli, a da Vinci (in earlier versions and drafts), even a Raphael might have done justice to this Flora, this 'classical impersonation of the Spring' and luminous creature.[2] But Maud's present image is a special, difficult kind of beauty, the very essence of what Yeats meant

[1] *Autobiographies*, p. 123.   [2] *Ibid.*

by Quattrocento art. For this image is of 'intellectual beauty', or '"the victory of the soul"' during a time when 'the Mother of God sat enthroned' amid the 'Soul's unity'.[1] This is what Quattrocento art could do, according to Yeats, to celebrate the marriage of earth and heaven. These are also the aesthetic properties of ideal becoming. A Botticelli had seemed to combine the motifs of Porphyry's Cave and the Holy Manger, both great emblems of the soul's entry into the world, in a 'Nativity' Yeats had seen in the National Gallery.[2] Such a finger might have fashioned this image from hollows and shadows, precisely as Yeats does. After all, Maud combined, for him, as we have seen, the pagan and Christian virtues of classic beauty and Madonna. The beauty he finds in this sixty-year elegance is truly their spiritual child, though he creates it out of near despair. He has it both ways. There is a contrast in the years and yet she is to him still transcendently beautiful. Otherwise, looking about him, he realizes that before the children both he and she are scarecrows, another rude jar to his reverie nearly objectified in the classroom.

So far then, after the introductory stanza, we have read three more that have dealt with the lonely singer, as Gentile might say, the lyric poet in his reveries filled with the pain of his passion before living change that mocks the permanent image of his dreams. If there is a beauty in the language that can describe Maud's present skeletal image, it derives from a poet-artist in torment before the imagined child and the actual aged woman who was never truly his. His corrective, so to speak, lies in the children who also sing and whom he would not frighten. Their singing, in contrast to his, does not retreat to dreams and subjective memories. It is a balancing part of their daily multifarious labours.

In the fifth stanza, Yeats turns from his first theme of art, as exemplified in the passion of the artist, explicitly the poet

[1] *A Vision* (1925), pp. 203–4.   [2] *Ibid.*, p. 202.

himself. He turns here not to his other major themes of religion and philosophy, but to the human becoming that both practise on — in the rôle of Madonnas or philosopher-teachers — the becoming that commands the greatest earthly affection, a mother's hopes. Such affection is fixed upon the growing babe, who, according to Porphyry and Wordsworth, has ventured from a better world of the pure soul to a lesser one. Yet a mother, no matter what the pain of birth and bruise of body, imagines in the healthy shape a coming burgeoning of soul in human activity, perhaps even greatness, which may never be achieved. As children learn cutting, sewing and neatness among their studies, so they prepare for responsible parenthood. Yet a mother's generative endeavour, considered alone, is no less painful to her than is his song to the solitary singer. This stanza implies that time has also provided other betrayals here, perhaps three : that of the babe, the mother and the mother-to-be who would make generation the narrowed beauty of her life. For maternal affection is born in pain, hemmed in by uncertainties, and might well be broken by the sight of the child grown old. Before these realities, the pleasuring of a mother's soul must depend upon more than the hopes of a bruised maternity. The child must be more than neat, the mother more than mother.

The sixth stanza discovers another kind of affection, that of the so-called wise teacher. As an example of mistaken wisdom or philosophy, or a kind of misdirected affection, the stanza has an overlapping relation to Stanza VIII and its philosophy of unity. The philosophic teacher, if he has not begotten a scarecrow-to-be or even become one himself, by his very specialization has created one to frighten birds of any heritage. As Yeats wrote at the time : 'Aristotle and Plato end creative system — to die into the truth is still to die — and formula begins. Yet even the truth into which Plato dies is a form of death, for when he separates the Eternal Ideas from Nature and shows them self-sustained he prepares the

Christian desert and the Stoic suicide.'[1] All three men fail as
philosophers and teachers. The ciphering child has turned
into the specialist who fails with Alexander, as did Aristotle
— a bircher; who separated reality into the one and the
many, as did Plato (and not Berkeley and Gentile); or who
reduces flow to rigid integer, as did Pythagoras. Such mis-
begotten wisdom destroys unity, never makes the jump
between subject and object, between pupil and culture, ideal
and nature — or sing-song and logic.

In Stanza VII we turn to religion as the objectification and
virtual denial of self. The focus is on saintliness, the perfection
sought after in the cloister rather than the worship of the
ordinary man. The image of the artist had been of a past life
negated by a real present. The mother's image had been a
singular projection of the present negated by a likely future.
That of the nun is of an eternity — bronze or marble and in
repose — which human life negates at each moment. The
flesh that kneels before candles or bronze and marble images is
not only bruised, it can also have its heart broken by a perfection that man can at best only strive for. Appropriately at
this point, Yeats looks back to all those Presences — those
projections of the spirit, those avenging angels which we
image forth: passion knowing the form of a Ledaean body
that Quattrocento art had glorified in Madonna and pagan
goddess; affection creating the vision of the grown child based
on the shape that innocently invests a newly arrived soul, or
affection expressed in the taming of nature, kings and music in
the fond hope that they will body forth design, reason and
mensuration; and piety emulating a Mary or Madonna that
ensures the eternal presence of God. All such Presences are
born of the self that images them forth — in pure subjectivity
or objectivity — and yet those Presences, while symbolizing
heaven, also mock the fragmentary, incomplete nuisances we
have become, no matter what our industry or labour.

[1] *Ibid.*, p. 183.

145

The proper beginning of the concluding stanza is then most certainly with the word 'Labour'. For it signifies both the birth-struggle, that never stops in earthly becoming, and that task to which all of us are consigned. Yet 'labour' may truly be said to blossom and dance in an ideal culture, or education, if you will. Here art and religion (if we can accept both nuns and mothers as worshippers) are unified by an ideal philosophy that does not merely divide, coerce or measure the world. In an ideal culture, the tendance of the soul need not sacrifice the body, for religion will be properly tempered with an artistic regard for self. Nor need beauty necessarily be got from a despair of contrasts, since religion may help us see beauty in even a partially obviated or dilapidated self. Nor will the wisdom that brings art and religion together be that of the guest who excludes himself from life's feast. This ideal of roundness — spiritual and physical, in any case ideal — Yeats had caught a glimpse of in the first stanza. Among the children, song, measurement, domestic chores and religion were one. And now he apostrophizes that unity.

From a nation's point of view, as complement to the child's, reading books and studying history and religion together may provide a total view of a district, the nation and even the world. They may also include Greek philosophers, the story of Christ, the Italian Renaissance, and a poet's memories. This unity of study provides a civic view of the nation where past, present and future are one much in the same way that bole (past), leaf (present) and blossom (future) merge in a chestnut tree. This 'great-rooted blossomer' is rooted in spirit or the ideal, which gives unity to multiplicity, does not separate them as Plato did, and, as object of a child's contemplation, keeps all his future studies and years living and unified. The chestnut tree, itself like a living body, the symbol of an ideal civic culture under the aegis of religion, also has its artistic complement. I speak of that other symbol taken from those ciphering and singing Montessori children of the first stanza. Song and number realize the complementary artistic ideal of the dancer whose 'gaze of motion' is constantly brightening with the increased grace of a child's proper becoming or growth. Here is 'aimless joy' and 'pure activity', yet also discipline. Like the image of the eighteen-year-old dancer that Yeats requested in 1926 from T. Sturge Moore as the design for a book-plate for Anne, this dancer would be just as likely to be pictured dancing between the earth and the moon.[1] She brings both together. She too is a symbol from life in motion — 'what a child sees' — not a Graeco-Roman cast on a shelf. The music is the formal complement of the soul during its dance of life. Musical number provides the dancer with a measured motion rather than arresting her or abstractly reducing her to counting fixed intervals on a stick or string.

Yet there is one more line and that line maintains the tragic plaint of wasted human endeavour apparent in even the original idea of the poem. Already in the question 'Are you the leaf, the blossom or the bole?' Yeats seems not only to have commended the ideal of a unified civic education — to the benefit of child and state — but he also suggests its inherent limitation. For if a child discovers himself at one with the organic, virtually timeless, growth of the nation, how can he know or understand the uniqueness of his own historical moment? Thus, in the last line, Yeats makes an even more insistent reservation on what might be called man's finest concept of education. The line reminds us that even ideally, even in the new friendly long Montessori classroom, the superchild-to-be must still face those limitations of his humanity, as have those burdened specialists, whether artists, mothers, philosophers or nuns. This last line merely repeats much more finely the paradox voiced by Gentile of a philosophy which in fulfilling itself cannot be realized, the

---

[1] *W. B. Yeats and T. Sturge Moore, their Correspondence, 1901–1937*, ed. Ursula Bridge, New York, 1953, pp. 60, 90, 91, 113.

paradox of an ideal identification of subject and object — the child and his culture — where the self is liable not to be discerned, where the child cannot know his infinite liberty, here in space. The lovely merge of dancer and dance, like the difficult beauty of a sixty-year-old woman, may yet also break hearts. As Gentile observed, 'He that increaseth knowledge increaseth sorrow'. After all then, there may be just the slightest touch of irony in the conclusion of that first Senatorial stanza. Then, too, the presence of Maud Gonne, whether as disappointed child, divine mother, soul's companion or beloved witness to Parisian springtime, lends fragile human grandeur to what might have otherwise been the irony of the inconsolable.

VII

In 1937, A. N. Jeffares, then a student at the High School on Harcourt Street, Yeats's old school, rang up Yeats and, as editor, asked for a poem as a possible contribution to the April issue of the *Erasmian*, the school publication. After some thought Yeats selected a poem called 'What Then ?' that looked to his own youthful designs, labour, later accomplishments and successes that had brought him friends, home, family and even some perfection in his own work — and these in the face of the buffoonish detractors that Dublin can always offer. Yet the refrain ending each stanza of the poem remained the same : '*What then?*' This sentiment had been the impetus of his own growth. As a scholar at the Godolphin School, Hammersmith, he had been virtually at the bottom of his class.[1] Nor had Yeats distinguished himself academically at the High School. He had, however, done something more. Lacking the patience for a grammatical adventure with the classics, he had readily surrendered himself

[1] Godolphin School Reports, 1878, in the possession of Mrs. W. B. Yeats.

to cribs and bad marks, yet, as John Eglinton has gone on to remind us :

> Yeats in the High School was a kind of super-boy, who enjoyed an enviable immunity from the various ignominies of school discipline.

.   .   .   .

His privileged standing among the boys was due, no doubt, to some arrangement with his father, who had applied certain educational principles to his children's upbringing, of which spontaneous development was the essential : and Yeats was really an unusually well read young man of about 19, with a conscious literary ambition.[1]

The point is best made in Yeats's own youthful remarks to J. B. Bury, editor of Gibbon : "'I know you will defend the ordinary system of education by saying that it strengthens the will, but I am convinced that it only seems to do so because it weakens the impulses'".[2]

Finally then, irreverently perhaps, one cannot help musing over Trinity's thoughts of granting Yeats a professorship in literature in 1913, he who could not have passed the entrance examination as a nineteen-year-old, and then, of course, going no further with that appointment. Nor, in the same year, does U.C.D. seem to have given the same matter much more thought. Nor can one forget the ever-buoyant remarks of the two present Irish literary greats, remarks directed at Yeats as a poet during the very gestation period of 'Among School Children'. The first was by Frank O'Connor, who said, 'Now, what do I find wrong with Yeats? I find this : that never, at any time or for any occasion whatsoever, does his art come into touch with life, with the world around us.'[3] Sean O'Faoláin merely endorsed O'Connor's fantasy when in the next month he called Yeats's poetry that of 'passing

[1] 'Yeats at the High School', *Erasmian*, xxx (June, 1939), p. 11.
[2] 'I Become an Author', *The Listener*, 4 August 1938, p. 218.
[3] 'What Is Irish Literature', *Irish Statesman*, 12 December 1925, p. 430.

moods', to be compared unfavourably with native Gaelic poetry, 'that of basic emotions'.[1]   One wonders what they came to think 'Among School Children' was about ?   Otherwise, in later saying that 'Man can embody truth but he cannot know it', Yeats was but ascertaining once again part of his own life's work :   the imaginative bodying forth of an ideal Irish culture while never ceasing to try to explain it to himself. Consequently, in even so exciting and exacting a problem as the education of the young, his final position in 'Among School Children' realistically remained that of metaphysical mystery.

[1] 'Irish and Anglo-Irish Modes in Literature', *Irish Statesman*, 9 January 1926, pp. 558–9.

WILLIAM BUTLER YEATS

*

A. D. HOPE

To have found at last that noble, candid speech
In which all things worth saying may be said,
Which, whether the mind asks, or the heart bids, to each
Affords its daily bread;

To have been afraid neither of lust nor hate,
To have shown the dance, and when the dancer ceased,
The bloody head of prophecy on a plate
Borne in at Herod's feast;

To have loved the bitter, lucid mind of Swift,
Bred passion against the times, made wisdom strong;
To have sweetened with your pride's instinctive gift
The brutal mouth of song;

To have shared with Blake uncompromising scorn
For art grown smug and clever, shown your age
The virgin leading home the unicorn
And loosed his sacred rage —

But more than all, when from my arms she went
That blessed my body all night, naked and near,
And all was done, and order and content
Closed the Platonic Year,

Was it *not* chance alone that made us look
Into the glass of the Great Memory
And know the eternal moments, in your book,
That we had grown to be?

SOME YEATSIAN VERSIONS OF COMEDY

*

HAZARD ADAMS

Joy and woe are woven fine.

BLAKE

IN THIS CENTENARY YEAR, as we pause to salute a great achievement, it is well to remind ourselves that Yeats wrote not only poems and plays but also two of the most remarkable books of his time — the *Autobiographies* and *A Vision*. Perhaps because we are still staggered by Yeats's poetic accomplishments we are inclined to overlook the fact that these works are, so to speak, books in themselves. Of course, we have read them with care, but usually as if they were mines of interpretation situated somewhere underneath the poetry. Because they have been so very helpful to us as mines, the qualities which they possess in themselves are not often remarked. One of their most absorbing qualities is the comic. Nevertheless, in a recent excellent study, *The Irish Comic Tradition*, Professor Vivian Mercier has disregarded both books; indeed Yeats has usually been considered an essentially tragic writer. There is nothing fundamentally wrong with such an assessment : all of us know that the tragic and the comic, rather than being incompatible, are necessary contraries. But the scales of Yeats criticism have long been tipped rather too far in the direction of high seriousness. The result is that without fail we have tended to discover behind Yeats's poetic ironies a brooding solemnity, and we have tended to treat it as more fundamental than the gesture of the language itself. Although I accept the essential tragedy in many of Yeats's poems, I must insist that when we examine *Autobiographies* and *A Vision* it will positively not do to pass through Yeats's outward gesture too rapidly. *Autobiographies* and *A Vision* are serious books, but their seriousness comes to us in a very complicated way and is perhaps more the act of coming than what comes. The books *are* gestures. That this is so should not surprise us when we consider the emphasis which Yeats himself put upon drama and gesture not only in art but in life as well.

The comic in *Autobiographies* and *A Vision* is more than casually related to Yeats's strong but peculiar sense of fate. Fatality is, of course, the source or vehicle of much tragedy. To couple it with comedy may call for explanation. Fatality in Yeats is curiously different from that irrepressible cosmic force in, say, Hardy. Yeats's vision is at all time dialectical, and one finds his idea of fatality inevitably attached to a curious freedom. Although Yeats refers to exterior fate in a prose passage I am about to quote, generally we can say that Yeatsian fate flows outward from within the individual; it is not primarily an outer force pressing down on the hero but something generated out of his human nature and even his own individuality.[1] Furthermore, the idea of fate has ultimately no meaning for Yeats without the contrary existence of the will. Yeats writes in *The Trembling of the Veil*:

Among subjective men (in all those, that is, who must spin a web out of their own bowels) the victory is an intellectual daily recreation of all that exterior fate snatches away, and so that fate's antithesis; while what I have called 'the Mask' is an emotional antithesis to all that comes out of their internal nature. We begin to live when we have conceived life as tragedy. (p. 116)[2]

[1] I am not referring here to what Yeats calls in *A Vision* the 'body of fate', which *is* the outer world and its events, but am using the word 'fate' to stand for something never directly named in his work except perhaps at the end of *A Vision*, where it is called peculiarly 'freedom'.

[2] All quotations from Yeats's autobiographical writings are taken from *The Autobiography of William Butler Yeats*, New York, 1953, published in England as *Autobiographies*, London, 1955. Page numbers following quotations refer to the New York edition.

L

We have here the dialectic of the gyres. The last sentence tips
the balance for tragedy just as critics of Yeats have so often
done, but we must remember that much of Yeats's writing
takes up where this quotation ends : what does one do after
one makes such a formulation of experience ? What does one
do after one has begun to live ? One must take a stance before
tragic truth. One must make one's laughter *contain* the tragic
perception, rather than allowing tragedy to smother one's
will :

> Their eyes mid many wrinkles, their eyes,
> Their ancient, glittering eyes, are gay.
>
> ('Lapis Lazuli')

Is it not important to remember, then, the following passage
from *Estrangement* ?

> Tragedy is passion alone, and rejecting character, it gets form
> from motives, from the wandering of passion ; while comedy is
> the clash of character. Eliminate character from comedy and you
> get farce. Farce is bound together by incident alone. In practice
> most works are mixed : Shakespeare being tragi-comedy. Comedy
> is joyous because all assumption of a part, of a personal mask,
> whether of the individualised face of comedy or of the grotesque
> face of farce, is a display of energy, and all energy is joyous. (p. 286)

The remark about farce here is interesting, particularly with
respect to *A Vision*, and I shall return to it. But I am more
concerned with the implied interweaving of comedy and
tragedy and with Yeats's association of the comic with the
mask.[1] In examining *Reveries over Childhood and Youth* we
might well note that the Yeats of that book is well masked,
indeed twice masked. He is masked first by the 'confessional'
nature of the work, which invites us by its own inner form to

---

[1] It is important to remember that Yeats means nothing derogatory
by his use of the word 'mask'. We associate masks perhaps with
criminals and Hallowe'en hobgoblins, or a puritanism within us associates
it with the impropriety of mimesis in the theatre, a sort of deception.
But Yeats's aesthetic stance makes the tools of drama the avenue not to
magical delusion but to ideal reality.

neglect judging it on the basis of biographical veracity and to remember as we read that the speaker himself is part of the construction. In this case he is a character thinking, and the book as a whole is the familiar romantic monologue of a created voice. But because the character is speaking of his past there is a further removal. The character re-created by the monologist is in turn the child, the young man, and the dramatist of about 1900. All of these, it is well to remember, are creations *from a point of view*. We might call the whole thing an intimate distancing, in which romantic expressiveness is balanced by what T. S. Eliot characterized as the necessary extinguishing of the personality. The whole book might be called an excellent example of Keats's 'negative capability' exhibited in autobiographical circumstances. Yeats's flowers come not upon the highway to be doted upon.

The source of Yeats's comedy is similar to that of fatalistic tragedy. It lies in the relation of the individual to fate; but rather than Hardy's brooding cosmic or natural force, Yeats's fate seems to be generated out of self.

I know now that revelation is from the self, but from that age-long memoried self, that shapes the elaborate shell of the mollusc and the child in the womb, that teaches the birds to make their nest; and that genius is a crisis that joins that buried self for certain moments to our trivial daily mind. There are, indeed, personifying spirits that we had best call but Gates and Gate-keepers, because through their dramatic power they bring our souls to crisis, to Mask and Image, caring not a straw whether we be Juliet going to her wedding, or Cleopatra to her death; for in their eyes nothing has weight but passion. We have dreamed a foolish dream these many centuries in thinking that they value a life of contemplation, for they scorn that more than any possible life, unless it be but a name for the worst crisis of all. They have but one purpose, to bring their chosen man to the greatest obstacle he may confront without despair. (pp. 164–5)

We must always remember that we ourselves contain the gates and gate-keepers here mentioned. We look through gates much as, according to Kant, we wear involuntarily the spectacles of time and space. Because he acknowledges this undesired wilfulness in us, Yeats often sees us fool-like and doltish in ridiculous conflict not only with our time and place ('body of fate') but also with the fate we ourselves apparently and mysteriously generate. Yeats's versions of comedy lie in his sense of the fundamental irrationality of life, glimpsed from a position as rational as we partly irrational creatures can make it. Unfortunately under the circumstances no position is ever either irrational or rational enough. Therefore, the speaker of Yeats's books becomes involved in farce as both observer and object of comedy, and the comedy is ironic.

In *Reveries Over Childhood and Youth* the Yeats recalled is a child, the Yeats speaking an adult. As the speaker views the child he generates an ironic distance not unusual in reminiscences of youth. There is something conventionally comic in observing childish activities from an adult point of view or observing adult life from the point of view of childhood. But it is clear that this manipulation of point of view in *Reveries*, which is apparently conventional, becomes less so in the later books, where the author watches the young man Yeats observing not adults from childhood but other adults. Finally in *A Vision* the author's curious treatment of himself as a character in the book controls the work's whole drama. The result of this sort of distance is not primarily tragic but curiously humorous. Indeed, if we look back at *Reveries* after reading the whole of *Autobiographies* we sense that the humour there is not quite the sentimental humour we conventionally thought it to be, that the author means more by the distance established in the discussion of childhood because he maintains it in the later books.

We must now examine what he does mean. In *Reveries* observations of the child lend considerable humour, and this fact is particularly interesting in the light of an assertion made in *The Trembling of the Veil* about 'imaginative men who must always, I think, find youth bitter' (p. 225) and an even more personal statement early in *Reveries* :

> Indeed I remember little of childhood but its pain. I have grown happier with every year of life as though gradually conquering something in myself, for certainly my miseries were not made by others but were a part of my own mind. (p. 7)

Bitterness is not, however, the tone of *Reveries*. Rather the child is shown confused by the irrationalities of his intercourse with adults. The speaker's tone is that of a wondering, searching contemplation of human nature. The child himself is the comic victim of rapid shifts of attitude, sometimes his own :

> . . . having prayed for several days that I might die, I began to be afraid that I was dying and prayed that I might live. (p. 3)

This childish changeability does not, as we might expect, disappear in the later books. Instead it seems to be characteristic even of adulthood. Nor is the child's inconsistency the only peculiarity of life. The world itself is strange :

> . . . everybody had told me that English people ate skates and even dog-fish, and I myself had only just arrived in England when I saw an old man put marmalade in his porridge. (p. 21)

So all that had been told him of the English was true ! And more ! But then his grandfather, though Irish, spoke approvingly of the eating of skates. How strange ! Perhaps the child is asking too much of the world. Perhaps he takes things too much at their face value :

> . . . because my grandfather had said the English were in the right to eat skates, I carried a large skate all the six miles or so from Rosses Point, but my grandfather did not eat it. (p. 31)

Is the moral here that words do not lead to deeds and that causality is complex ? Does the child discover anything quite so precise as all that ? He discovers certainly that his grandfather did not eat the skate. Does he conclude, too, that the world is irrational ?

In an unexpectedly irrational world, perhaps it is the naïvely rational creature who is its victim or dolt because he is out of step with experience. Certainly adults misunderstand the child as much as the child misunderstands them :

> Several of my uncles and aunts had tried to teach me to read, and because they could not, and because I was much older than children who read easily, had come to think, as I have learned since, that I had not all my faculties. (p. 14)

The speaker often remembers his childish incapacities :

> My father was still at Sligo when I came back from my first lesson and asked me what I had been taught. I said I had been taught to sing, and he said, 'Sing then' and I sang
>
> > Little drops of water,
> > Little grains of sand,
> > Make the mighty ocean,
> > And the pleasant land.
>
> high up in my head. So my father wrote to the old woman that I was never to be taught to sing again. (p. 15)

In the face of these peculiar adult acts it is no wonder that thought becomes unmanageable for the child. But there is also something working within the child himself that is responsible :

> My thoughts were a great excitement, but when I tried to do anything with them, it was like trying to pack a balloon into a shed in a high wind. (p. 25)

Indeed, the irrationality of the 'real' world of adulthood seems to become even for the older narrator its central form, and the experience of it in childhood seems permanently to have affected his adult attitudes towards people and the supernatural. There is no doubt that, as he looks back, the speaker of *Autobiographies* relishes the remembrance of what seems to be wild eccentricity in others. He likes to think of this wildness as characteristically Irish. His remembrance of people has a mythical quality beginning as early as the appearance of an Irish schoolmaster in his English school :

There was but one interruption of our quiet habits, the brief engagement of an Irish master, a fine Greek scholar and vehement teacher, but of fantastic speech. He would open the class by saying, 'There he goes, there he goes,' or some like words as the headmaster passed by at the end of the hall. (p. 25)

Wild eccentricity Yeats associates with freedom, but because Yeats also believes in a fate generated from within, he sees that freedom must be positively asserted against some other aspect of the self. Therefore he detects in the people he mythicizes and most admires a certain theatricality. He recalls in various episodes the theatricality of his Pollexfen grandfather and several of the Yeatses, including his father. The Middletons, on the other hand, lacked 'the instinctive playing before themselves that belongs to those who strike the popular imagination' (p. 10), and Yeats's reverie seldom includes them. The theatrical sense is what separates Yeats's comic heroes from those unconsciously heroic and world-defying grandparents, uncles, and aunts of James Thurber.

In the many reminiscences of his studies in and experience of the occult, this love of the great character is combined with that comic self-disparagement recognizable in the treatment of his own youth. In the midst of a serious description of a seance there appears the following comment:

I was now struggling vainly with this force which compelled me to movements I had not willed, and my movements became so violent that the table was broken. I tried to pray, and because I could not remember a prayer, repeated in a loud voice —
'Of Man's first disobedience and the fruit
Of that forbidden tree whose mortal taste
Brought death into the world and all our woe . . .
Sing, Heavenly Muse.' (p. 64)

The ridiculousness here plays off Yeats's upbringing against conventional life, but in the most unexpected way, making his incapacity not pathetic but comical and in some curious way even possibly admirable. There is no pose implied by Yeats's quoting Milton in his excitement. Rather there is quite the opposite — an unwilled gesture — a sort of desperation in his recognition that *something* must be said. The speaker sees, alas, no theatricality in these early past selves. He would like to see it, but the world and himself get in the way. Or, to put it another way, he has been rudely thrust out upon the stage without a proper part. A little different are incidents and thoughts described in *The Trembling of the Veil* :

I had various women friends on whom I would call towards five o'clock mainly to discuss my thoughts that I could not bring to a man without meeting some competing thought, but partly because their tea and toast saved my pennies for the 'bus ride home ; but with women, apart from their intimate exchanges of thought, I was timid and abashed. I was sitting on a seat in front of the British Museum feeding pigeons when a couple of girls sat near and began enticing my pigeons away, laughing and whispering to one another, and I looked straight in front of me, very indignant, and presently went into the Museum without turning my head towards them. Since then I have often wondered if they were pretty or merely very young. Sometimes I told myself very adventurous love-stories with myself for hero, and at other times I planned out a life of lonely austerity, and at other times mixed the ideals and planned a life of lonely austerity mitigated by periodical lapses. (pp. 93–4)

Here the young man either fails to 'act' or locks his theatricality in his own fantasy, finds no mask. Behind this story we must remember the voice of its teller, the dramatic masked Yeats, a speaker with the requisite stage presence, consumed by his part. The actor must be able to communicate his maskedness. As Dr. Johnson long ago pointed out, we never assume the play to be 'real'. Indeed we want to know that the players are players so that we may admire them, escaping out of the sense of the disagreeable or agreeable into a sense of the beautiful. For Yeats aesthetic distance is a state of mind relevant to the contemplation not merely of works of art but of all life itself.

The young Yeats described is present in *Autobiographies* partly in order to allow the speaking actor to blow off dramatic steam. The point is not merely that egoistic masking is necessary to us all but that the mask is a sort of ideal. (Therefore, when in *A Vision* Mary Bell holds up the egg which will hatch the great rough beast of the new era, Denise de l'Isle Adam [a pseudonym] comments, 'She has done very well, but Robartes should have asked me to hold it, for I am taller, and my training as a model would have helped.' [p. 53]) Behind this sort of gesture, often farcical, as above, lies a very serious conception enunciated most clearly in *Estrangement* :

There is a relation between discipline and the theatrical sense. If we cannot imagine ourselves as different from what we are and assume that second self, we cannot impose a discipline upon ourselves, though we may accept one from others. Active virtue as distinguished from the passive acceptance of a current code is therefore theatrical, consciously dramatic, the wearing of a mask. (p. 285)

Romantic imaginative creativity is here given a curious twist. In order truly to create, the individual must seek a mask, an opposite perhaps impossible to attain, and thus freedom is 'fated' in so far as our natures are not freely chosen. All such activity defies the logic of society as well as of language : 'Style, personality — deliberately adopted and therefore a mask — is the only escape from the hot-faced bargainers and the money changers' (p. 279). Indeed, logic is the villain. 'Logic is a machine, one can leave it to itself; unhelped it will force those present to exhaust the subject, the fool is as likely as the sage to speak the appropriate answer' (p. 279).

When Yeats describes others in the *Autobiographies* it is a similar theatricality expressed with some strange irrational *élan* that he most admires. Of Madame Blavatsky Yeats remembers that Henley said to him, 'Of course she gets up fraudulent miracles, but a person of genius has to do something' (p. 107). Yeats's meeting with her emphasizes her eccentricity, not the crazy heroism of Thurber's grandfather, insisting upon *his* own world and brandishing his sword against the Sciota River or breaking the spirit of his electric car, but that of a great lady on a stage :

... I was kept a long time kicking my heels. Presently I was admitted and found an old woman in a plain loose dark dress : a sort of old Irish peasant woman with an air of humour and audacious power. I was still kept waiting, for she was deep in conversation with a woman visitor. I strayed through folding doors into the next room and stood, in sheer idleness of mind, looking at a cuckoo clock. It was certainly stopped, for the weights were off and lying upon the ground, and yet, as I stood there the cuckoo came out and cuckooed at me. I interrupted Madame Blavatsky to say, 'Your clock has hooted me.' 'It often hoots at a stranger,' she replied. 'Is there a spirit in it ?' I said. 'I do not know,' she said, 'I should have to be alone to know what is in it.' I went back to the clock and began examining it and heard her say, 'Do not break my clock.' (pp. 106–7)

The reminiscing Yeats admires nothing more than a person about whom a good story can be told. A good story seems to be one which contains a grain of comic irrationality or at least something unsuspected by logic. Madame Blavatsky provided that sort of story :

When I first began to frequent her house, as I soon did very constantly, I noticed a handsome clever woman of the world there, who seemed certainly very much out of place, penitent though she thought herself. Presently there was much scandal and gossip for the penitent was plainly entangled with two young men, who were expected to grow into ascetic sages. The scandal was so great that Madame Blavatsky had to call the penitent before her and to speak after this fashion, 'We think that it is necessary to crush the animal nature ; you should live in chastity in act and thought. Initiation is granted only to those who are entirely chaste,' but after some minutes in that vehement style, the penitent standing crushed and shamed before her, she had wound up, 'I cannot permit you more than one.' (p. 109)

The turnabout spoken in the grand style Yeats inevitably recalls. He also always remembers the paradoxical quip, true beyond apparent logic. So he quotes with great admiration Wilde's words about Shaw : 'Mr. Bernard Shaw has no enemies but is intensely disliked by all his friends'. He follows Wilde's lead himself in a letter of 1911 to T. Sturge Moore : 'When a man is so outrageously in the wrong as Shaw he is indispensable, if it were for no other purpose than to fight people like Hewlett, who corrupt the truth by believing in it'.[1]

He remembers also Madame Blavatsky saying that people sell their souls to the devil 'to have somebody on their side'. He delights in her description of religions :

'That is the Greek Church, a triangle like all true religion,' I recall her saying, as she chalked out a triangle on the green baize, and then as she made it disappear in meaningless scribbles, 'It spread out and became a bramble bush like the Church of Rome.' Then rubbing it all out except one straight line, 'Now they have lopped off the branches and turned it into a broomstick and that is protestantism.' (p. 110)

Precisely what kind of theatricality is characteristic of the great 'actors' Yeats observes ? It is difficult to say, because Yeats, the actor in his book, quite consciously and for the sake of drama obfuscates the issue. The heroic, almost mythical figures of *Autobiographies* have a sort of discipline, but how it is achieved remains a mystery to the speaker. Yeats describes his own search for it :

Discovering that I was only self-possessed with people I knew intimately, I would often go to a strange house where I knew I would spend a wretched hour for schooling sake. I did not discover that Hamlet had his self-possession from no schooling but from indifference and passion-conquering sweetness, and that less heroic minds can but hope it from old age. (p. 57)

We can agree that the speaker of these words has schooled himself in theatrical discipline. Much of *Reveries* is therefore composed of (1) a great actor's recollections of his own past

[1] *W. B. Yeats and T. Sturge Moore : Their Correspondence, 1901–1937*, London, 1953, p. 19.

fumblings for the mask of nonchalance and (2) remembrance of those in his life who lived their theatricality with glorious abandon, whether willed or fated. Such a gesture is apparently necessary to creative life, and it is essentially comic.

By the time that Yeats came to write *A Vision* he seems to have raised the idea of heroic theatricality and cosmic irrationality to principles of human existence. These ideas actually control the form of the work. In 1928 he was involved in the now well-known exchange of letters on epistemology, or more specifically John Ruskin's cat, with T. Sturge Moore. In one of these letters he wrote:

> If Kant is right the antinomy is in our method of reasoning; but if the Platonists are right may one not think that the antinomy is itself 'constitutive', that the consciousness by which we know ourselves and exist is itself irrational? I do not yet put this forward as certainly the thought of my instructors, but at present it seems the natural interpretation of their symbols.[1]

This sort of statement needs a great deal of qualification and perhaps some correction if it is to become philosophically responsible. Nevertheless it is quite helpful to us as we look at *A Vision* and its comedy. The comedy of *A Vision* arises constantly out of the idea that we cannot adequately know all things by logic or indeed by means of any symbolic system available to us.[2] The comedy is often farcical in Yeats's sense; that is, it is comedy with character eliminated and full of grotesquerie.

A Vision is not a discursive work with the aim of communicating a philosophical or pseudo-scientific system of thought. Its so-called 'system' must be abstracted up and out of it with the greatest care, for the book as a whole has a dramatic shape and a recognizable, though complicated, gesture. Taken in

[1] *W. B. Yeats and T. Sturge Moore: Their Correspondence, 1901–1937*, London, 1953, p. 131.
[2] I have discussed this matter in 'Symbolism and Yeats's *A Vision*', *Journal of Aesthetics and Art Criticism*, xxii, 4 (Summer, 1964), pp. 425–436.

this way the introductory material of the book must be considered as intimately related to the more technical parts. In *A Vision*, as in *Autobiographies*, the speaker is contained by the total form of the book, and his gesture is a fictional one. Within this form, Yeats the speaker reminisces about Yeats the questor for mysterious cosmic knowledge. At the same time Yeats the speaker creates fabulous farcical stories about the discovery of the system of thought he is about to expound. These stories seem to reflect in life what the system puts to us more abstractly, the idea that the 'antinomies cannot be solved'.[1] The characters in the stories about Michael Robartes and the preparation of the cosmic egg to hatch the new cultural cycle are characterless characters. They are, in fact, nearly allegories representing aspects of their author's being. The world they inhabit is irrational, the author's treatment of them ridiculous, though at bottom the issues raised are quite serious. All the characters are driven, in the Yeatsian sense, towards mask and image.

There is not enough space here to make a long analysis of the introductory sections of *A Vision*, and one example of what Yeats is doing must therefore suffice.[2] In *Stories of Michael Robartes and his Friends* a man named John Bond tells a very strange story of falling in love with Mary Bell, wed to an elderly man who early in their marriage decided to devote his life to some philanthropic endeavour, namely teaching cuckoos to make nests. This virtually mad, certainly hopeless effort everyone in the story seems to take seriously enough, and indeed there is in the end a sort of Don Quixotish heroism about the old gentleman. John Bond and Mary Bell between them make him believe on his deathbed that one of his more intelligent students has at last succeeded in weaving

[1] Quoted from Yeats's 'Genealogical Tree of Revolution', in A. N. Jeffares, *W. B. Yeats: Man and Poet*, London, 1962, p. 351.
[2] For a longer discussion see my *Blake and Yeats: The Contrary Vision*, Ithaca, 1955, pp. 162–99.

a nest. The absurdity of the ideal and the seriousness of it from the old man's point of view emphasize the strangeness of those many human efforts we all know about which are perhaps only a little less absurd. John Bond and Mary Bell are names taken from William Blake's 'William Bond' and 'Long John Brown & Little Mary Bell', the latter of which is one of Blake's most raucous poems about sexual relations and their failure when the 'selfhood' triumphs over the desire to annihilate the self in love. There is much giving of the self in John Bond's story. It does not result in a closer apprehension of reality on the part of any of the characters, but it does result in a limited sort of satisfaction. The old man dies content. Mary Bell has helped him to contentment through her efforts to produce a cuckoo's nest from her own hands and therefore she is to a degree content herself, and John Bond, an expert on birds, has been of service to both.

But more important even than these things is the epistemological problem of inner fate implied by the whole matter of teaching, or trying to coax cuckoos, who do not naturally build nests, to an unnatural effort. This matter is, in fact, taken up in *Autobiographies* :

> When Locke's French translator Coste asked him how, if there were no 'innate ideas', he could explain the skill shown by a bird in making its nest, Locke replied, 'I did not write to explain the actions of dumb creatures', and his translator thought the answer 'very good, seeing that he had named his book *A Philosophical Essay upon Human Understanding*.' Henry More, upon the other hand, considered that the bird's instinct proved the existence of the Anima Mundi, with its ideas and memories. Did modern enlightenment think with Coste that Locke had the better logic, because it was not free to think otherwise ? (p. 160)

A few pages later, Yeats tells us that he himself keeps canaries and at one time provided them with an artificial nest, 'a hollow vessel like a saucer', so that they were not in need of the wild bird's skill. The canaries would twist stems of grass around the nest. Yeats observed the mother and father birds taking care of the young, and he has observed his own children, concluding:

When a man writes any work of genius, or invents some creative action, is it not because some knowledge or power has come into his mind from beyond his mind ? It is called up by an image, as I think . . . but our images must be given to us, we cannot choose them deliberately. (p. 164)

We cannot, like the cuckoos, get very interested in nest-making if we are not nest-making creatures. But we are poem-makers, perhaps — or at least some of us are — and Yeats seems here to express a romantic individualistic version of that old idea called possession by the Muse. In any case, revelation is 'from the self', but from an 'age-long memoried self'. In the farcical story of *A Vision* in which Yeats recounts his experience with the mysterious instructors, he casts himself much as he remembers himself in *Autobiographies*, incapacitated by an irrational reality in which the whole direction of modern society with its logical education refuses to believe. The instructors come to him from within and yet from some strange 'other' world as well. They are some part of himself, and yet he cannot control them or even communicate adequately with them. The results are farcical events — his wife falls into a trance in a restaurant because the instructors think them to be in a garden, the instructors complain about Yeats's slowness and literalness of mind, Yeats tries to drive away his wife's dream that she is a cat by barking like a dog. These events are very funny, verging sometimes upon the slapstick. The result is quite similar to that of the comedy in *Autobiographies*. It emphasizes the limits of man's control over himself and the naïveté of man's faith in simple 'reality'. It suggests that man inhabits a world where he will always look a bit foolish and will always confront something beyond his powers to understand. As a result, the gesture that man makes towards his situation is his most important function. Yeats recommends a fine balance of tragic irony and ironic comedy, the laughing lip praised by the red man in *The Green Helmet*,[1] the glittering eyes of the Chinese sages in 'Lapis Lazuli', gay joy in the contemplation of theatrical eccentricity, willing acceptance of the joke upon oneself, even when that joke is a cosmic one. All of these stances imply the necessity of discovering what dignity one can salvage from cosmic farce :

I think that the true poetic movement of our time is towards some heroic discipline. . . . When there is despair, public or private, when settled order seems lost, people look for strength within or without. Auden, Spender, all that seem the new movement, *look* for strength in Marxian Socialism, or in Major Douglas ; they want marching feet. The lasting expression of our time is not this obvious choice but in a sense of something steel-like and cold within the will, something passionate and cold.[2]

At first glance steel-like coldness seems antithetical to the comic, but perhaps if we study comedy carefully we shall see that it is not. In any case, the comedy which Yeats offers us is ironic comedy, laughter emanating from a mask of cold ideality. It leads oddly enough to a great sense of humanity which is nowhere better shown than in the ironic conclusion of *A Vision*. There, the absurd relationship between himself and his instructors having been set forth, Yeats admits to the limitations of his powers to interpret the instructors' message. Indeed does the message contain knowledge at all ? Sitting in his chair, meditating upon the symbols of gyre and cone, he discovers, like Faust, that ultimate knowledge will not be his. For a moment he grieves, but

Then I understand. I have already said all that can be said. The particulars are the work of the *thirteenth sphere* or cycle which

---

[1] The relevant lines are :
... And I choose the laughing lip
That shall not turn from laughing, whatever rise or fall ;
The heart that grows no bitterer although betrayed by all ;
The hand that loves to scatter ; the life like a gambler's throw.
[2] *The Letters of W. B. Yeats*, ed. Allan Wade, London, 1954, pp. 836–7.

is in every man and called by every man his freedom. Doubtless, for it can do all things and knows all things, it knows what it will do with its own freedom but it has kept the secret. (p. 302)

Yeats seems almost to exult in this conclusion. It does after all represent the achievement of a kind of knowledge — though ironic like that in which Kant takes pleasure — but more important it completes a total gesture and concludes the ironic comedy of which it is a part.

Reveries over Childhood and Youth ends with a statement not unrelated to it :

For some months now I have lived with my own youth and childhood, not always writing indeed but thinking of it almost every day, and I am sorrowful and disturbed. It is not that I have accomplished too few of my plans, for I am not ambitious, but when I think of all the books I have read, and of the wise words I have heard spoken, and of the anxiety I have given to parents and grandparents, and of the hopes that I have had, all life weighed in the scales of my own life seems to me a preparation for something that never happens. (p. 65)

Indeed this passage appears very much the antithesis of comedy, but by a sort of negative appraisal one can see, I think, that the statement is meant to reveal that there is a possible contrary to its speaker : a masked figure who cares not a fig for 'preparation' or for some great day, a figure who believes in the 'now' of things, in momentary gay gesture and in drama, a figure who believes that there are things more important than all that is laboriously achieved by material effort or consumed by the mill of the mind. In *Autobiographies* this contrary figure, a perhaps coarse and indecorous artist, insists on a considerable substance of comedy, serious as it may be, some of it satirizing the too-solemn, insufficiently masked young man remembered by the speaker, much of it remembering with affectionate awe great comedians among old acquaintances and their momentary acts.

Beautiful lofty things : O'Leary's noble head ;
My father upon the Abbey stage, before him a raging crowd :

'This Land of Saints', and then as the applause died out,
'Of plaster Saints'; his beautiful mischievous head thrown back.
('Beautiful Lofty Things')

The comic is a necessary aspect of Yeats's art that should not be neglected. Its apprehension is necessary to any tragic perception we discover in Yeats's work. On the great poet's tombstone famous words advise the passing horseman to 'Cast a cold eye/On life, on death'. Let us remember that the warm eye laments and overflows. It is the cold eye, high on the mountain or on horseback, that, seeing abroad, glitters.

YEATS AS ANTHOLOGIST

*

JON STALLWORTHY

I

NOTHING STIRS UP THE DUST of the literary arena so much as an anthology, and there can be few better examples of this than *The Oxford Book of Modern Verse.*[1] Now that the dust of controversy has fallen away, it is possible to reconstruct the moves and countermoves of this minor, but entertaining, fragment of literary history.

In the summer of 1930 Humphrey Milford, Publisher to the University of Oxford, proposed to the Georgian poet Lascelles Abercrombie that he should compile an *Oxford Book of Modern Verse.* His reply has survived only in an extract quoted in a memo from Milford to Kenneth Sisam, the distinguished Anglo-Saxon medieval scholar who was at that time Assistant Secretary to the Delegates of the University Press, at the Clarendon Press, Oxford :

	Oxford University Press
	Amen House
26 July 1930	Warwick Square London E.C.4

Oxford Book of Modern Verse

Lascelles Abercrombie writes (25 July) :
'An Oxford Book of Modern Verse ? I thought you had one, and a terrible thing it is. But a book to represent 1900 onwards —

---

[1] I am grateful to the Delegates and the Secretary to the Delegates of the Oxford University Press for permission to examine and reproduce letters from their files ; also to the Oxford University Press for permission to quote extracts from Dorothy Wellesley : *Letters on Poetry from W. B. Yeats to Dorothy Wellesley* (1940).

that would be a delightful pie to cook, and I would love to have a finger, or even two, in it. Certainly I'll come and see you about it when I get back.'

H I M

Abercrombie was almost certainly thinking of *The Oxford Book of English Verse*, A.D. 1250–1900, chosen and edited by Sir Arthur Quiller-Couch, which included poems by Binyon, Blunt, Gosse and Yeats, but none of his own. He agreed to edit the new anthology, and was to be assisted in his researches by Milford's niece, Anne Bradby, later to become better known as Anne Ridler. All appears to have gone well, if slowly, until 1934 when the poet and playwright Charles Williams, an editor at the London office of the Press, wrote in a memo to Milford :

> [Oxford University Press
> Amen House

2 October 1934   Warwick Square London E.C.4][1]

L.A : O.B. Modern Verse

I saw L. A. yesterday. He was in considerable distress over the book, both personal and moral. It has begun to dawn on him (i) that none of his poetic acquaintances are going to love him afterwards, (ii) and more bitterly, that he hasn't really the time to exercise a proper judicious choice, and that his reputation may suffer (he said, as regards both i and ii that it was 'going to take a long time to live down'), and (iii) that he's hardly going to find time to do it all. I pointed out the financial advantages, and alluded to our difficulty. But I was so convinced that we should gain little advantage from having him put his name, and so dubious whether his name will — now — help very much, that I consented — subject to higher approval — to relieve him of the lists and see if we can manage another way. And I am very strongly of opinion that it would be profitless to try and force it through him. He swears he would like to be of any little use he can, but the whole task — it is now clear — he would muddle.

This leaves me with two alternatives : (i) to try and get another Name (ii) to do without a Name, and rely merely on the modernity

---

[1] Addresses in square brackets indicate that a letter or memo has been transcribed from a carbon copy on unheaded typing paper.

... a fairly unknown name might excite no feeling on any side —
moderns or traditionalists or what not. I have had a growing feeling
that L.A.'s book might be crabbed merely as L.A.'s, and I think
there is a good deal to be said for not prejudicing anyone in advance
— if the *Oxford Books* and *Modern Verse* can together make up
sufficient force in the title for sales.

If we come to human possibilities, I can think of two. One is
Dylan Thomas. We rather reluctantly declined some very modern
poems of his some time ago ; and he has been to see me two or
three times and shown me some more of his stuff — chiefly short
stories. I passed these on to Curtis Brown, who thought enough
of them to talk of financing him for a novel. He tells me that he
came to know Eliot, and Faber and Faber are probably publishing
a book of poems. He does reviewing for the *Morning Post* and the
Bookman. I do not know what his capacities as a selector may be ;
his own verse is very physiologically modern.

The other possibility is, of course, Anne herself. She's done a
lot of work already, and would finish it off as well as anyone I can
think of.

My own immediate feeling is to let her go on with it, under her
name ; to introduce L.A. into the preface as having given advice
with the older poets ; and perhaps to ask Dylan Thomas to look
through the stuff and give any comments that occurred to him. . . .

C.W

Though Milford was 'doubtful about the best policy',
Sisam felt strongly 'that a name is very important for these
books ; that there is little difference between anonymous,
Dylan Thomas and Anne Bradby . . . a name well known to
the reviewers and suggesting readability seems to me to be
essential for the project'.

Charles Williams accordingly drew up a list of possible
editors.

[Oxford University Press
Amen House
Warwick Square London E.C.4]

Oxford Book of Modern Verse

Names then.

Names are of two classes — (i) the greater (ii) the lesser. Of
the greater, Cumberlege plumped for *Yeats*, and there is no doubt

he would be the one name which would awe all sides. He is 69, but when I met him last year he was vivid and entertaining. He would have to be offered much more money down, I suppose (£250 or £300 ?), but he has a 'modern' manner, is admired by the moderns, and his name will last when he is dead. I doubt if he'd take him [*it ?*] on, but I could write.

T. S. Eliot is probably tied up to Faber, but again he would be generally acceptable. I should think his time however would be too occupied.

De La Mare I dont feel much drawn to.

Aldous Huxley ? (I'm rather attracted by the idea !)

(ii) Lesser names will hardly 'frighten reviewers'. I feel fairly clear that *Dobree* wouldn't — not as a selector of modern verse . . . *Robert Graves* might want too much trouble, and from our point of view might be too ec-centric [*sic*].[1] I see *G. M. Young* reviews poetry and criticism, and is rather amusing and good : is he too crowded with *Victorian England* ?

There, for the moment, my mind fails. I lean to (i) Yeats (ii) Aldous Huxley ; and of the names that won't frighten to (i) Read (ii) Young. My own acquaintance, the *Human Parrot* Belgion, passed through my mind, but he'd frighten less.

C.W

11 October 1934

Sisam and R. W. Chapman, then Secretary to the Delegates of the Press, also voted for Yeats, who was thereupon approached through his literary agent, A. P. Watt & Sons, and agreed to undertake the task. A memo from Milford to Chapman, dated 8 November 1934, begins : 'I forgot to mention yesterday that Watt said Yeats was keen to include Americans'. At this point Sisam issued a *caveat* to Milford :

. . . You are dealing with an editor who has himself passed from the popular to the very select audience. At Amen House I think you are all inclined to the highbrow attitude in poetry, so he will get no leaven of commonplace from the contact. Therefore, better tell him at the outset that a popular book which ordinary people can enjoy is intended : that, even if 'The Fiddler of Dooney' is

---

[1] He had, after all, published in collaboration with Laura Riding *A Pamphlet Against Anthologies* (1928).

inferior to his latest bits of hard and high thinking, you (at least in your capacity of publisher) expect him to fiddle. After all, Yeats has immediately reminded you through a literary agent that even the most spiritual poets need money. He could hardly be offended if you, in your capacity as publisher, don't take a loftier line . . .

There is no record of this being passed on to Yeats, who in March 1935 wrote to Olivia Shakespear :

The proof sheets and typescripts I am correcting are for the Cuala edition of *Dramatis Personae*, as I call the coming instalment of autobiography. After that will come the proof-sheets of *A Vision* and then my work as editor of *The Cambridge* [*sic*] *Book of Modern Verse*. I can never do any kind of work (apart from verse) unless I have a clear problem to solve. My problem this time will be : 'How far do I like the Ezra, Eliot, Auden school and if I do not, why not ?' Then this further problem 'Why do the younger generation like it so much ? What do they see or hope ?' I am to write a long introduction.[1]

II

In May 1935 a Memorandum of Agreement was signed whose first clause laid down :

That the Editor agrees to compile a volume of between five hundred (500) and six hundred (600) pages in length in the style of the Oxford Book of English Verse which shall contain poems representative of the period nineteen hundred and thirty-five (1935) by British, Irish and American poets and which as at present arranged shall be entitled

THE OXFORD BOOK OF MODERN ENGLISH VERSE

The Editor agrees to use where practicable his personal influence in applying for permission to use therein copyright matter and to supply an introduction, list of acknowledgements and indices to the said volume.

In his reading for the anthology Yeats came upon the poems of Dorothy Wellesley. Early in June Lady Ottoline

[1] Wade dates this letter 'shortly after . . . March 4'. See *The Letters of W. B. Yeats*, London, 1954, p. 833.

Morrell introduced them, and so began a friendship that was to last until Yeats's death. On 17 June he wrote to her of his progress : 'For the moment I am studying you, Edith Sitwell, Sacheverel Sitwell and Sackville West together'.[1] On 6 July he was asking her : 'Do you know the work of Elinor Wylie ? Since I found your work I have had as sole excitement here "Eagle and Mole", a lovely heroic song.'[2] Curiously, this did not appear in his final selection. The same letter told how he had

re-read all Edith Sitwell and found her very hard to select from, poem is so dependant upon poem. It is like cutting a piece out of a tapestry. If you have strong preferences among her poems please tell me. I have made my choice but feel very uncertain. I take back what I said of your friend Sackville West, having found 'The Greater Cats', that has the irrational element rhetoric never has. It is very moving.[3]

On 4 July[4] Yeats had written to his agent :

Being now clear of my illness I am working at the 'Oxford Book of Modern Verse'. Would you mind asking Mr. Milford if I can begin from the death of Tennyson instead of the arbitrary 1900.

This new date will enable me to put Gerald [*sic*] Hopkins at the beginning, instead of in a period with which he has no connection except that he remained unpublished for so many years. It will also enable me to bring in Dowson and some others who belong to the Modern Movement, though they died before 1900.

This very reasonable request was passed to Milford, who in turn passed it to Sisam, who commented on 9 July :

I am in favour of Yeats' suggestion, provided he goes back to 1892 only to show a development, i.e. he does not treat all poets

[1] Dorothy Wellesley, *Letters on Poetry from W. B. Yeats to Dorothy Wellesley*, London, 1940, p. 5.   [2] *Ibid.*, p. 7.   [3] *Ibid.*, p. 8.
[4] The date of this letter (which, to the best of my knowledge, exists only in this extract quoted in a letter dated 5 July from Watt to Milford) must remain tentative. This extract, that on pp. 177–8, and Yeats's letters of 24 October, 15, 19 and 27 November 1935 — all here published for the first time — are © Michael Butler Yeats and Anne Yeats 1965 and reproduced by their kind permission.

between 1892 and 1900 on the same basis as those from 1900 onwards; but takes from 1892 to 1900 those poets whom he thinks
important for the purpose of his book, because they represent a
developing rather than a dying tradition.

Accordingly, Yeats was given the permission he wanted.

On 26 July we find him writing to Dorothy Wellesley:
'Your praise of the poem by Edna St. Vincent Millay — I have
only known her so far in Anthologies and have liked one or
two things — has made me order all her books.'[1]   He evi-
dently found nothing there that he liked well enough to include
in his own anthology.   During the middle of August he and
his daughter Anne paid a visit to Penns in the Rocks, Dorothy
Wellesley's home.   She remembers that

the fortnight was a busy one, interrupted only by games of croquet
with his daughter and mine. We sat, indoors or out, surrounded
by the piled volumes of contemporary poets, for I was anxious to
persuade him to reconsider some of his selections and omissions for
The Oxford Book of Modern Verse, and especially his decision to
omit nearly all the war poets, including Wilfred Owen. On this
point he remained adamant . . .[2]

A week later, and back in Dublin, he writes complaining

I am tired, I have spent the day reading Ezra Pound for the
Anthology — a single strained attitude instead of passion, the
sexless American professor for all his violence.

I delight in a young poet called George Barker (Faber & Faber)
a lovely subtle mind and a rhythmical invention comparable to
Gerard Hopkins . . .[3]

On 11 September Yeats's agent relayed to Charles Williams
a further progress report:

I have been working on the Anthology for the last three or four
months. I went to London three weeks ago and read or smelt 45
books of poetry in the British Museum as I could not get them
anywhere else. I have now completed about 400 of the 500 pages
I am aiming at. I shall have finished the collection by the end of the
month. I shall want a couple of weeks after that to look it over,

---

[1] Dorothy Wellesley, *op. cit.*, p. 13.
[2] *Ibid.*, p. 21.   [3] *Ibid.*, p. 25.

put things in and take things out.   One of my difficulties at the moment is that three books I want badly are out of print ; if I can't borrow them, or get them from a second-hand bookseller I shall have to pay another visit to the British Museum.   I wonder if Mr. Charles Williams could help me, as they are on the list of books suggested to me by his firm :—

Isaac Rosenberg	Poems 1922
Coppard	Collected Poems
Roberts	These Our Matins

Does the Oxford University Press want to publish for Christmas or for next Spring ?

17 September found Yeats writing to Dorothy Wellesley : 'I am absorbed in the Anthology, excited mainly by certain philosophical poems [of W. J. Turner's]. . . . Some of the poems are exquisite.   I choose the word deliberately — exquisite as a flower or a seabird.'[1]   Five days later she asked him

Are you including Flecker's 'Old Ships' and 'The Dying Patriot' ?   Do consider from the Shropshire Lad : 'Be still, my soul, be still ; the arms you bear are brittle'.   Have you found the passage from Bridges called 'Come se quando' ?   It concerns the starry heavens and was I thought in Shorter Poems.   Wilfred Owen, 'Strange Meeting', and other names occur to me, Edward Thomas, Stella Gibbons.[2]

Of the poems she suggests, only 'Old Ships' found its way into the anthology :   Yeats represented Edward Thomas by one short poem, and included nothing by Wilfred Owen and Stella Gibbons.   On 1 October he writes to Dorothy Wellesley : 'I found I had given more from you than from anybody else and this would not do, people would think it was friendship, especially as, I think, you come immediately before T. S. Eliot'.[3]   This anticipates his final calculation of the number of pages per poet : 'T. S. Eliot $14\frac{1}{2}$ pages, Turner 17 pages, Lady Dorothy $17\frac{1}{2}$ pages, Edith Sitwell 19 pages but nobody will count'.[4]   Events were to prove him wrong.

---

[1] Dorothy Wellesley, *op. cit.*, p. 30.
[2] *Ibid.*, p. 31.   [3] *Ibid.*, p. 34.   [4] *Ibid.*, p. 42.

At last the first fruits of his labour arrived in the form of a list (dated 9 October 1935) of poets and the number of poems by each to be included. Comparing this with the final list of contents, we learn that he originally intended to include one more poem by the following : Abercrombie, Blunt, Bridges, Roy Campbell, de la Mare, Drinkwater, Lady Gregory, Hardy, Henley, Hodgson, Housman, Hughes, Kipling, Nichols, Edith Sitwell, Dorothy Wellesley ; two more poems by Brooke ; three more by Day Lewis and Strong ; four more by Barker, and four 'extracts' by Eliot ; five more by Masefield ; seven more and three 'extracts' by Pound. This preliminary list, however, shows one poem fewer by Blunden, Dowson, Field, Madge and Turner than were finally chosen ; two poems fewer by Lawrence ; three fewer by MacNeice ; and four fewer by Margot Ruddock. Seven poets feature in the preliminary list but not the book : Elizabeth Daryush, Graves, John Gray, Edna St. Vincent Millay, R. L. Stevenson, Sir William Watson and Elinor Wylie. Four who appear in the book do not feature in the preliminary list : Boyd, Trench, Waley and Yeats himself. It should be stressed that there were several reasons other than aesthetic ones for these changes.[1] Some poets, for example, could not accept Yeats's choice of their work, others wanted to charge too much.

The preliminary list was presumably accompanied by a detailed list of authors and titles, for two days later we find Charles Williams writing to Yeats :

W. B. Yeats Esq.,	[Oxford University Press
'Riversdale',	Amen House
Willbrook,	Warwick Square London E.C.4]
Rathfarnham, Dublin.	

11 October 1935

Dear Mr Yeats,

The letters asking for permission are being typed here, and we hope to dispatch them to you this week. We will take steps to ask

[1] See Yeats's Introduction to *The Oxford Book of Modern Verse*, p. xlii.

for the Bridges and Daryush poems direct, and Gerard Hopkins [*these three were Oxford authors*] is certainly at your disposal ; you need not trouble about any of them.   About the Watson poems there may be some difficulty ;   Lady Watson does not, I think love the Oxford Press.   Perhaps she will give you what she might not give us ;   I wonder, if you need him, whether a personal letter might not be more successful than our formal draft.

We rely upon you to be generous to us (which is, in fact, no more than to be just to yourself) with your own poems.   Blame us in the Introduction if you choose ;   we could bear it quite proudly, and there also you will be as long as possible, I hope ;   it is an important part of the making of the book.

I am not quite sure, from Watt's letter, and after looking through your lists, whether they cover the whole book, or whether there are more to come.   A few other names occurred to me, but I realize you may be working on them now.   I take the risk of seeming officious, however, and send a brief list.

One entry perplexed me, and no-one here can help.   'Pater : The Mona Lisa'— *was* there such a poem ?   I knew — stupidly, perhaps — nothing but the prose purple of the essay on Leonardo.

The 'brief list' ran as follows :

John Davidson.	If Dowson & Johnson go in, might he not have a place ?
Charles Doughty.	He is beginning to be more widely read and studied.
Wilfred Owen.	He will be generally expected, both by old and young.
T. E. Hulme.	May not be important, but he was the first of or the leader of a movement, and I think might be desired.

Richard Aldington ?
F. S. Flint ? (Myself, I dont know him)
H.D ?
Robert Frost
Stephen Rose Beret [*sic*]

The last three are American, but you have some Americans, and the exclusion of these might grieve our countless U.S.A. readers.

None of these are to be taken as pressed against your conscience ;   they are no more than questions.

To this Yeats replied :

> Riversdale,
> Willbrook,
> Rathfarnham,
> Dublin.
> October 24 1935

Dear Mr Williams

I must apologise for not replying sooner to your letter. I had a slight operation which kept me to my bed for a short time. You speak of my ommissions of certain Americans ; H.D. Robert Frost, and Benet (your typist has written 'Stephen Rose Beret ; there are two Benets, one Stephen Vincent, the other William Rose.) I am acting on the advice of T. S. Eliot who said 'dont attempt to make your selection of American poets representative, you cant have the necessary knowledge and will be unjust ; put in the three or four that you know and like'— or some such words. I am taking his advice and am explaining so in my introduction. As a matter of fact this will be far better for the popularity of the book as I shall not have to condemn certain popular figures. I am putting in all the people well-known on this side of the water through residence or accident, with perhaps one exception, that exception is H.D. I have known her for many years, known her and admired her, and it was a real distress to me in looking at her work after ten or fifteen years to find it empty, mere style. Aldington also is a friend of mine, but I have always known that if I did an Anthology I would have to reject his work, just as I have had to reject everything except one poem by Squire, a friend to whom I owe certain obligations. When you get my introduction you will find why I reject Wilfred Owen and certain other war poets. I had John Davidson in but withdrew him on finding I had too much matter ; I may have to restore him. I was his contemporary and we never put him on a level with Dowson and Johnson. Hulme I have left out precisely because he was the mere leader of a movement.

Now about Doughty ; it will amuse you to hear that A. E. Housman refused me leave to quote even from his LAST POEMS (which he generally allows) because of my supposed enthusiasm (or that of your publishing house) for Hopkins (with Doughty as runner-up). I have had to turn infidel and deride both as if they were relics of the True Cross, and I am not quite infidel where Hopkins is concerned ; Doughty I cannot abide except in prose. . . .

I hear that Faber and Faber are bringing out an anthology and as the entire contents seem to have been approved by Laura Riding we are apparently in for a war of the books.

Yours
W. B. Yeats

Williams received no answer to his query regarding 'Pater: the Mona Lisa', though he had unknowingly answered it himself. Yeats wrote in his Introduction: '. . . I begin this book with the famous passage from his [*Pater's*] essay on Leonardo da Vinci. Only by printing it in *vers libre* can one show its revolutionary importance.'

The next three letters in this series provide an amusing illustration of the devious tactics that seem sooner or later to be inevitable in the preparation of an anthology.

Robert Nichols Esq.,
3 Upper Cheyne Road,
Chelsea, S.W.3.

[Oxford University Press
Amen House
Warwick Square London E.C.4]
12 November 1935

PRIVATE

Dear Mr Nichols,

Extremely unofficially and by a roundabout method your poems called A SPANISH TRIPTYCH came into my hands, and more unofficially than ever, I feel I ought to murmur to you that I have caused them to be dispatched where they should come under Mr Yeats' eye. You will understand that for obvious reasons other poets ought not to know of this, and of course no one can say anything to Mr Yeats. But I could not resist telling you.

Yours sincerely,
[Charles Williams[1]]

H. Watt Esq.,
Messrs A. P. Watt & Sons,
Hastings House,
Norfolk Street, Strand, W.C.2.

[Oxford University Press
Amen House
Warwick Square London E.C.4]
12 November 1935

Dear Mr Watt,

. . . There have come into my hands, by a roundabout process, two or three poems by Mr Robert Nichols, which I know he would

[1] As this and subsequent letters have been transcribed from carbon file copies, they are unsigned.

very much like considered. Since Mr Yeats is putting in something of his, and since I had a respect for some of his work, I have allowed myself unofficially to send them on to you. You will understand that neither Mr Nichols nor any of us here are doing more than allow them to slide under Mr Yeats' eye. But I gather that he thinks them better than are actually chosen, and a poet has perhaps some claim to have his own opinion considered. So long as there are not too many of them.

Yours sincerely,
[Charles Williams]

Riversdale,
Willbrook,
Rathfarnham,
Dublin.
November 15 1935

Dear Mr Williams

The poems you sent from Nichols I have either read or read poems exactly like them, I consider them unreadable [*last word crossed out*] vague, rhetorical, empty. Nichols and I have had some correspondance and I have a letter from him finally agreeing to a group of poems which pleases me without greatly displeasing him. I have his letter, dated October 26th, agreeing. He has no power of criticism. He suggested to me certain poems and some of these I have included. My selection gives a certain representation of his personality and his development, to some extent it dramatises both ; I do not think it would be possible to add to it, or to subtract from it without weakening the effect. He keeps pressing upon me poems which would blur the outline and add nothing but their own vagueness. I would sooner leave him out altogether than include any of the enclosed poems.

The list of Nichols' poems which I originally sent to you is not the list that Nichols and I have agreed upon.

Yours
W. B. Yeats

Four days later Yeats wrote again to Williams, this time on a different topic.

Nov 19 [1935]   Riversdale,
                                                                     Willbrook,
                                                              Rathfarnham,
                                                                        Dublin.

Dear Mr Williams

I go to Majorca on Nov 24 soon after I am gone my wife will send you the contents of the Anthology (the Introduction is written but may not be typed in time — I have to dictate my illegible script — I may have to finish by dictating to a friend in Majorca). Can you give me any idea when your firm will publish the book?

I enclose a poem which please return. I did not put it in the Anthology as I thought it would exclude the book from school libraries & for all I know you are counting on that public. I brought the poem to England & read it out to Dulac, Turner, Mrs Sackville West, Dorothy Wellesley & others, (cut as in the copy I send) all said it was a masterpiece & that it ought to go in. I have decided to throw the responsibility on you — on one side the school-libraries, on the other universal curiosity about the Primrose Path. Please say if the poem should be left out or not. I give another translation of the poem but not so good

                                                                         Yours
                                                                    W. B. Yeats

The next letter shows this to have been a translation by Oliver St. John Gogarty, which I am unable to trace, of Villon's '*Les Regrets de la belle Heaulmière*'.

W. B. Yeats Esq.,   [Oxford University Press
Riverside,   Amen House
Willbrook,   Warwick Square London E.C.4]
Rathfarnham, Dublin.   26 November 1935

Dear Mr Yeats,

Thank you for your letters, for returning the Nichols poems, and for the poem by Mr Gogarty which you sent. After a very great deal of careful consideration Mr Milford himself and those of us who have read the poems, are inclined on the whole to think you were right in your first decision. It is no doubt a nuisance that a publisher has to consider so many groups among the public, but that is beyond praying for, and if this Anthology was barred from the places where young people gathered together it might seriously limit both its use and its sales (after all they have Swinburne's translation of the *Fair Armouress*, though I do not say that it is so good). Regretfully therefore we return you the poem, accepting, with a conviction that you will blame us, the responsibility which you throw on us.

I am rather glad that you wrote as you did about the Nichols poems. I read them through and could not convince myself that they succeeded. It was therefore a relief when I found that you took that view. But I am sorry that the trumpets with which he began should have died under so cloudy a sky.

Yours very sincerely,
[Charles Williams]

To this Yeats replied the following day.

Nov 27 [1935]

Riversdale,
Willbrook,
Rathfarnham,
Dublin.

Dear Mr Williams

I think you are quite right, & the author thinks so too. I thought after reading it to London friends that perhaps I no longer understood the public & that therefore I had better consult you

I have finished my introduction (about thirty pages) finished except for verbal revisions which I will do in Majorca. My wife thinks it is [the] best bit of prose I have written for years

Yours

W. B. Yeats

I leave for Majorca to-morrow. The Anthology is complete so far as I can make it so — my wife has still some letters to write, some poems to type that I could not get in print

The typing of poems and securing of authors' permissions appear to have taken a further five months, and as late as April 1936 Yeats was still prepared to add to his selection. In reply to Dorothy Wellesley's remark, 'I found some really interesting poems by Laura Riding in some quarterly of which I cannot remember the name', he writes :

You are right about Laura Riding. I had rejected her work in some moment of stupidity but when you praised her I re-read her in 'The Faber Book of Modern Verse' & delighted in her intricate intensity. I have written to her to apologise for my error & to ask leave to quote 'Lucrece and Nara', 'The Wind Suffers', 'The Flowering Urn'. She will refuse, as Graves has, but as a matter of honour I must ask.[1]

Laura Riding, in fact, did not refuse, but made conditions that Yeats did not feel able to accept —

must see introduction, must see list of contents, must not take anything already in any other anthology. I have written very politely but pointing out that I am a despotic man & offering nothing. I have already over spent by about fifty pounds the five hundred pounds the Oxford Press set aside to pay authors.[2]

On 1 May, however, Charles Williams was able to write to Kenneth Sisam :

The MS arrived from Watt yesterday. It goes to you today by registered post ; including the Introduction, but not including any Acknowledgements. I have written to Watt asking about this list.

You will remark that Mr Gogarty is better than I feared. The whole book varies most amazingly from the most imbecilic simple poems of Masefield and Drinkwater to Mr Empson. You cannot however, say that it has not a great deal of very popular stuff in it.

C.W

The anthology, at last, was sent to press, and the summer and autumn of 1936 were taken up with proof-reading and sorting out the permissions that Yeats had passed to his publishers in a sorry tangle. Reading the galleys he was 'astonished at the greatness of much of the poetry, & at its sadness. Most of the "moderns" — Auden, Spender, etc. seem thin beside the more sensuous work of the "romantics".'[3] On 15 November he wrote to Ethel Mannin.

My dear Ethel, I have asked the Oxford University Press to send you a copy of my anthology of modern verse which comes out next Thursday. I hear that the first edition has been subscribed

---

[1] Dorothy Wellesley, *op. cit.*, p. 64.
[2] *Ibid.*, p. 67.   [3] *Ibid.*, p. 81.

twice over so it will not be a copy of the first edition, but probably you are like me and care but little what edition you read. I will write your name in it when we meet. The introduction may interest you — a little of my favourite thoughts are there.[1]

On Thursday 19 November *The Oxford Book of Modern Verse* was published.

III

The Times reviewer the following morning welcomed the anthology enthusiastically :

By a happy inspiration the Oxford Press has chosen whom many would choose as the greatest living poet for the editor of the volume which brings down to the present day the series of Oxford Books of Verse.

Mr Yeats contributes not only some of the finest poems in the book, but also an introduction which is a brilliant and penetrating essay on English poetry during the last half century.

. . . Those who would cavil at his principles of selection, or at the high arguments with which he justifies them, may reflect that any ordinary man can be mechanical, and that greatness, even where it is wilful, is given us to learn from, not to teach.

The *Spectator* reviewer on the same day sounded a very different note :

. . . No one is going to deny the attraction of Mr Yeats's name on the title-page ; no one can fail to be curious about the attitude to contemporary poetry of its most eminent living exponent. But, in selecting him to edit the last of the Oxford Books for many years to come, the Delegates of the Clarendon Press may not unreasonably be accused of opportunism of a kind that tempts newspaper editors to print the opinions of the Church on the Modern Novel and of Modern Novelists on the Church.

After a statistical 'breakdown' of the space allotted to each of the ninety-five poets represented in the anthology, the reviewer turned his guns on to the editor :

[1] *The Letters of W. B. Yeats*, ed. Allan Wade, p. 867.

Unfortunately, Mr Yeats's fragmentary introduction throws very little light on his method of selection. It is a curious, tantalising and unintegrated piece of work, too perfunctory and shapeless to satisfy the reader who expects a critical survey of modern verse and not sufficiently conclusive to justify Mr Yeats's predilections.

To this reviewer's charge that 'Kipling and Pound are poorly represented because the Clarendon Press would not pay for their work', Yeats replied in a letter to the *Spectator* on 4 December: 'The book has been immensely expensive because all the contents are copyright. As I had a fixed sum for payment of authors I decided on my own responsibility that I could not afford more of these expensive writers.'

The Times Literary Supplement, reviewing the book on 21 November under the heading MR YEATS SELECTS THE MODERN POETS / A TIME OF LITERARY CONFUSION, sided more with its sister newspaper than with the *Spectator*.

. . . Let us be grateful to the Oxford Press for giving Mr Yeats and ourselves this opportunity instead of committing the task to someone who would have chosen a more objectively 'representative' selection . . .

Mr Yeats's is an anthology which reflects its maker . . .

The reviewer went on to criticize certain of Yeats's omissions — notably Wilfred Owen — and to express surprise at the number of pages allotted to Gogarty and Dorothy Wellesley. Of the Introduction he said that 'Mr Yeats, eloquent without allowing his cadences (as they do occasionally in his prose) to run away with his thought, reduces that confusion [*of contemporary literature*] to an intelligible order'.

The criticisms so far levelled at the anthology, however, were but snipers' bullets as compared to the salvo that was to follow. Lord Alfred Douglas now sent Yeats a telegram, with copies to the leading newspapers and literary figures of the day:

Your omission of my work from the absurdly-named Oxford Book of Modern Verse is exactly typical of the attitude of the minor to the major poet. For example Thomas Moore, the Yeats of the 19th century, would undoubtedly have excluded Keats and Shelley from any anthology he had compiled. And why drag in Oxford ? Would not shoneen Irish be a more correct description ?

Douglas followed up his telegram with a letter[1] to Milford at the Oxford University Press :

> 1, St. Ann's Court,
> Nizells Avenue,
> Hove 2,
> Sussex.
> Nov. 28, 1936.

Dear Mr Milford,

I wonder why you asked an Irish minor poet to do the '*Oxford*' Book of Modern English Verse. I have just heard from Sir Arthur Quiller-Couch to whom I sent a copy of my telegram to Yeats. This is what he says :

> Jesus College
> Cambridge
> Nov. 27, 1936

'Dear Lord Alfred,

It must be the "Oxford" that stirs your gall. You should take it as a high compliment that you are not in Mr Yeats' gallery. He was a poet once : but adulation has turned his head, and Lord ! *What* an anthology and *what* a Preface.
> Yours sincerely,
> Arthur Quiller-Couch'

As Sir Arthur says, I ought to take it as a high compliment that I am not in your ridiculous anthology which will remain as a monument of the ineptitude of the 'Oxford University Press', as conducted by you, for all time. I am lucky, because if Yeats had asked me I could not very well have refused to allow some of my work to be quoted, and I could not possibly have guessed that the anthology would be so hopeless. Poor Oxford ! It has to suffer all over the

[1] This is reproduced by kind permission of Lord Alfred Douglas's Literary Executor, Mr. Edward Colman. Part of Sir Arthur Quiller-Couch's letter was quoted in the *Daily Express* of 2 December 1936. Q's 1939 revised edition of *The Oxford Book of English Verse* included three poems by Lord Alfred Douglas.

world for the young microbes of the Union who won't fight for their country and for the 'Oxford (American) Group' and now comes your idiot anthology.

Yours sincerely,
Alfred Douglas

Yeats, accustomed no doubt to the more savage vendettas of his native land, seems not at all disturbed by the furore when he writes to Dorothy Wellesley on 9 December 1936:

> The Oxford University Press has congratulated me on my 'courage' in stirring up 'such a hornet's nest' & offers me a further advance on royalties. Most of my critics are very vindictive, a sure sign that I have some where got down to reality.[1]

This echoes his admirable advice after the publication of *Selections from the Poems of Dorothy Wellesley* earlier that year:

> But, my dear, you must be prepared for silly reviews until you are so old that you are beyond caring & then they will only take another form of silliness. For twenty years I never sent a book for review in Ireland knowing that any review here would be an attack. The more alive one is the more one is attacked.[2]

On 21 December he wrote to her again.

> My Anthology continues to sell & the critics get more and more angry. When I excluded Wilfred Owen, whom I consider unworthy of the poets' corner of a country newspaper, I did not know I was excluding a revered sandwich-board Man of the revolution & that some body has put his worst & most famous poem in a glass-case in the British Museum — however if I had known it I would have excluded him just the same. He is all blood, dirt & sucked sugar stick (look at the selection in Faber's Anthology — he calls poets 'bards', a girl a 'maid,' and talks about 'Titanic wars'). There is every excuse for him, but none for those who like him.[3]

On 1 January he comments on some of the other charges brought against the anthology.

[1] Dorothy Wellesley, *op. cit.*, pp. 121–2.
[2] *Ibid.*, p. 97.   [3] *Ibid.*, p. 124.

Recent attacks have concentrated on my putting in you & Gogarty — the last because he sings a brave song & so makes a whinging propaganda look ridiculous. You because you are a woman of rank (their hatred is, to use a phrase of Balfour's intemperate youth, 'a fermentation of their desire to lick your boots') & because I have left out Wilfred Owen who seems to me a bad poet though a good letter writer. One American fury mentions neither you nor Owen but denounces Gogarty & Wilfred Blunt (Wilfred Blunt did several anti-pacifist things including Bull-fighting).[1]

In a postscript to this letter he adds :

I have just had a letter from an enraged English schoolmaster denouncing me for saying nothing in my introduction about Rupert Brooke who is 'the truest and, if he had lived, unquestionably would have been the finest poet ever produced by England'. He then complains that 'towards the end' I find room for 'some of the most senseless twaddle he has ever read'. This is of course Auden, Day Lewis, etc.[2]

The anthology certainly continued to sell — 'in spite of universal denunciation from both right and left, fifteen thousand . . . in three months', he told Mrs. Llewelyn Davies.[3] The denunciation, of course, was not universal. The Clarendon Press received a touching card from Powys Mathers, to whom a complimentary copy had been sent :

> 48 Upper Mall, W.6
> 20
> P. Wing
> West London Hospital
> 4. I. 37

Gentlemen,

I want to thank you most sincerely for sending me 'The Oxford Book of Modern Verse'. I received it here on Xmas Eve, and it turned what would otherwise have been a dull and wistful season into a period of excitement and delight. It makes a cast in iron of the mind and development of its selector ; I understand him better, and my contemporaries better, and am the richer for one or

[1] *Ibid.*, pp. 128–9.   [2] *Ibid.*, p. 130.
[3] *The Letters of W. B. Yeats*, ed. Allan Wade, p. 886.

two introductions. To have got to know Walter James Turner really well was alone worth a whole forest of candle-fruited trees.

Yours faithfully

P.M.

Perhaps the last word on *The Oxford Book of Modern Verse* should be the admirably balanced review by S. [tuart] N. H. [ampshire] in the *Oxford Magazine* of 4 February 1937.

It is the prose, not the verse, which makes this book magnificent and exciting. The Introduction is a contribution to any future anthology of English prose, the rest does not even afford the raw material for an adequate anthology of modern verse. 'He gave to lyric poetry a new cadence, a distinction as deliberate as that of Whistler's painting, an impulse moulded and checked like that in certain poems of Landor, but different, more in the nerves, less in the blood, more birdlike, less human. . . . Every metaphor, every thought a commonplace, emptiness everywhere, the whole magnificent'— this about Bridges ; nowhere else in the book — always excepting Yeats' own contribution — does one find anything of such quality ; meditation in language at once simple, splendid and restrained is suddenly interrupted by direct personal utterance — which is the peculiar genius of his later poetry : his diction is so saved from the stifling voluptuousness which is the common characteristic of his early work and that of his contemporaries. But his taste seems to have strangely failed to keep pace with his imagination : he looks in his contemporaries for the qualities of his own early verse — richness of sound and imagery, a facility for easy, insistent rhythms, exotic epithets and smooth cadences . . .

Yeats stands out in this book as a poet of the highest genius developing his talent in isolation against a background of more or less clever literary men writing poetry about poetry. . . . Perhaps no anthologist could avoid proving some such conclusion : but the background might have been made less insignificant. But then the Introduction might never have been written. The deafness and the grandeur seem to be inseparable.

YEATS

*

BRENDAN KENNELLY

HE SUMMONED VOICES from the urgent past
    To scatter darkness now and still to come,
The die of poetry was quickly cast
And truth beat faintly as a distant drum;
Assiduously, he hawked and scoured his heart
For perfect subtleties of right and wrong,
Nobly resolved to play the maker's part,
Retrieving something lost to myth and song.

He chronicled his blind and bitter land,
Stretched always on the rack of love or hate,
Unyielding woman, peasants, heroes and
Angry men who shaped a country's fate;
Explored at length the unrelenting dark,
Impelled by piercing searchlights of desire,
Discovering his city, did not shirk
The burden of the architect of fire.

He hammered on truth's anvil till he made
Such images as must endure,
Immortalised the house that has decayed,
The fallen lintel, rotted roof and floor;
Became what he created in his blood
Through years of thinking in the marrowbone —
Man and poet contracted into God
Beyond the certainties in book and stone.

THE VARIORUM EDITION OF YEATS'S PLAYS [1]

*

RUSSELL K. ALSPACH

IN 1956, SHORTLY AFTER COMPLETING the manuscript of *The Variorum Edition of the Poems of W. B. Yeats*, I began working on a variorum edition of the plays of Yeats that I finished in the spring of 1964. The book is dedicated to the memory of Peter Allt with whom I had collaborated on the poetry-variorum from 1947 until his tragic death in 1954. My purpose in this paper is to discuss some of the major editorial and bibliographical problems encountered during the years of composition from 1956 to 1964.

The first was that of a basic text. For the poetry this problem was easy : shortly before his death Yeats had revised his poetry and signed pages for a de luxe edition to be published by Macmillan and Company Ltd. But World War II intervened and it was not until 1949 that the handsome, two-volume, final revised edition of the poetry was published. Ready to hand, therefore, was an authoritative basic text for the poetry-variorum.

But there was no such final revised text of the plays. The best seemed to be the London Macmillan edition of *The Collected Plays of W. B. Yeats* (1952). The plays in this edition and its New York Macmillan counterpart of 1953, with the exception of *A Full Moon in March*, *The King of the Great Clock Tower*, *The Herne's Egg*, *Purgatory*, and *The Death of Cuchulain*, were reprintings with few and unimportant changes of *The Collected Plays of W. B. Yeats* (1934) that Yeats had carefully revised. The user of the variorum-plays must use

[1] © Michael Butler Yeats and Anne Yeats, and Macmillan & Co. Ltd.

his own judgment in assessing the slight textual changes between the editions of 1934 and 1952, as well as those between the edition of *Nine One-Act Plays* in 1937[1] and the edition of the collected plays in 1952.

The second problem was page set-up. Because the set-up of the poetry-variorum had apparently met with approval, I decided to use it again, and although it could not be strictly followed in all the plays (some of these I discuss below), I was on the whole satisfied with it. A sample page — the first page of 'Cathleen ni Houlihan' — will make the set-up clear.

CATHLEEN NI HOULIHAN

1902

Persons in the Play

Peter Gillane	Bridget Gillane, *Peter's wife*
Michael Gillane, *his son, going to be married*	Delia Cahel, *engaged to Michael*
	The Poor Old Woman
Patrick Gillane, *a lad of twelve, Michael's brother*	Neighbours

Interior of a cottage close to Killala, in 1798. Bridget is standing at a table undoing a parcel. Peter is sitting at one side of the fire, Patrick at the other.

1. *Peter.* What is that sound I hear?

2. *Patrick.* I don't hear anything. [*He listens.*] I hear it
3. now. It's like cheering. [*He goes to the window and looks*

PRINTINGS[1] *Samhain*, October 1902; **8, 16, 17, 22, 29, 34, 36, 42, 45, 69, 84, 89, 97.**
DATE [lacking] **S-22, 34-69.**
EPIGRAPH 'Young she is, and fair she is, and would be crowned a queen,
      Were the King's son at home here with
         Kathaleen-Ny-Houlihan !' **8.**

[1] The textual evidence suggests that Yeats probably did little more than select the nine plays.

DEDICATION   To the Memory of William Rooney **8.**

DRAMATIS PERSONAE.   / [heading lacking] / Peter . . . **S, 17, 22, 42;**
Dramatis Personae / Peter . . . **8;** Persons / Peter . . . **16;** Characters / Peter . . . **29.**

STAGE DIRECTIONS   Scene.— *Interior* . . . **S;**   Scene *Interior* . . . **8;**
Scene : *Interior* . . . **16, 22, 29, 42–69;**   Scene : *Interior* . . . *1798,*
Bridget . . . . **17.**

NAME OF SPEAKER   ['The Poor Old Woman' for 'Old Woman' throughout] **16.**

TEXT TITLE . . . Hoolihan **S–16.**
    1. . . . is the sound . . . ? **97A.**

    ¹ I have not collated the version of the lyrics (lines 182-185, 190-197, 288-293,
313-316) that Yeats quoted in his letter to *The United Irishman*, 5 May 1902, because I did not feel that they represented anything but a casual version. *The United
Irishman* letter is reprinted in full on pp. 235-236.

The material above the line dividing the page is the basic
text — *The Collected Plays of W. B. Yeats*, London, 1952 —
with which the variants below the line are collated and keyed.
'Printings' lists the publications of the play;   the numbers
refer to the numbered bibliography at the beginning of the
book.   The remainder of the material below the line is self-
evident.

The plays are in the order of *The Collected Plays* of 1952,
and are set up in a fashion generally similar to the example
above, but some needed special treatment.   The first such was
'The Countess Cathleen', the initial play in the book.

'The Countess Cathleen' was published originally in *The
Countess Kathleen and Various Legends and Lyrics* (1892).¹
It was republished in *Poems* (1895) ;² in *The Poetical Works of
William B. Yeats* (1907) ;³ in *The Collected Works in Verse
and Prose*, III (1908) ;⁴ by itself titled *The Countess Cathleen*
(1912) ;⁵ in the Tauchnitz edition (1913) ;⁶ in *Selected Poems*

    ¹ London.
    ² London.   Revd. and rptd. 1899, 1901, 1904, 1908, 1912, 1913, 1919,
1920, 1922 (2), 1923, 1924, 1927, 1929.
    ³ New York and London.   Vol. II, Dramatical (Dramatic 1912)
Poems.   Rptd. 1909, 1911 ;   revd. and rptd. 1912 ;   rptd. 1914, 1916,
1917, 1919, 1921.   ⁴ Stratford-on-Avon, in eight volumes.
    ⁵ London.   Revd. and rptd. 1916 ;   rptd. 1916, 1920, 1922, 1924.
    ⁶ *A Selection from the Poetry of W. B. Yeats*.   Leipzig.   Rptd. 1922.

(1921) ;[1] in *Plays and Controversies* (1923, 1924) ;[2] with *The Land of Heart's Desire* (1924, 1925) ;[3] in *The Collected Plays of W. B. Yeats* (1934, 1935) ;[4] and in *The Collected Plays of W. B. Yeats* (1952, 1953).[5]

Yeats revised 'The Countess Cathleen' frequently. The revision for the second printing, *Poems* (1895), was so drastic that intelligible collation was virtually impossible. I decided, therefore, to print the original version, 1892, complete on the verso pages and to print above the line on the recto pages the basic text of 1952, with collations of all other printings — that of 1895 to that of 1934 — below the line. Even so, the additions and deletions were so great that the collations frequently extend for several extra pages before they can be brought into some harmony again with the basic text. Similarities between the original version and the basic text I showed by bracketed line-numbers in the verso margins ; identities by unbracketed line numbers.

The sample pages that follow illustrate the set-up and arrangement. The first is a verso page and will face the second, a recto page. In these pages the original version is much closer to the basic text than is true elsewhere. (It should be noted that the sample pages contain no identities although lines [831]–757 and [832]–758 are close.)

[769]   755. *First Merchant.*   Now are our days of heavy labour
                done.

         756. *Second Merchant.*   We have a precious jewel for
                Satan's crown.

[1] New York.
[2] London ; New York. Rptd. London, 1927.
[3] *The Countess Cathleen and The Land of Heart's Desire.* London, 1924 ; *The Land of Heart's Desire and The Countess Cathleen.* London, 1925.   [4] London ; New York.
[5] London ; New York. Rptd. London, 1953.

[831]   757. *First Merchant.* We must away, and wait until she
              dies,
[832]   758.   Sitting above her tower as twin grey owls,
[833]   759.   Watching as many years as may be, guarding
[834]   760.   Our precious jewel — waiting to seize her soul.

[835-836] 761. *Second Merchant.* And we shall not wait long. I saw
              a look
[836]   762.   That seemed the dimness of the tomb in her,
[837]   763.   And she walks slowly, as with leaden slippers,
        764.   And has her eyes fixed often on the ground,
        765.   As though she saw the worms a-beckoning.

[840]   766. *First Merchant.* Away ! Now leap we feathered
              on the air.

                              [*They rush out.*]

                    End of Scene IV

823. *Cathleen.* I have no thoughts ; I hear a cry — a cry.
824. *Aleel* [*casting the pen on the ground*]. I have seen a vision under
              a green hedge,
825.   A hedge of hips and haws — men yet shall hear
826.   The archangels rolling Satan's empty skull
827.   Over the mountain-tops.
        First Merchant. Take him away.
        [*Teigue and Shemus drag him roughly away so that he falls
        upon the floor among the Peasants. Cathleen picks up parch-
        ment and signs, then turns towards the Peasants.*
828. *Cathleen.* Take up the money, and now come with me ;
829.   When we are far from this polluted place
830.   I will give everybody money enough.
        [*She goes out, the Peasants crowding round her and kissing
        her dress. Aleel and the two Merchants are left alone.*
831. *Second Merchant.* We must away and wait until she dies,
832.   Sitting above her tower as two grey owls,
833.   Waiting as many years as may be, guarding

834.   Our precious jewel ;   waiting to seize her soul.
835. *First Merchant.*   We need but hover over her head in the air,

---

823.   ... thoughts :   I ... **5–33.**
Directions at 824.   [... *the parchment on* ...] **5–49, 63.**
824.   I had a vision ..., **5–33.**
826.   ... Archangels ... **46–80.**
827.   ... mountain tops ... **48, 63.**
Directions after 827.   [... *up the parchment* ... *signs, and then* ...]
        5–33;   [... *up the pen and* ...] **52.**
828.   ... money ;   and ... me. **5–33.**
Directions after 830.   [... *around* ...] **71A.**
830a. *Second Merchant.*   Now are our days of heavy labour done, (done.
        6–33)
830b. *First Merchant.*   We have a precious jewel for Satan's crown.
831.   *Second Merchant.* ... away, and ..., **5–33.**
832.   ... as twin gray ..., **5.**
833.   Watching as ... **5–33.**
835.   ... air **49;**   ['We need' lacking] **67.**

Compounding the collation problem of 'The Countess Cathleen' was the shift Yeats made from five scenes in the original, 1892, printing to four acts in the second, 1895, printing. He kept the four acts until 1912 when he restored the five-scene arrangement that he retained through the final version. Because of this shift from five scenes to four acts and back again, I decided that collation would be more understandable if I numbered the lines consecutively throughout the play with no break between scenes or acts, but with scene- and act-changes marked both above and below the line.

Yeats revised each of the printings from 1895 to 1908 ; he revised rather extensively, besides restoring the five scenes, for the printings of 1912 :   *The Countess Cathleen* (June),[1] *The Poetical Works of William B. Yeats*, Vol. II, *Dramatic Poems* (August),[2] and *Poems* (September).[3]   Yeats scholars and bibliographers have as a rule assumed that the revision of 1912

---

    [1] See note 5, p. 196.
    [2] The revised edition of the 1907 Poetical Works, II.   See note 3, p. 196.   [3] See note 2, p. 196.

was, except for quite minor changes, the final version.[1] But examination of the Tauchnitz edition, published quite early in 1913,[2] proves the assumption wrong. Besides making this wrong assumption, Yeats scholars have overlooked Yeats's statement in the Preface to the Tauchnitz edition, that '. . . the play ['The Countess Cathleen'], . . . differs from any published version, . . .'[3] It is the Tauchnitz version of 1913 that is the earliest almost-final version of the play.

One of the main revisions for the Tauchnitz edition is in Scene IV. As Yeats wrote this scene for the three 1912 printings, it went as follows :

Scene IV

Scene. — *A wood near the Castle, as in Scene II.*
The Spirits pass one by one carrying bags.

First Spirit. I'll never dance another step, not one.
Second Spirit. Are all the thousand years of dancing done ?
Third Spirit. How can we dance after so great a sorrow ?
Fourth Spirit. But how shall we remember it to-morrow ?
Fifth Spirit. To think of all the things that we forget.
Sixth Spirit. That's why we groan and why our lids are wet.

The Spirits go out. A group of Peasants pass.

First Peasant. I have seen silver and copper, but not gold.
Second Peasant. It's yellow and it shines.
First Peasant.   It's beautiful.
　The most beautiful thing under the sun,
　That's what I've heard.
Third Peasant.   I have seen gold enough.
Fourth Peasant. I would not say that it's so beautiful.
First Peasant. But doesn't a gold piece glitter like the sun ?
　That's what my father, who'd seen better days,
　Told me when I was but a little boy —
　So high — so high, it's shining like the sun,
　Round and shining, that is what he said.

[1] For example, Allan Wade, in *A Bibliography of the Writings of W. B. Yeats.* Second edition, revised, London, 1958, items 93–100.
[2] *Ibid.*, item 103.
[3] P. [5]. The preface is dated October 1912.

Second Peasant. There's nothing in the world it cannot buy.
First Peasant. They've bags and bags of it.

> *They go out. The two Merchants follow silently.*

When he revised the scene for the Tauchnitz edition he took out the six Spirits and moved Aleel's song beginning 'Impetuous heart, be still, be still', from Act (Scene) I (lines 122–7) — where it had been from the 1895 printing up to and including the three 1912 printings — to the end of this almost-final version of Scene IV. The scene now read as follows:

> Scene. — *A wood near the Castle, as in Scene II.*
> *A group of peasants pass.*

First Peasant. I have seen silver and copper, but not gold.
Second Peasant. It's yellow and it shines.
First Peasant.   It's beautiful.
  The most beautiful thing under the sun.
  That's what I've heard.
Third Peasant.   I have seen gold enough.
Fourth Peasant. I would not say that it's so beautiful.
First Peasant. But doesn't a gold piece glitter like the sun?
  That's what my father, who'd seen better days,
  Told me when I was but a little boy
  And but so tall it's shining like the sun,
  Round and shining, that is what he said.
Second Peasant. There's nothing in the world it cannot buy.
First Peasant. They've bags and bags of it.

> *They go out. The two Merchants follow silently.*
> *Then Aleel passes over the stage singing.*

Aleel. Impetuous heart, be still, be still,
  Your sorrowful love can never be told,
  Cover it up with a lonely tune.
  He who could bend all things to His will
  Has covered the door of the infinite fold
  With the pale stars and the wandering moon.

Another striking alteration for the Tauchnitz version likewise concerned the Spirits, who, besides talking the foolishness noted above in the 1912 Scene IV, are present also in the 1912 Scene III talking equal nonsense until Yeats exorcized them for the Tauchnitz edition. All in all, the Tauchnitz edition is practically the final version of the entire play and is reprinted first in the seventh English edition, 1913, of *Poems* (1895),[1] then in the first 1916 so-called 'impression' of the 1912 *Countess Cathleen*,[2] and thereafter.

I also used the verso-recto page arrangement of 'The Countess Cathleen' in a number of other plays where it seemed the best way to show clearly how a play developed and where, as in 'The Countess Cathleen', it helped avoid excessive and confusing collation. The method seemed especially appropriate for those plays that have verse and prose versions : e.g., *The Only Jealousy of Emer* (verse) and *Fighting the Waves* (prose), *The Hour-Glass* (verse and prose), *The King of the Great Clock Tower* (verse-and-prose and verse). I followed the same arrangement, in part, for *On Baile's Strand* where in the first three printings that portion of the text corresponding in general to lines 1–458 of the final version show differences so great that intelligible collation would again have been virtually impossible ; I used it for *The Resurrection* because of the marked differences between the first printing in *The Adelphi* and subsequent printings. In all cases I showed, as I had for *The Countess Cathleen*, similarities between the verso-page version and the basic text by bracketed line-numbers in the verso margins, and identities by unbracketed line-numbers.

For *The Green Helmet*, that also has verse and prose versions, I chose another arrangement. The first two printings were prose[3] and all others verse. The problem was different here in that the poetry versions were little more than a casting into verse of the prose versions. I decided that the play's development would be more obvious if I divided the page into three parts : the top part would have the lines of the basic text, the middle part the corresponding lines of the two prose

---

[1] Wade, *op. cit.*, item 100.   [2] *Ibid.*, item 93.
[3] The prose versions are titled *The Golden Helmet*. See Wade, *op. cit.*, items 74 and 78.

texts with variations between them marked within these lines, and the bottom part the collations of the other printings with the basic text. The following sample page illustrates this arrangement. The bracketed line-numbers in the left-hand margin of the middle part of the page serve the same purpose as previously mentioned.

92.   And thinking that if we told it we should be a laughing-stock
93.   Swore we should keep it secret.
        Laegaire.   But twelve months upon the clock —
94. *Conall.* A twelvemonth from the first time —
        Laegaire.   And the jug full up to the brim :
95.   For we had been put from our drinking by the very thought
        of him —
96. *Conall.* We stood as we're standing now —
        Laegaire.   The horns were as empty —
        Conall.   When
97.   He ran up out of the sea with his head on his shoulders again.

---

[92]   flagon, and we laughed, and we said we will tell nobody about
[93]   it. We made an oath to tell nobody. But twelve months after
[93, 94]   when we were sitting by this table, the flagon between us —
[94]   *Leagerie.* But full up to the brim. (brim — **34**)
[95]   *Conal.* The thought of that story had put us from our drinking.
                (drinking — **34**)
[96]   *Leagerie.* We were telling it over to one another. (another — **34**)
[97]   *Conal.* Suddenly that man came in with his head on his shoulders
[97, 98]   again, and the big sword in his hand. He asked for **30, 34.**

---

92. . . . laughing stock **38–45** (1911) ; . . . laughing-stock, **50**
93. . . . clock. **38, 39, 43–69.**
94. . . . twelve month . . . time. (time — **F**)
    Laegaire. And . . . brim. (brim, **F**) **38–F** ;
    . . . twelve month (twelvemonth **50, 69A**) . . . time.
    Laegaire. And . . . : **43–69.**
95. . . . him. **38, 39, 43–69.**
96. . . . now.
    Laegaire. The . . . empty.
    Conall.   When **38, 39, 43–69.**

Another editorial and bibliographical problem — one that is met constantly when studying editions of the plays, as well as of the poems — was Yeats's habit of revising for one edition and ignoring another though the printing dates might very nearly coincide.[1] This erratic behaviour is noticeable especially in English *vs.* American editions. Two examples will show the confusion that results. The revision of 1912 of 'The Countess Cathleen' was, as I said, printed only three times when it was again and almost-finally revised for the Tauchnitz edition of 1913.[2] But Yeats continued using the revision of 1912 in the 1914, 1916, 1917, 1919 and 1921 reprintings of *The Poetical Works of William B. Yeats*, II, Dramatic Poems, published in New York. And to compound the confusion he used in the 1921 American *Selected Poems* the 1913 Tauchnitz version of the play.[3] The bewildered student could well ask himself, if he were studying and comparing the play in the 1921 reprint of *The Poetical Works*, etc., (1912), and the 1921 *Selected Poems*, which version Yeats preferred.

My second example of 'another editorial-bibliographical problem' is 'Deirdre', whose bibliographical history presents several curiosities. Its initial printing was 1907 ;[4] later in the same year it was published in America.[5] Here again American reprints are ignored in revisions, for although the Stratford collected edition of 1908[6] was 'Deirdre's' next appearance in print, the revisions therein were not made for the 1909 and 1911 American reprints of the 1907 American edition.

Another curiosity about the American 'Deirdre' is that some of the stage directions are unique to the 1907 American edition and its reprints. One of the most striking of these is a lengthy insertion of directions after Deirdre and Naisi have entered the guesthouse and the musicians have finished the

[1] I have written about this in relation to the poetry. See 'Some Textual Problems in Yeats', *Studies in Bibliography*, ix, Charlottesville, Va., 1957, pp. 51–67. [2] See p. 200, above.
[3] This despite the fly-title on p. [49] of *Selected Poems* that reads 'The Countess Cathleen / (1893, revised 1911)'.
[4] *Deirdre*. London and Dublin. [5] See note 3, p. 196.
[6] See note 4, p. 196. 'Deirdre' is in vol. II.

song (line 148) that begins '"Why is it," Queen Edain said,' (line 125) :

[*The sky outside is still bright so that the room is dim in the midst of a wood full of evening light, but gradually during what follows the light fades out of the sky ; and except during a short time before the lighting of the torches, and at the end of all, the room is either dark amid light or light amid the darkness. The lighting and the character of the scenery, the straight trees, and the spaces of sky and mountain between them suggest isolation and silence.*

The musicians almost throughout remain near the brazier, but show the effect upon their minds of what is happening by their movements and the expression of their faces.]

It is almost as if Yeats didn't trust American companies to play 'Deirdre' without more explicit aid from him than he thought English companies needed.

A third curiosity about 'Deirdre' is the patchings that Yeats did from time to time and that he thrice printed by themselves. The first is in a note to the initial printing — London and Dublin, 1907 — and consists of nine lines ; the second, entitled 'A Different Version of Deirdre's Entrance', is in Appendix II of volume II of the Stratford edition of 1908 and consists of 56 lines ; the third, called 'Alterations in Deirdre', printed in *Samhain* for November 1908 and as a separate 4-page leaflet shortly afterwards, consists of 127 lines. These I have collated with the basic text and printed complete in the notes to the play.

Finally, I had the problem of where to put Yeats's notes about the plays. I decided that rather than placing them all in an Appendix, I would put the notes about a particular play at the end of that play and the general notes about the plays in an Appendix, cross-referencing all notes not only to each other but also to the Prefaces and Dedications that I placed in another Appendix.

So much for the major editorial and bibliographical problems I encountered. Other, but lesser, problems do not justify discussion here; but a last and general comment would be that the chief impressions one gets from a chronological study of Yeats's plays are the same impressions one gets from a similar study of the poetry: he was never content, he revised constantly, and he almost always improved.[1]

[1] This essay is the basis of the Introduction to *The Variorum Edition of the Plays of W. B. Yeats.*

PASSION AND CUNNING: AN ESSAY ON THE POLITICS OF W. B. YEATS

*

CONOR CRUISE O'BRIEN

I

THE DAY THE NEWS of Yeats's death reached Dublin I was lunching with my mother's sister, Hanna Sheehy Skeffington. Hanna was the widow of Frank Skeffington, pacifist and socialist, who had been murdered on the orders of a British officer, Bowen-Colthurst, in Easter Week 1916. She was not consistently a pacifist; she was an Irish revolutionary; Madame MacBride and Countess Markievicz were among her close political friends, Countess Markievicz being, however, politically the closer. Physically she looked a little like Queen Victoria and — a comparison that would have pleased her better — a little like Krupskaya. Mentally she was extremely and variously alert. Her conversation, when politics were not the theme, was relaxed, humorous and widely tolerant of human eccentricity; when politics were the theme she always spoke very quietly and economically, with a lethal wit and a cutting contempt for 'moderates' and compromisers. Hers was the kind of Irish mind which Yeats could call — when he felt it to be on his side — 'cold', 'detonating', 'Swiftian', or when — as in this case — it was not on his side, 'bitter', 'abstract', 'fanatical'.[1]

On this day I tried to tell her something of my generation's sense of loss by Yeats's death. I was genuinely moved, a little

[1] An unpublished letter from Yeats to my father, dated October 1927, contains an extremely angry reference to her 'ungraciousness and injustice' in some controversy.

pompous, discussing a great literary event with my aunt, a
well-read woman who loved poetry.

Her large, blue eyes became increasingly blank, almost to
the polar expression they took on in controversy. Then she
relaxed a little : I was young and meant no harm. She almost
audibly did not say several things that occurred to her. She
wished, I know, to say something kind ; she could not say
anything she did not believe to be true. After a pause she
spoke :

'Yes,' she said, 'he was a Link with the Past.'

I had been speaking of the poet ; she was thinking of the
politician.

At the time I thought this attitude exasperating and even
ludicrous. Who cared about Yeats the politician ? What
mattered was the poetry ; the fact that Yeats had been at sea
in politics — as I then thought — was irrelevant. Yeats the
poet was all-in-all.

This opinion was characteristic of my generation — which
is partly why I cite it — and, as that generation is now middle-
aged, it is now perhaps the dominant one. On re-reading
Yeats's poetry, and some of his prose — and reading some of
the prose for the first time — I no longer think this opinion
quite adequate. I no longer believe Yeats's political activities
to have been foolish or fundamentally inconsistent or his
political attitudes to be detachable from the rest of his personality, disconnected from action, or irrelevant to his poetry.
His politics were, it now seems to me, marked by a considerable
degree of inner consistency between thought and action, by
a powerful emotional drive, cautious experimentalism in
action, and, in expression, extravagances and disengagements
which succeeded one another not without calculation and not
without reference to the given political conjuncture of the
moment.

It is true that warrant — rather too much warrant — can
be found in his poetry for the conventional picture of the

208

impractical poet drawn to politics by romantic love and generous emotion, and recoiling ruefully from each political failure to poetry, his proper sphere :

> All things can tempt me from this craft of verse :
> One time it was a woman's face, or worse —
> The seeming needs of my fool-driven land ; (1909)

And again :

> I think it better that in times like these
> A poet's mouth be silent, for in truth
> We have no gift to set a statesman right ; (1916)

And again :

> Dear shadows, now you know it all,
> All the folly of a fight
> With a common wrong or right. (1927)

And finally :

> I never bade you go
> To Moscow or to Rome.
> Renounce that drudgery,
> Call the Muses home. (1938)

Such apolitical or anti-political pronouncements, scattered over thirty years of Yeats's writing, represent 'the true Yeats' for three large classes of Yeats's admirers: those who are bored by Irish politics, those who are bored by all politics, and those who are frightened by Yeats's politics. 'We have no gift to set a statesman right' is particularly popular because it sets a neat and memorable dividing line between literature and politics. Yet the poet who wrote it was exercising a political choice : he was refusing to write a war-poem — probably solicited for the cause of the Allies in the First World War, a cause which did not move Yeats. He politely and elegantly refused to be drawn. That the aphorism produced in the process was not, for him, a guiding maxim he was to prove a few months later when he wrote a series of noble war-poems in a cause which did move him, that of Ireland. He who had no gift to set a statesman right was no longer troubled by this disability when he wrote after the executions of the leaders of the 1916 Rebellion :

> You say that we should still the land
> Till Germany's overcome ;
> But who is there to argue that
> Now Pearse is deaf and dumb ?
> And is their logic to outweigh
> MacDonagh's bony thumb ?

When the Muses came home, they came full of politics ; there is a far higher proportion of poems with political themes in the last book than in any other, and the last four poems of all, when there was no longer time for politeness or pretence, carry a burden of politics. Throughout his life as a writer Yeats had abiding, and intensifying, political interests and passions. It is misleading to make him essentially non-political, on the strength of certain disclaimers, refusals and ironies. The fact that General Ludendorff carried out a number of tactical withdrawals did not necessarily make him a pacifist.

This essay is concerned, not primarily with Yeats's 'political philosophy',[1] but with the forms of his actual involvement, at certain critical times, in the political life of his own day. Yeats's biographers have recounted some of his political activities — and in some of what follows I am indebted in particular to the late J. M. Hone's *W. B. Yeats* ; Dr. Richard Ellmann's *Yeats, the Man and the Masks* ; and Dr. A. N. Jeffares's *W. B. Yeats, Man and Poet*. But a

---

[1] On that aspect see J. M. Hone, 'Yeats as a Political Philosopher', *London Mercury* (April, 1939) ; Grattan Freyer, 'The Politics of W. B. Yeats', *Politics and Letters* (Summer, 1947) ; Donald Torchiana, 'W. B. Yeats, Jonathan Swift and Liberty', *Modern Philosophy* (August, 1963). The last two also discuss his political activities, but the stress is more on theory and less on practical political choices — in an Irish context — than is the case with the present essay. The two lines of approach give significantly different results.

biographer may feel that he cannot — without toppling his book over — give the detail necessary to situate a given action, or inaction, in the political context of its time. In biographies, as in literary histories, we necessarily find, instead of the complexities of actual political conjunctures, a generalized 'political background', lacking the texture and the weight of real politics. It is often assumed, I think, that this does not matter much in the case of a writer like Yeats because his politics, if they existed, were probably rather vague and generalized themselves. In what follows I shall present some reasons for believing that Yeats's politics were less vague than is commonly supposed.

II

At the bottom of it all was the Anglo-Irish predicament. The Irish Protestant stock from which Yeats came was no longer a ruling class but still a superior caste, and thought of itself in this way.[1] When he wrote towards the end of his life of 'the caste system that has saved the intellect of India'[2] he was almost certainly thinking not so much of India as of Ireland. His people were in the habit of looking down on their Catholic neighbours — the majority of those among whom they lived — and this habit Yeats never entirely lost. But when he went to school in England Yeats was to find, as Parnell and others had found, that this distinction had lost much of its validity. Unsophisticated Englishmen — including all the young — made no more distinction between 'Protestant-Irish' and 'Catholic-Irish' than they did between Brahmin and untouchable. The Irish were known by their

[1] Yeats belonged, not to the 'Ascendancy' in the strict sense of the word, but to the Protestant middle-class of merchants and professional people : *une famille de bonne bourgeoisie protestante*, in the words of Paul-Dubois. But, like many members of this class, he preferred, particularly in his later years, to think of himself as belonging to an aristocracy. The family tree, it seems, had been 'burnt by Canadian Indians' (*Explorations*, p. 347).　　　　[2] *On the Boiler*, Dublin, 1939.

brogue — which in Yeats's case must have been quite marked at this stage — and they were all comic, inferior and 'mad'[1] (among the sophisticated classes these same categories found gentler nuances : witty, impractical, imaginative). The Irish Protestant thus acquired two basic bits of information : the important thing about him, in relation to Ireland, was that he was a Protestant; in relation to England, that he was an Irishman. This duality was the characteristic feature of the community to which Yeats belonged. 'Everyone I knew well in Sligo', he wrote, 'despised Nationalists and Catholics but all disliked England ...'[2]

For proud and sensitive natures, exposed at this period to the English view of the Irish, a political reaction was predictable, starting from the premises : 'I, an Irishman, am as good as any Englishman. Ireland is therefore as good as England. Yet England governs herself; Ireland is governed by England. Can this be right?'

Parnell thought not; Yeats's father thought not; Yeats thought not.

It used to be widely assumed in Ireland that Yeats became entangled in politics by Maud Gonne. This is of course wrong; Yeats had been drawn into politics before he ever heard of Maud Gonne, and the most active phases of his political life were to come after he had quarrelled with Maud Gonne. Yeats entered politics under the influence of John O'Leary, the Fenian convict and exile, who returned to Ireland in 1884. Yeats now became what he was to remain all his life — as he was to repeat towards the end — 'a nationalist of the school of John O'Leary'.

What was the school of John O'Leary? Its central doctrines were those of classical, uncompromising Irish Republicanism : 'the tone', as O'Leary himself said, 'of Wolfe Tone' — but scarcely less important were certain limitations

---

[1] See *Reveries over Childhood and Youth*, London, 1916.
[2] *Ibid.*

placed, by O'Leary himself, on the practical application of the doctrine. 'There are things', he used to say, 'that a man ought not to do to save his country.' It was a phrase that Yeats was often to repeat. The 'certain things' included, along with some pleasant personal taboos — 'a man ought not to cry in public for his country' — some of practical political importance. The school of John O'Leary withheld its endorsement from parliamentary action, frowned on agrarian agitation, and vehemently condemned acts of individual terrorism.

Now in the 'eighties these, and no others, were the methods effectively used to weaken the foundations of English rule. The successful application of agrarian ostracism had just given a new word — boycott — to the languages of the world, and the dynamite of the Clan na Gael had reinforced the arguments of Parnell's disciplined parliamentary party so that Englishmen were beginning, for the first time in their lives, to feel that self-government for Ireland was a question within the bounds of practical politics. 'Violence', as William O'Brien so rightly said, 'is the only way of securing a hearing for moderation.' O'Leary had little use for O'Brien's kind of moderation and no use for the kinds of violence O'Brien had in mind. The Dublin Fenians whom O'Leary led — and whom Yeats was to join — spent their time not in causing but in preventing acts of terrorism. Their task, it seems, was to keep an organization in being for the day when a general rising would become a practical possibility. The distant future was to show that their work was not in vain, but in the 'eighties insurrection seemed — and was — a very remote contingency. In the 'eighties, the people who were hanged were political and agrarian terrorists ; the people who were beaten by the police and put in jail were the 'moderate' agrarian nationalists of the Plan of Campaign. O'Leary's group, shunning alike agrarian action, terrorism and moderation, was left alone by the police.

The school of John O'Leary, then, was in the 'eighties

and 'nineties extreme but not dangerous. This combination has a natural appeal to two of Yeats's most enduring characteristics : his pride and his prudence. With the power he knew to be in him he had much to be both proud and prudent about. The prudent Yeats, the sound calculator of chances, is as it seems the manager of the poet. A poet, if he is to survive long enough to be recognized as a great poet, has need of such a manager. The poet is drawn to nationalism by a deep sense of injured dignity and by a hatred proportionate to his power : hatred always strong in him, and (with pride) the strongest of his political emotions. 'There are moments', he wrote, 'when hatred [of England in the context] poisons my life and I accuse myself of effeminacy because I have not given it adequate expression.'[1] Yeats the manager was always there to see that he gave it just the right degree of expression for any given time. One can imagine him saying to the poet trembling on the verge of national politics : 'Oh well, if you must you must, but for God's sake don't do anything — like getting jailed or killed — that would stop your poetry. I'll tell you what — I'll arrange an introduction to John O'Leary.'

Yet there were some things no manager could have arranged. How could it come about that the extremist politician most likely to attract the manager, should also have the magnificence — in moral stature, in style of speech and in personal appearance — which could hold the poet :

Beautiful lofty things : O'Leary's noble head ;

Or what manager could have arranged that the young woman, ablaze with politics,[2] who called on him, with an introduction from the O'Leary's, on that fateful winter day in 1889 should be the most beautiful woman of her time :

[1] *A General Introduction for my Work* (1937). The important passage from which this is taken is quoted at greater length on pp. 270-1.

[2] ...'It was you was it not', Yeats wrote to O'Leary, 'who converted Miss Gonne to her Irish opinions ? She herself will make many converts' (1 February 1889). *The Letters of W. B. Yeats*, ed. Allan Wade, London, 1954, p. 108.

Pallas Athene in that straight back and arrogant head :
All the Olympians ; a thing never known again.

One has to remind oneself that O'Leary and Maud Gonne
were historical figures and not simply invented by Yeats, like
Michael Robartes and Owen Aherne :

As if some ballad-singer had sung it all.

Yeats's long and splendidly unhappy relation to Maud
Gonne had, of course, profound effects on his life and work
but I do not find that it had any proportionate effect, at least
directly, on his political alignment. It is true that it was after
he met her — and probably at her instance — that he actually
joined the Fenian brotherhood, but they were O'Leary's
Fenians, he was already closely associated with them, and
joining them committed him, as we have seen, to little of
practical consequence.[1] There was also a sound practical
argument for going with the Fenians. 'In this country',
O'Leary had told him, 'a man must have upon his side the
Church or the Fenians, and you will never have the Church.'[2]

His letters, just after he first met Maud Gonne, do show
some trace of her specific influence. He wrote to Katharine
Tynan, about the murder in America of a supposed informer
by members of the Clan na Gael : 'He seems to have been a
great rascal. It was really a very becoming thing to remove
him ... a Spy has no rights.'[3] These ferocious sentiments are
definitely not 'school of John O'Leary' ; they are characteristic of Maud Gonne, whom Yeats had met six months before.
The difference was that Maud Gonne perhaps meant them,
and might conceivably have acted on them ;[4] Yeats probably
did not mean them and certainly would not have acted on
them. His letter went on : 'There ! You will be angry with

---

[1] He seems never to have taken the Fenian oath (Hone, *W. B. Yeats*,
p. 145).   [2] *Autobiographies*, p. 209.
[3] To Katharine Tynan, 25 July 1889. (*Letters*, p. 151.)
[4] In practice, when an occasion offered, she did not.

me for all these dreadful sentiments. I may think the other way tomorrow.'

In practice, where Maud Gonne differed from O'Leary — as she did in favouring agrarian agitation — Yeats does not seem to have followed her, although he did intercede for her with O'Leary.[1]

Maud Gonne did not affect Yeats's political course at this time so profoundly as is usually assumed. What did affect it were events which took place two to three years later — the fall and death of Parnell.

III

'The modern literature of Ireland,' Yeats told the Swedish Academy in 1925, 'and indeed all that stir of thought which prepared for the Anglo-Irish war, began when Parnell fell from power in 1891. A disillusioned and embittered Ireland turned from parliamentary politics ; an event was conceived and the race began, as I think, to be troubled by that event's long gestation.'[2]

Elsewhere he speaks of Four Bells, 'four deep tragic notes' in Irish history, the first being the war that ended in the Flight of the Earls (1603), the fourth being the death of Parnell in 1891.

'I heard the first note of the Fourth Bell forty years ago on a stormy October morning. I had gone to Kingston [*sic*] Pier to meet the Mail Boat that arrived about 6 a.m. I was expecting a friend, but met what I thought much less of at the time, the body of Parnell.'[3]

The friend was, of course, Maud Gonne, who came over on the boat that brought Parnell's body back to Ireland.

---

[1] Maud Gonne, *A Servant of the Queen*, pp. 206–7 ; *Scattering Branches*, p. 49.

[2] Lecture on accepting the Nobel Prize. Text in *Autobiographies*, p. 559.

[3] Commentary on the poem 'Parnell's Funeral'. Text in *The Variorum Edition*, London, 1957, p. 834.

Few historians, I think, would challenge Yeats's estimate, in his Swedish address, of the impact of Parnell's fall and death, or his summary account of a process in which he himself played an important part. His historical sense was keen, as his political sense also was. For he not only saw in retrospect the crucial importance of the fall and death of Parnell. He saw it *at the time*, immediately, and he saw in it his opportunity and took that opportunity. He had not been a follower of Parnell's before his fall — the 'school of John O'Leary' forbade it, and his father's influence was also against it[1] — and he does not seem to have become intensely interested in Parnell until the moment of his fall. Since, in later life, he made Parnell a symbol, almost a god indeed, in whose name he as priest excommunicated prominent public figures of the day, it is interesting that in his letters of the time there is no note of grief at his fall or even at his death. The first note is one of rather gleeful excitement at an event and an opportunity; the creation of a vacuum. 'This Parnell business', he wrote to O'Leary after the divorce case, 'is most exciting. Hope he will hold on. As it is he has driven up into dust and vacuum no end of insincerities. The whole matter of Irish politics will be the better of it.'[2] In a later letter to O'Leary Yeats expresses an optimism, which sounds a little artificial, about Parnell's chances and gives some not entirely random reasons for being on Parnell's side : the priests and the 'Sullivan gang' were on the other side. Then Parnell died. Yeats wrote a poem about him on that day for the press that evening. The poem was called 'Mourn and then Onward'.[3] It concluded :

> Mourn — and then onward, there is no returning
> He guides ye from the tomb ;

[1] J. B. Yeats admired Butt and thought Parnell 'not a great man' (*Letters*, 20 September 1915).
[2] Undated (?) letter (probably December 1890) quoted in Ellmann, p. 102. Not in the selection of *Letters* edited by Allan Wade.
[3] Full text in *The Variorum Edition*, p. 737. The poem was never republished by Yeats.

His memory now is a tall pillar, burning
Before us in the gloom !

There is not much gloom in the covering letter with which
the poet sent this dirge to his sister :

I send you a copy of United Ireland with a poem of mine on
Parnell written on the day he died to be in time for the press that
evening. It has been a success.
The Funeral [which Yeats did not attend] is just over. The
people are breathing fire and slaughter. The wreaths have such
inscriptions as 'Murdered by the Priests' and a number of Wexford
men were heard by a man I know promising to remove a Bishop
and some priests before next Sunday. Tomorrow will bring them
cooler heads I doubt not.[1]

Yeats, according to Dr. Ellmann, 'had grasped instinctively
that the time had come for him to act'. The word 'instinctively' may be misleading. Yeats in later life, when he had
no more use, for the moment, for nationalist political activity,
used to write as if his political activity at this time had been
a sad mistake, committed mainly because of his passion for
Maud Gonne. Critics and biographers have tended to follow
him in exaggerating, as I believe, the importance of the Gonne
factor in his politics. This influences presentation : thus
Dr. Ellmann reserves the entrance of Maud Gonne into his
narrative for the moment of Parnell's death, although the
natural moment to have brought her in would, one would
have thought, have been the time at which Yeats first met her
and fell in love with her, almost three years before. Keeping
her back intensifies the drama but blurs the politics. It helps
to perpetuate Yeats's myth of himself as 'a foolish passionate
man', whereas the weight of the evidence suggests that he
was something much more interesting : a cunning passionate
man.[2] In this case the cunning was more in evidence than the

[1] *Letters*, p. 179.
[2]   'That I may seem though I die old
   A foolish passionate man.'
The use here of the word 'seem' seems to have been overlooked by some
critics.

passion. Yeats was still almost unknown. He had been glad
to get space, through O'Leary's influence, in a paper like *The
Gael* — the organ of the Gaelic Athletic Association — and
was sometimes in danger of being squeezed out by a big foot-
ball-match. Now he had an opportunity of reaching, with
powerful impact, at a time of maximum national emotion, the
widest possible Irish audience. *United Ireland* was Parnell's
last paper and Irish people everywhere must have fought for
copies of its issue of 10 October, to see what it had to say
about the death of the Chief. And they found there the poem
and the name of W. B. Yeats. There can have been few —
and hardly any on the Parnellite side — who were not more
moved by 'Mourn and then Onward' than Yeats was. A
name almost unknown the day before became known to most
of Ireland overnight.

I can see no reason to suppose that, in writing this poem
and above all in getting it to the press with the necessary
celerity, Yeats was just reacting instinctively or trying to
please Maud Gonne. He had an eye for an opportunity — a
politician's eye, and a politician's sense of timing.[1]

Some will perhaps find offensive the suggestion that Yeats
used Parnell's coffin for a platform. Parnell, who made his
own name out of the Manchester Martyrs, would have approved Yeats. Parnell knew, as Pearse knew, by Rossa's
grave, that in Ireland there is no better platform than a hero's
coffin.

Yeats had seen Parnell, after consolidating his Irish fief,
impose himself on the politics of the United Kingdom.
'Mourn and then Onward' was not exactly a bid for the mantle
of Parnell — a garment which was just then, as Yeats well
knew, being thoroughly torn in pieces — but may reasonably

[1] Those who doubt the existence of an element of calculation in
Yeats's behaviour at this time should consider a sentence in a letter of his
advising a young Irishwoman to write about 'Irish legends and places':
'It helps originality and makes one's verses sincere, and gives one less
numerous competitors.' (31 January 1889). *Letters*, p. 104.

be interpreted as an attempt, by bringing poetry into the political vacuum left by Parnell's death, to become as a poet something like what Parnell had been in politics : a virtual dictator in Ireland : a power, and sometimes an arbiter, in England. If so, it was not a wild aim, and Yeats in large measure made it good. Not that power, in itself, was the object as it is for the man who is primarily a politician, but that the power already in him needed living-space. The poet Yeats wanted elbow-room and an audience, and the politician Yeats saw to it that he got them.

Ireland was now, as he said, 'like wax' and he set about shaping it. In later years — after the fighting had begun — the phrase 'the litherary side of the Movement' came to be used derisively, but in the 'nineties and in the early years of the new century 'the litherary side of the Movement' was the only side that was moving, and its leader was Yeats. In helping to found the Irish Literary Society in London and the National Literary Society in Dublin, and the theatre which later became the Abbey Theatre, the politician Yeats was about the poet's business, using for the ends of poetry the political energy diverted by the fall of Parnell. Later, he liked to talk as if he had been duped, and wrote bitterly of evenings spent with 'some small organizer' pouring his third glass of whisky into the spittoon.[1] One may feel that, if anyone was duped, it was more likely to be the unfortunate 'small organizer' than Yeats, the big organizer. But there is no need to speak of dupes at all ; both Yeats and the 'small organizer' were serving, in their different ways, the dignity of the nation to which they both belonged. For the small organizer the end was a political one, and poetry a means ; for Yeats the end was a poetic one, and the means political. They had to part in the end but there is no need now to regret, or to quarrel over, the road they travelled together.

[1] *Autobiographies*, p. 355.

IV

They parted, of course, in 1903, with the marriage of Maud Gonne to Major John MacBride. Nature, deferential to the poet, made this 'the year of the big wind' in which great trees blew down all over Ireland, including Lady Gregory's park at Coole. It was the great turning point in Yeats's life, in politics as well as in other ways. The fact that he broke — for a time and in a way — with Irish politics after Maud Gonne's marriage has naturally contributed to the romantic belief, encouraged by himself, that his politics were 'just Maud Gonne'. The evidence does not warrant this conclusion. As we have seen he had made his political choice before he met Maud Gonne, and his entry into effective politics dates, not from his meeting with Maud Gonne, but from the political opportunity created by the fall of Parnell. The most that can be said of Maud Gonne — politically — is that she deepened his political involvement, and probably kept him politically involved for some time after he would otherwise have quit. For her he had written *Cathleen ni Houlihan,* and she had played the part so that a member of the audience could write this : 'The effect of *Cathleen ni Houlihan* on me was that I went home asking myself if such plays should be produced unless one was prepared for people to go out to shoot and be shot ... Miss Gonne's impersonation had stirred the audience as I have never seen another audience stirred'.[1]

After the curtain fell on *Cathleen ni Houlihan* (1902) it could fairly be said that Yeats's work for the Irish revolution had been accomplished. It seems, in retrospect, considerate of Maud Gonne to have married in the following year.

The poet — having acquired in his political years a name,

[1] Stephen Gwynn, quoted by A. N. Jeffares, *W. B. Yeats : Man and Poet*, p. 138. This is not at all an isolated judgment : P. S. O'Hegarty stated that to him and his revolutionary contemporaries *Cathleen ni Houlihan* was 'a sort of sacrament' ('W. B. Yeats and the Revolutionary Ireland of his Time' in *Dublin Magazine,* July–September, 1939).

an audience and the dramatic society that was about to become the Abbey Theatre — now turned aside from Irish politics. He did not cease — he never ceased — to be an Irish nationalist but his nationalism now became aristocratic and archaizing, instead of being popular and active. Aristocratic nationalism was not, in Ireland, practical politics because the aristocracy was almost entirely Unionist, that is to say antinational. This did not matter to Yeats who had had enough, for the moment, of practical politics. In his new aristocratism he was releasing a part of his personality he had been forced to try to suppress during the years of political activity. In those years this Irish Protestant had necessarily emphasized his Irishness, minimizing or denying the separate and distinct tradition which the word Protestant implies. The Protestant now re-emerged with an audible sigh of relief. It had been stuffy in there, and getting stuffier. For, in the first years of Yeats's involvement in active politics, there had been special circumstances making political life among Irish nationalists tolerable for a Protestant: by 1900 these special circumstances had disappeared. The fall of Parnell had produced, as well as a 'clerical' party, led by Dillon, an anti-clerical Parnellite party led by John Redmond. Parnellite circles — to which Yeats had directed his first appeal, and which probably made up the larger part of his audiences — were distinguished by a scarcity of priests and a minimum of priestly authority. The glee with which Yeats in his letters chronicles threats against priests is significant. It was not that he necessarily hated priests himself — though he certainly did not like them — but that an atmosphere of priestly authority, in which for example priests tended to be arbiters of taste, was inimical to Protestant and poet. This atmosphere was temporarily dissipated in a considerable part of Ireland, including Dublin, in 1891, and Yeats must have found the going relatively easy then. By 1900, however, with the reunification of the Irish party and the burying of the Parnellite hatchet — which was an anti-clerical hatchet — the clergy had recovered most of their former authority, and life among nationalists must have become proportionately depressing for Protestants.[1] It was already depressing enough, for reasons of class. Yeats has left us a collective picture of his political associates of the 'nineties : 'Men who had risen above the traditions of the countryman, without learning those of cultivated life, or even educating themselves and who because of their poverty, their ignorance, their superstitious piety, are much subject to all kinds of fear'.[2]

This is a classical statement of the Irish Protestant view of the rising Catholic middle-class. From this class Yeats was now recoiling and the violence of his recoil did much to determine the political direction of his later years.

'One thing that Marxist criticism has not succeeded in doing,' as George Orwell pointed out, 'is to trace the connection between "tendency" and literary style.'[3] Orwell goes on, in the essay on Yeats, to reveal, unconsciously, some

[1] How little the trend to reconciliation between the factions was to Yeats's taste may be gathered from the following : 'John Dillon [leader of the anti-Parnellite faction] is making the first speech he has made before a popular Dublin audience since the death of Parnell ... [he] is very nervous. ... I am almost overpowered by an instinct of cruelty : I long to cry out, "Had Zimri peace that slew his master ?"' (*Autobiographies*, p. 366.) Yeats has been represented as himself seeking to make peace between Parnellite and anti-Parnellite. This is true only in the sense that he and Maud Gonne, in helping for example to organize the centenary commemoration of the 1798 rebellion (a commemoration in which parliamentarians of both sections took part) reflected what J. M. Hone described, I believe correctly, as an endeavour on the part of the Irish Republican Brotherhood to assume control not only of Fenian propaganda but also of the Irish Parliamentary Party which was still torn by internal dissension (*W. B. Yeats*, p. 146). The support of the former anti-Parnellites — being the majority of the Irish people — was essential to the success of any Irish movement. But the quotation from the *Autobiographies* (above) shows how Yeats continued to feel about the anti-Parnellite parliamentarians — of whom Dillon was not only the most eminent but also the most moderate.
[2] 'The Cutting of an Agate' (1907) in *Essays and Introductions*, p. 260.
[3] 'W. B. Yeats' in *Critical Essays*, London, 1943.

of the reasons for that failure. He seeks, in Yeats's work, 'some kind of connection between his wayward, even tortured, style of writing and his rather sinister vision of life'. He finds this connection, as far as he finds it at all, in Yeats's archaisms, affectations and 'quaintness'. This does not fit very well, for the 'quaintness' was at its height in the 'nineties, when Yeats's vision of life was, from either an Orwellian or a Marxist point of view, at its least sinister : when he was identified with the popular cause in his own country and when, in England, he sat at the feet of William Morris and looked on Socialism with a friendly eye. Unfortunately for Orwell's thesis, it was precisely at the moment — after the turning point of 1903 — when Yeats's vision of life began to turn 'sinister' — aristocratic and proto-Fascist — that he began to purge his style of quaintness, and his greatest poetry was written near the end of his life when his ideas were at their most sinister. A Marxist critique which starts from the assumption that bad politics make for bad style will continue 'not to succeed'. The opposite assumption, though not entirely true, would be nearer to the truth. The politics of the left — any left, even a popular 'national movement' — impose, by their emphasis on collective effort and on sacrifice, a constraint on the artist, a constraint which may show itself in artificialities of style, vagueness or simple carelessness. Right-wing politics, with their emphasis on the freedom of the *élite*, impose less constraint, require less pretence, allow style to become more personal and direct.

It is not necessary to claim that these generalizations are universally valid ; they were, I think, valid for Yeats and for many of his generation and that immediately following. Snobbery — 'abhorring the multitude' — was then a more acceptable, and therefore comfortable, attitude than it now would be. A hero of François Mauriac's, after a day spent among workers in some Christian Socialist movement, used to change into black silk pyjamas in the evening and read

Laforgue, *pour se désencanailler.* Yeats after 1903 *se désen-
canaillait* in the company of Lady Gregory and her circle.
Now that he had withdrawn for the time from active politics,
politics became explicit in his poetry. His bitterness about
Maud Gonne's marriage took a political form :

> Why should I blame her that she filled my days
> With misery, or that she would of late
> Have taught to ignorant men most violent ways,
> Or hurled the little streets upon the great,
> Had they but courage equal to desire ?

If the snobbery endemic in his class and generation takes
in his writing from now on an almost hysterical intensity, it is
I think that he felt himself to have undergone, in his political
years, a kind of contamination, a loss of caste, through 'the
contagion of the throng' and that, in the end, he had suffered
a deep injury to his pride. 'One must accept' — he had written to Lady Gregory near the end of his political involvement
— 'the baptism of the gutter.'[1] 'The foul ditch' and 'the
abounding gutter' became recurring symbols of disgust in his
later poetry. In the same letter in which he accepted the
baptism of the gutter, he spoke of trying to get someone to
resign from something 'in favour of MacBride of the Irish
Brigade' — the man whom Maud Gonne was to marry three
years later :

> My dear is angry that of late
> I cry all base blood down,
> As though she had not taught me hate
> By kisses to a clown.

There were moments when he felt ashamed of this hate,[2]
but it proved enduring. Hatred of England had been with
him early ; hatred of 'the base' in Ireland now joined it.

---

[1] 10 April 1900. (*Letters*, p. 338.) In later years he liked to tell the
story of the speaker at the Socialist picnic : 'I was brought up a gentleman and now as you can see associate with all sorts'.

[2] Cf. 'The People' (1916).

The two hates represented an abnormal intensification of the normal dualism of the Irish Protestant. They formed an unstable and potentially explosive combination : a volcanic substance which would from time to time erupt through the surface of Yeats's public life.

V

Although Yeats withdrew in a sense from Irish politics about 1903, this did not mean that Irish politics withdrew from him. His theatre, because of *Cathleen ni Houlihan*, had just become a kind of Holy Place of Irish nationalism and his new frame of mind — fortunately for the theatre — was far from that of a custodian of such a Holy Place. Militant nationalists, of whom the most vocal Dublin leader at this time was Arthur Griffith, the founder of Sinn Fein, naturally wanted the theatre to serve the cause actively, as it had done with *Cathleen ni Houlihan*. They also — and with them a wider Dublin public — insisted that it must not 'play into the enemy's hands' by presenting a 'degrading' image of Irish life. Here nationalist pressures and Catholic pressures — which often worked against each other, as Parnell and the Fenians knew — converged in turbulent menace. Plays that showed Irishmen as sinful — or even, for example, coarse in speech — were hurtful to many militant nationalists as denigrating the inherently virtuous and refined character of 'the Irish race'[1] (a phrase much in use at the time) ; to many militant Catholics such plays were both inherently immoral and scandalous and also offensive by the suggestion that the Catholic education of the Irishman left something to be desired. 'An insult to Ireland' cried the first set of voices, and the second set responded : 'an insult to Catholic Ireland'.

[1] Those who find it hard to understand such hypersensitivity should look through the back files of *Punch*. It was natural — though silly — that some Irish people, depressed by being seen as Caliban, should insist on getting from 'our own theatre' a much more flattering reflection.

'Audience', telegraphed Lady Gregory on the first night
of *The Playboy of the Western World,* 'broke up in disorder
at the word *shift.*'[1]

It seems in retrospect surprising — and it is a tribute to
the courage, tenacity and skill of Yeats and Lady Gregory —
that the theatre should have been able to survive at all under
the combined pressure — only fitfully applied it is true — of
the two most powerful forces in Irish life.[2] Yeats had many
battles to fight and fought them with gusto. 'Into the dozen
or so fairly important quarrels in the theatre movement from
1903 to 1911 he threw himself with something like abandon.
The issue was in almost every case national art versus nationalist propaganda.'[3]

The art that he defended in his theatre was that which belonged to 'life' as against, in his words, 'the desire which
every political party has, to substitute for life a bunch of
reliable principles and assertions'.[4]

He never, as we say in Dublin, said a truer word. He was
here taking his stand as an artist, in defence of the life of art in
his country. For him then — and for us now — the politics
of the matter come on a much lower level. But it is with that
lower level — in which he took an ever-renewed interest —
that we are concerned here. On that level the defence of
'national art' against 'nationalist propaganda' represented a
political shift; for Yeats, in *Cathleen ni Houlihan,* had produced one of the most powerful pieces of nationalist propaganda ever written. Yeats could be an excellent propagandist
when he wanted to, and he often did want to. 'You have
been liable at times, only at times,' his father wrote to him

[1] Hone, *W. B. Yeats*, p. 217.
[2] To be fair to the much-maligned Abbey audiences the survival was
also due to the recognition by small — but qualitatively significant —
sections of Catholics and nationalists that the Playboy rioters had made
fools of themselves.
[3] Ellmann, p. 179.
[4] Quoted in Hone, p. 194.

anxiously, 'to a touch of the propaganda fiend.'[1] And he
himself was later to affirm more sweepingly : 'I have been
always a propagandist . . . '.[2] Those who looked to him
and his theatre for nationalist propaganda, and did not get it,
had therefore some reason to feel confusion and disappoint-
ment. The fact was that their cause — the nationalist cause
— did not sufficiently stir Yeats at this particular time (between 1903 and 1916) to make him write (or encourage others
to write) in a way which would have had the effect they
desired — as he had written before and as he was to write
again. The nationalist in him was dormant, the aristocrat
wide awake, dominating the mob from the stage.[3] For those
in whose blood-stream *Cathleen ni Houlihan* was still working
this was an unfortunate conjuncture ; for those who detested
all that that play stood for, it was an auspicious one. The
young men from Trinity came to the Abbey to defend artistic
freedom by singing *God Save the King*.[4]

There is one important apparent break in the otherwise
consistently aristocratic line of thought and action which he
pursued in these years and — with the partial exception of
certain nationalist flare-ups — throughout his life from about
1903 to the end. This apparent break is constituted by the
stand he took on the great Dublin Lock-out, when in 1913 the
Dublin employers, led by William Martin Murphy, tried to
starve the Dublin workers into submission[5] in order to break

[1] J. B. Yeats, *Letters* (11 December 1913).
[2] Letter to Ethel Mannin, 4 March 1935 (*Letters*, p. 831). He added :
'though I have kept it out of my poems and it will embitter your soul
with hatred as it has mine'.
[3] His always latent hostility to 'the crowd', including his own
audience, was generously stimulated when, on a night in 1905, some
members of an Abbey audience hissed Maud Gonne on her appearance
after her separation from Major MacBride. 'He felt that never again
could he touch popular politics.' (Hone, p. 210.)
[4] Not at all to Yeats's pleasure.
[5] This is not just a rhetorical flourish. 'You will recollect, when
dealing with a company of this kind,' said Murphy in an address to his
tramway workers on 19 July 1913, 'that every one of the shareholders,

Jim Larkin's Irish Transport and General Workers' Union. Few who had read Yeats's writings, or considered his attitude to public questions in the preceding ten years, could have expected him to come out on the side of Larkin's men. William Martin Murphy, if he had had time for Yeats and for his poetry, might plausibly have claimed that if ever there was a man who

> ... taught to ignorant men most violent ways

that man was Big Jim Larkin. He could also have contended — and proved his case, certainly to the satisfaction of a Dublin court of the time — that it was actually Larkin's policy to :

> ... hurl the little streets upon the great.

For this Larkin himself, if not all his followers, had 'courage equal to desire'. 'My advice to you', Larkin had told his men, 'is to be round the doors and corners, and if one of our class should fall, then two of the others should fall for that one. We will demonstrate in O'Connell Street [Dublin's principal thoroughfare]. It is our street as well as William Martin Murphy's. We are fighting for bread and butter. We will hold our meeting in the streets, and if any one of our men fall, there must be justice. By the living God if they want war they can have it.'

A conservative admirer of Yeats could reasonably have expected to find him, in such a war, on the side of public order, the rights of property and the rule of the educated. What Yeats did, however, was to come out explicitly and vehemently against the activities of the employers' principal allies — police, press and clergy. His protest — in the form

to the number of five, six or seven thousand, will have three meals a day whether the men succeed or not. I don't know if the men who go out can count on this.' (Quoted in *1913: Jim Larkin and the Dublin Lock-out*, Workers' Union of Ireland, Dublin, May, 1964.)

of a letter to Larkin's *Irish Worker* — is important enough, in the context of the present discussion, to be quoted in full :

I do not complain of Dublin's capacity for fanaticism whether in priest or layman, for you cannot have strong feeling without that capacity, but neither those who directed the police nor the editors of our newspapers can plead fanaticism. They are supposed to watch over our civil liberties, and I charge the Dublin Nationalist newspapers with deliberately arousing religious passion to break up the organisation of the workingman, with appealing to mob law day after day, with publishing the names of workingmen and their wives for purposes of intimidation.

And I charge the Unionist Press of Dublin and those who directed the police with conniving at this conspiracy. I want to know why the *Daily Express*, which is directly and indirectly in-citing Ulster to rebellion in defence of what it calls 'the liberty of the subject' is so indifferent to that liberty here in Dublin that it has not made one editorial comment, and I ask the *Irish Times* why a few sentences at the end of an article, too late in the week to be of any service, has been the measure of its love for civil liberty ?

I want to know why there were only (according to the press reports) two policemen at Kingsbridge on Saturday when Mr. Sheehy Skeffington was assaulted and a man prevented from buying a ticket for his own child ? There had been tumults every night at every Dublin railway station, and I can only assume that the police authorities wished those tumults to continue.

I want to know why the mob at North Wall and elsewhere were permitted to drag children from their parents' arms, and by what right one woman was compelled to open her box and show a marriage certificate ; I want to know by what right the police have refused to accept charges against rioters ; I want to know who has ordered the abrogation of the most elementary rights of the citizens, and why authorities who are bound to protect every man in doing that which he has a legal right to do — even though they have to call upon all the forces of the Crown — have per-mitted the Ancient Order of Hibernians to besiege Dublin, taking possession of the railway stations like a foreign army.

Prime Ministers have fallen, and Ministers of State have been impeached for less than this. I demand that the coming Police Inquiry shall be so widened that we may get to the bottom of a conspiracy, whose like has not been seen in any English-speaking town during living memory. Intriguers have met together somewhere behind the scenes that they might turn the religion of Him who thought it hard for a rich man to enter into the Kingdom of Heaven into an oppression of the poor.[1]

'It may be surmised', wrote the late J. M. Hone about this letter, 'that Yeats was not actuated solely by humanitarian zeal.'[2] It may indeed — as we shall see — but Hone's comment needs itself to be treated with some reserve. Hone was a friend of Yeats, and in tune with his political views, but his conservatism was of a colder and more intellectual stamp than Yeats's. It is clear from Hone's references to the lock-out — he pays tribute to Murphy's services to 'Dublin' — that the employers, rather than the workers, commanded such store of sympathy as he possessed.[3] The very use of the words 'humanitarian zeal' conveys as much. Granted his premises this was a logical position. But Yeats was not logical in this chilly way. He was an enthusiast, in the old sense of the word ; he was not only capable of generous indignation — he positively revelled in it, as he was to show again and again. We may — and I do — accept the view that Yeats on this occasion was not actuated *solely* by humanitarian zeal, but we need more stress on the 'solely' than Hone, in the context, seems to imply. The events of the Dublin Lock-out — including the events which Yeats described — aroused strong emotions and there can be no doubt that Yeats's indignation was genuine, and that it sprang, in part, from those human feelings which, when we find them inconvenient, we call 'humanitarian zeal'.

Yet, as Hone suggests, feelings of this kind would hardly

[1] 'Dublin Fanaticism', *Irish Worker*, 1 November 1913 ; reprinted in *1913: Jim Larkin and the Dublin Lock-out*.

[2] *W. B. Yeats*, p. 268. Hone's reference to the letter is brief and he does not quote it.

[3] Typically, he refers to the events which followed the lock-out, decided on by the Dublin employers of members of the Irish Transport and General Workers' Union, as 'the great strike led by Larkin which paralysed the life of Dublin'.

by themselves explain the phenomenon of the letter. There is no reason to suppose that Yeats was either peculiarly accessible, or peculiarly resistant, to such feelings. He could, like most other politically-minded people, modulate the expression of such feelings — and perhaps even, to some extent, the feelings themselves — in accordance with his judgment of the social and political context in which the 'crimes' or 'regrettable incidents', as the case might be, occurred. Thus, in later years, Yeats did not, as we shall see, allow his humane feelings to overpower his political judgment in connection either with the repressive measures of the first Free State government, or with the penal achievements of the Fascist governments. Nor, in these later contexts, did he show the marked specific concern for civil liberties which he shows here. It is true that he became more conservative — and more than conservative — as he grew older, but a conservative, aristocratic, pattern had already, by 1913, become quite distinct. The concern about the 'oppression of the poor' in this letter does not fit more easily into this pattern than the apparent Christian piety of the last sentence fits into the pattern of Yeats's religious ideas.

The explanation of the letter which Hone suggests is, as far as it goes, helpful. This is that Yeats was already violently incensed against Murphy on an artistic issue — Murphy's opposition, in his powerful paper *The Irish Independent*, to the housing, by Dublin Corporation, of the Lane collection of paintings, in the manner proposed by Lane. When Murphy attacked Lane, Larkin praised Lane. Yeats, it is hinted — no more than a hint is given — came to the support of Larkin for similar reasons to those that made Larkin come to the support of Lane. The poet was naturally no more disposed in favour of the labour leader than the labour leader was predisposed in favour of the art-connoisseur, but all three had a common enemy in the person of the arch-philistine and arch-bourgeois : William Martin Murphy. This is illuminating, and the

reminder that Murphy had been a prominent anti-Parnellite
is also highly relevant. If this were all, however, the
letter would be little more than an incident in something
like a personal feud, with little relevance to the wider
pattern of Yeats's politics. I believe, however, that this
is not all, and that the letter is both more relevant to that
pattern, and more consistent with it, than appears at first
sight.

'Yeats', according to Hone, 'chose to regard Martin
Murphy as a representative type and leader of the middle-class
which had begun to rise to power under the shadow of the
Land League . . .'[1] Both Yeats and Hone are rather vague
about this middle-class; it is possible to be a little more
specific. The Land League (1879–81), with its successor movements, had profoundly weakened the influence, formerly
overpowering, of the old Protestant landed Ascendancy, with
which Yeats liked to identify himself; it threatened also the
privileged social position — and sometimes directly hit the
incomes — of the Protestant middle-class to which Yeats did
in fact belong. The boycott, in which the people had received
and absorbed effective instruction from Land League times on,
was certainly not intended by its organizers as a lever to help
in bringing about the emergence of a Catholic middle-class,
but it is probable that that is one of the ways in which it
actually worked. People who sold goods to, or had dealings
with, boycotted farmers, land-agents, etc., were themselves
boycotted; those who attempted to break the boycott in this
way had a high propensity to be — in politics — Unionist
and — in religion — Protestant. It may be imagined that a
'Nationalist' shopkeeper would not be backward in urging
the boycott of a 'Unionist' competitor: in this way a socio-
political movement could shade over to a communal-religious
one. This process is still a reality of life, within the experience
of the present writer, in parts of Northern Ireland. I remember

[1] 'This,' Hone adds rather cryptically, 'Murphy certainly was not.'

being gently chided, by a group of nationalist friends in a Northern city, for not staying at 'the nationalist hotel'; in fact they not only chided me, but with two telephone calls, neatly transferred my hotel-political allegiance.[1] These friends were quite conscious about their intent: to shift as much economic power as possible from 'their' hands into 'ours'. They had not the air of having invented the idea and I believe that it was an important, though seldom mentioned, feature of Irish life generally for many years. Conditions between the institution of the boycott and the First War — that is during the first phases of Yeats's active life — must have been particularly propitious to it. Yeats, in associating as he did — rather strangely at first sight — the 'new middle-class' with the agrarian agitation, had this set of phenomena in mind. For the class from which Yeats had come — Protestant merchants and professional people — 'the shadow of the Land League' meant the boycott in its wide variety of forms, as an instrument for the transfer of economic power out of their hands into those of the more astute, energetic and rapacious of the conquered caste, now beginning to form a 'new middle-class'.[2]

Yeats was not wrong in seeing in the 'Sullivan gang' — that clan from Bantry, Co. Cork, of which the economic head was William Martin Murphy and the political head Tim Healy — representative leaders of this new class. The qualities of acumen and energy all Ireland, friend and foe, conceded to them; the quality of unscrupulous rapacity was persistently attributed to them by their numerous enemies.

[1] 'The nationalist hotel' was not a political centre, but the only hotel owned by a Catholic. The owner gave no sign of objecting to the political *status quo* and even, for business reasons, kept 'Protestant Bibles' in the hotel rooms.

[2] The Land League was primarily an agrarian body but it and its successor bodies extended their operations to urban areas. Michael Davitt boasted that a 'run' organized by the League broke the Munster Bank in Cork: the Plan of Campaign certainly brought economic life to a standstill in the town of Tipperary.

They had not been particularly closely associated with the Land League but they were associated with the varieties of religious-communal, economic and social activity which I have been describing as arising from the successful operation of the boycott. The Land League itself had not been clerically inspired or dominated — far from it — but in its successor body, the National League, the clergy began to play a direct and recognized political part.[1] After the Parnell divorce case the 'Sullivan gang', led by Healy and backed by Murphy's money, emerged as the spearhead of the clerical attack on Parnell. Other, more important, leaders who went against Parnell — John Dillon and William O'Brien — carefully eschewed the 'moral issue' and tried to spare Parnell. It was left to Healy and his clan, with the active support of the clergy, to hammer away at this issue, often in scurrilous language, and to Parnell's undoing. To the young Yeats — whose dislike of the 'Sullivan gang' antedated these proceedings — the spectacle of the plebeian Healy taunting the falling aristocrat was a powerful symbol. Paradoxically, the Parnell Split closed — for a time — the schism in his political soul between the 'Protestant/aristocrat' and the 'Irish nationalist'. The unified nationalist movement of 1880–90 — a movement in which the 'Sullivan gang' had followed Parnell — had been putting pressure on England, and there Yeats approved them, but they were also putting pressure on the superior caste in Ireland, and that he very much disliked. When Parnell and the 'Sullivan gang' flew apart, this tension in Yeats was relaxed. Parnell was fighting England and — no longer the Ascendancy, which began to discern merits in him for the first time — but the Catholic middle-class, encouraged by the clergy and led by the 'Sullivan gang'.

We know with what intensity this struggle revived in

---

[1] This was by decision of Parnell himself at a time when he wanted to brake the revolutionary tendencies of the movement. See the present writer's *Parnell and his Party*.

Yeats's mind in 1913 when, in the poem 'To a Shade', he apostrophized the ghost of Parnell. The line

Your enemy an old foul mouth

refers to a collective Sullivan orifice — the tongue of Healy and the teeth of Murphy. The immediate occasion for the attack — the art-gallery controversy — was aesthetic, but the roots of the controversy, and its emotional charge, were social and political and — in the communal sense — religious. It is true that the poet attacked the 'Sullivan gang' for its philistinism — and Murphy's *Irish Independent* was indeed, and long remained, a philistine bastion — but he had hated them long before any artistic controversy arose; in any case the Sullivan clan were certainly intellectually well above the level of the Irish middle-class as a whole (both Protestant and Catholic) and, aesthetically, did not lag conspicuously behind the upper class generally.[1] It was not primarily as art-critics but as representatives of a class — the new middle-class — and exponents of a method — clerical pressure — that they were obnoxious.

Yeats's intervention in the 1913 industrial conflict came just at the moment when the leader of the obnoxious class brought the obnoxious method to bear. Murphy, supported in this by Archbishop Walsh, had enlisted clerical aid to prevent children of the Dublin workers from being sent to the homes of English sympathizers. From the Archbishop's point of view the children's departure involved a danger to their faith: from Murphy's point of view it represented a danger to his economic blockade. If the children were not on hand, to go hungry — and be seen and heard to go hungry — then the men might be able to hold out and Larkin would win. So the cry 'the faith in danger' was used to starve the children.

---

[1] It is true that, as in comparable situations elsewhere, the new middle-class as a whole was inferior to the old one in education as in money. In the novels of Somerville and Ross we catch glimpses of this new class, as they appeared to two pairs of brightly observant Ascendancy eyes.

Yeats's attack is directed first and foremost at Murphy's use of 'religion'. His first charge is against 'the Dublin nationalist newspapers' — which were led by Murphy's *Irish Independent* — for 'deliberately arousing religious passion to break up the organisation of the workingman ...' The other charges are all ancillary to this — charges of connivance in Murphy's methods of defending the faith, and some details of these methods.

One can discern, then, in this letter, honest disgust at an odious piece of cruel hypocrisy, a human desire for a crack at Murphy, and the wish to illuminate a particularly unlovely example of the social influence of the Catholic clergy. Concern for the workers is also present, but it must be noted that this, in itself, had not been sufficient to arouse Yeats to intervene. The lock-out (of some workers) and strike (of others) and the police brutalities had begun in August, and protests began soon after. Yeats did not, however, protest until after the publication (21 October) of the letter from the Catholic Archbishop of Dublin in which he told the workers' wives that, if they allowed their hungry children to go to England to be fed, they could 'no longer be held worthy of the name of Catholic mothers'.

Yeats's indignation at the 'saving of the children' was spontaneous, comprehensible and creditable. It does not constitute — appearances to the contrary — an isolated pro-working-class outbreak, unique in his career. It was in no way inconsistent with his 'Protestant/aristocratic' position to attack the leaders of the rising Catholic middle-class, and their clerical allies, or to defend their victims. These leaders and that alliance had long inspired in him distrust and repugnance — feelings which 1913 fanned into flame. These feelings in themselves were habitual in the class from which he himself sprang. Other members of that class could, however, muffle the expression of these feelings when, as now, it suited their economic interest to do so — that is the meaning of the charge of 'connivance' which Yeats directs against the (Protestant) *Irish Times* and *Daily Express*. Yeats himself could do some muffling at times, but when the provocation was great — as now — he had to give vent to his feelings, against the formidable alliance of savings and prayers :

> What need you, being come to sense,
>   But fumble in a greasy till
> And add the halfpence to the pence
>   And prayer to shivering prayer, until
> You have dried the marrow from the bone ?
>   For men were born to pray and save :
> Romantic Ireland's dead and gone,
>   It's with O'Leary in the grave.[1]
>
> ('September 1913')

VI

Most of the leaders who planned the Rising which proved — three years later — that romantic Ireland was not yet dead and gone, belonged to the general class which Yeats distrusted ; not to the climbing 'Sullivan gang' section of it, but to the 'clerks and shopkeepers' whom he thought of as 'the base' ; the leaders included the basest of the base — from Yeats's point of view — Major MacBride himself. They had all been engaged for years in the kind of politics on which he had turned his back. But in 1916 they were shot by the English :

> All changed, changed utterly :
> A terrible beauty is born.

The poems 'Easter 1916', 'Sixteen Dead Men', 'The Rose Tree' and 'On a Political Prisoner' drew strength from the complexity as well as from the intensity of the emotions involved — the sense — which became explicit years after — of his own share in the 'gestation' of the event ;[2] the presence

---

[1] John O'Leary died in 1907.
[2] 'Did words of mine send out
  Certain men the English shot ?'

in the event of the strongest love and the strongest personal
hatred of his life ; an old hate, and even a kind of disgust,
for much of what the insurrection meant

> Blind and leader of the blind
> Drinking the foul ditch where they lie . . .

an even older and deeper hate for those who crushed the insurrection ; and finally a prophetic sense of the still more
bitter struggle yet to come :

> But who can talk of give and take,
> What should be and what not
> While those dead men are loitering there
> To stir the boiling pot ?

By the time when 'Easter 1916' and 'The Rose Tree'
were published, in the autumn of 1920, the pot had boiled over.
The Black-and-Tan terror was now at its height throughout
Ireland. To publish these poems in this context was a political
act, and a bold one : probably the boldest of Yeats's career.
Yeats could be fearless on issues where artistic integrity was
involved — as he showed for example in facing the riots over
The Playboy of the Western World in 1907 — and also when
clerical meddling aroused his anger. But in national politics,
even where he felt passionately, he usually acted prudently.
And even at this point, although he acted with unusual bold-
ness, he did not allow himself to be carried away. What he
published in 1920 concerned an historical event of four years
earlier ; even on that event he did not publish, in England,
the poem 'Sixteen Dead Men' which, with its 'boiling pot',
had the most explicit bearing on contemporary politics. He
did not publish, at all, the poem 'Reprisals' written against
the Black and Tans and addressed to the ghost of Lady
Gregory's son, killed in the Great War :

> Flit to Kiltartan Cross and stay
> Till certain second thoughts have come
> Upon the cause you served, that we

Imagined such a fine affair :
Half-drunk or whole-mad soldiery
Are murdering your tenants there.
Men that revere your father yet
Are shot at on the open plain.
Where may new-married women sit
And suckle children now ? Armed men
May murder them in passing by
Nor law nor parliament take heed.
Then close your ears with dust and lie
Among the other cheated dead.[1]

Yeats did, however, speak, at the Oxford Union in February 1921, in favour of Sinn Fein and against the Black and Tans.

Yeats's indignation was spontaneous : his method of giving expression to that indignation in his published writings seems calculated.[2] By publishing the 1916 poems in 1920 he placed himself openly 'on Ireland's side' in the fight with England but he closed no doors in terms of contemporary politics. For it was known, in 1920, that Ireland was going to get some form of self-government. If the rebels were beaten, it would be the Home Rule (with partition) of the British Act of 1920. If the rebels won, it would be the Republic proclaimed in 1916. The two poems that Yeats chose to publish covered, as it happened, both eventualities neatly. The spirit of the Proclamation of the Republic was in them :

'But where can we draw water,'
Said Pearse to Connolly,
'When all the wells are parched away ?

---

[1] Full text in *The Variorum Edition*, p. 791. It has been stated that he intended to publish this 'but cancelled the publication on hearing that it would distress Robert's widow'. (Hone, *W. B. Yeats*, p. 338.)

[2] He could hardly, of course, have published any of them in the United Kingdom in war-time, but could have published at least 'Easter 1916' in America ; it was written in September 1916, and the United States did not enter the war until the following April. 'Easter 1916' was printed at the time in an edition of twenty-five copies for distribution among friends, but the series was withheld from the sight of the general public until 1920. (Hone, *W. B. Yeats*, p. 301.)

> O plain as plain can be
> There's nothing but our own red blood
> Can make a right Rose Tree.'

But there were also in them the doubts and reservations which most Irishmen had felt about the Proclamation of 1916 : the doubts and reservations of those for whom Home Rule and the Act of 1920 represented an acceptable settlement :

> Was it needless death after all ?
> For England may keep faith
> For all that is done and said.
> We know their dream ; enough
> To know they dreamed and are dead ;
> And what if excess of love
> Bewildered them till they died ?

In the event the Anglo-Irish Treaty brought to Ireland the realities of the Act of 1920 with some of the trappings of 1916. This Treaty set up, not the Republic proclaimed in 1916, but a Free State within the Empire and without the six counties of the north-east. Many — probably more than half — of those who had been fighting the Black and Tans while Yeats had been publishing his 1916 poems, felt that this was a betrayal, as Yeats's Pearse and Connolly might have felt :

> Maybe a breath of politic words
> Has withered our Rose Tree . . .

Those who felt in this way tried to reject the Treaty and carry on the struggle. The majority of the people, tired of war, had voted, in effect, for the acceptance of the Treaty. The Free State Government, with the aid of British artillery and armoured cars, now set about liquidating the Republican forces. Whether it had behind it, in this effort, all of those who had given it its majority may be doubted. It certainly had behind it all the wealthier elements in the country, including almost all the Anglo-Irish, and it had W. B. Yeats, nominated by President Cosgrave to the Senate of the Irish Free

State in December 1922. The Civil War had now been raging for six months.

The Free State forces, in destroying the Republican forces, were obliged to use some of the same methods as the Black and Tans (flogging, shooting of hostages), but applied these with greater efficiency, based on far better intelligence, and with proportionately less accompanying publicity.[1] It was a pattern that was to be repeated — perhaps copied — after the mid-century, in many ex-colonies, and came to be assailed as neo-colonialism. Many of those who had denounced the excesses of the Black and Tans were plunged in deeper horror by what happened during the Civil War and in its aftermath. These included Lady Gregory, whose journals tell a story :[2]

During the Civil War: Jan. 23 [1923] These floggings in my mind. I wrote to Yeats in protest. The young men taken away were flogged, as well as those left, 'with a thonged whip'. I was not surprised to hear Hogan's house at Kilchreest has been destroyed. Hatred must grow — 'death answering to death through the generations like clerks answering one another at the Mass'.

After the Civil War: Aug. 23 W. B. Yeats here yesterday. I say the fault of the Government is this hatred of the Republicans they show in their speeches. He says it is justified or at least excused by the information they have had from America that it is to be said, in case 'of a Republican defeat', that the elections were not carried out fairly and assassinations are threatened. But with the Republicans saying the prisoners are flogged or tortured they probably have the same hatred ...

Nov. 10. ...There had been some talk about the hunger strike, Esmonde saying the Government would not yield. And this is Yeats's view. I had some talk with him after we came home, the first time I had seen him close and again this morning. He says the Government cannot give in. That if they had let Miss Mac-

---

[1] A friend who read this in draft objected to this comparison and pointed out that the Free State forces, unlike the Black and Tans, did not use indiscriminate terror against the civilian population. This is a valid point, though even the Black-and-Tan terror was not *altogether* indiscriminate.

[2] *Lady Gregory's Journals, 1916–1930*, ed. Lennox Robinson, London, 1946.

Swiney die, when she began it, this new hunger strike would not have begun, but they had a sentimental feeling for her for her brother's sake.[1] We talked a long time this morning. I had had a bad night and thought it over a long time, and had come to a determination of writing to the papers about it, asking that the crime or accusation against these four hundred men remaining on [hunger] strike might be told out, that we might know if consenting to their suicide is in accordance with the conscience of Christian nations and the law of God. I meant to go and consult 'A. E.' about them. But Yeats is violently against any protest, says it is necessary to the stability of Government to hold out, says they cannot publish the accusations because many are on suspicion, or as they think certainty, but they have not evidence that can be shown. ...

I ask if that might not come under an amnesty at the conclusion of the war, for the Government themselves signed death sentences during it. But he says no, and he says the Government cannot publish the real reason for the detention of this thousand, they themselves are in danger of being assassinated by some among them.

I asked if they could not, on their side, try to get rid of the Oath [of allegiance to the Crown]; that would do away with the real cause of trouble, the keeping of Republicans out of the Dail. He said they cannot in the present state of English feeling, it would be useless to ask for it, and besides we may probably want English help in getting the Loan. And the Senate can make no move in the matter. ...

Nov. 11. ...Went on to Jack Yeats [the painter, the poet's brother] ... Lennox Robinson ... said: 'Can we not do anything about the hunger strikers? Write a letter perhaps.' Strange, because I had not spoken of my own restless night or my talk with Yeats. So we walked and planned and at last went into the Arts Club and wrote a letter. We thought Stephens [James] and Jack Yeats might join in signing it. He called in Cruise O'Brien[2] from another room to ask if the *Independent* [pro-Government paper]

---

[1] Mary MacSwiney was the sister of Terence MacSwiney, the famous Lord Mayor of Cork, who had died on hunger-strike as a prisoner of the British. The Government may or may not have had a sentimental feeling for her; some of its members probably had; all of them knew that to let her die as her brother had died would discredit them in the eyes of most of their countrymen.

[2] Father of the present writer; at this time a leader-writer on the *Independent*.

would put it in. He thought so, made one or two slight alterations, thinking it showed a slight prepossession against the Government; then I came back to Merrion Square [to Yeats's house]. Later Lennox Robinson telephoned that Jack Yeats had refused to sign, 'he is much too red to do so', and asked if we should still send it on with our own names and Stephens' who has agreed. I said 'Yes'. It may perhaps bring letters or suggestions from others and possibly save some lives. Then I told Yeats (W. B.) what I had done and proposed leaving his house for the hotel, as he might not approve. He would not allow that and after talking for a while thought perhaps we had done right. Of course one won't have any gratitude from either side. But I slept better.

Nov. 16. On Monday night 'A. E.' and Lieutenant 'X' were with Yeats. I looked in but didn't stay. Yeats said they had talked of the prisoners. 'X' said they were not on hunger strike, were being fed. And that the stories of ill-treatment are not true — gave instances, thinks it 'likely only half a dozen men will die'. Dreadful, I think, even if that half-dozen were not of the bravest.[1]

VII

Yeats was now an established public figure. Having become a Senator in December 1922, he received an honorary Doctorate from Trinity College in 1923 and the Nobel Prize for Literature in the same year. The Yeatses had now a house in Merrion Square: 'the Berkeley Square of Ireland', as he said. He was soberly pleased about his political position and prospects. 'We', he wrote of himself and his fellow Senators, 'are a fairly distinguished body and should get much government into our hands.'[2] His political ideas were now explicitly reactionary: 'Out of all this murder and rapine,' he wrote in 1922, 'will come not a demagogic but an authoritarian government.'[3] And again: 'everywhere one notices a drift towards

[1] While refusing to protest publicly about the Government's policy on hunger-striking, Yeats may have interceded privately. Patrick McCartan informed Mr. Terence de Vere White, many years later, that 'I got Mrs. Green, W. B. Yeats and others to intercede for them, but it was futile'. (White, *Kevin O'Higgins*, London, 1949, p. 179.)

[2] To Edmund Dulac, 1 December 1922. (*Letters*, p. 694.)

[3] To Olivia Shakespear, May 1922. (*Letters*, p. 682.)

Conservatism, perhaps towards Autocracy'.[1] His ideas for
Ireland were explicitly linked with the rise of Fascism in
Europe :

> We are preparing here, behind our screen of bombs and smoke,
> a return to conservative politics as elsewhere in Europe or at least
> to a substitution of the historical sense for logic. The return will
> be painful and perhaps violent but many educated men talk of it
> and must soon work for it and perhaps riot for it.
>
> A curious sign is that 'A. E.' who was the most popular of men
> is now suffering some slight eclipse because of old democratic
> speeches — things of years ago. I on the other hand get hearers
> where I did not get them because I have been of the opposite
> party. ... The Ireland that reacts from the present disorder is turn-
> ing its eyes towards individualist [*i.e.* Fascist] Italy.[2]

This letter was written just before Yeats's nomination to
the Senate of the Free State and just after Mussolini's March
on Rome (22 October 1922).

Many of Yeats's contemporaries and of his younger admirers and subsequent writers about him refused to take all
this very seriously.[3] The Dublin to which Yeats belonged —
in so far as he belonged to Dublin at all — the Dublin of the
Arts Club, liked to treat Yeats's politics as a joke, and this
tradition went a long way back. More than twenty years
before, when Yeats and Maud Gonne were stirring up opinion
against Queen Victoria's visit to Ireland, Percy French had
made the Queen protest :

> And there must be a slate, sez she,
> Off that Willie Yeats, sez she.

[1] To the same. October 1922. (*Letters*, p. 690.)
[2] To H. J. C. Grierson, 6 November 1922. Dr. Ellmann quotes
(pp. 248–9) a public speech in the same vein nearly two years later
(2 August 1924).
[3] Thus, Mr. Arland Ussher has said that 'Yeats, in spite of his desire
to be a public figure was more apolitical than any fully responsible
person alive' (*Three Great Irishmen*, p. 91). Another critic has said that
even his 'superficially political poems' are 'not really so'. (M. L.
Rosenthal, in *The Nation*, 23 June 1956.) It is hard to see how these
judgments can be reconciled with the known facts of Yeats's life and
work.

He'd be betther at home, sez she,
Frinch-polishin' a pome, sez she,
Than writin' letthers, sez she,
About his betthers, sez she,
Paradin' me crimes, sez she,
In the Irish Times, sez she.

This mood of affectionate raillery persisted, and perhaps did something to protect Yeats from possible adverse consequences of his political involvement. My father, at the Arts Club, used to poke gentle fun at Yeats's 'Fascism', parodying him as referring in a speech to 'that very great man, Missolonghi' and then, when corrected, saying majestically: 'I am told the name is not Missolonghi but Mussolini — but, does it ... really ... matter?'[1]

Yeats enjoyed, and even encouraged, this kind of joke about himself and others:

And thought before I had done
Of a mocking tale or a gibe
To please a companion
Around the fire at the club,
Being certain that they and I
But lived where motley is worn ...

For those who admired Yeats, but were made uneasy by his politics, the idea that his politics were vague, ill-informed and funny offered a way out: a way out, left open by Yeats himself. Yet his politics had this much serious about them: that practice and theory tended to concur. The poet admired Mussolini and his colleagues from afar:[2] the Senator admired, and worked with, Ireland's strong man, Kevin O'Higgins.[3]

[1] I am not sure that it was parody. Dr. Sheehy Skeffington recalls it as an anecdote, and believes it to be true.

[2] 'Students of contemporary Italy where Vico's thought is current through its influence upon Croce and Gentile think it created, or in part created, the present government of one man surrounded by just such able assistants as Vico foresaw.' (Introduction to *The Words upon the Window-pane* (1931); *Explorations*, p. 355.)

[3] O'Higgins's biographer, Mr. Terence de Vere White, while noting that it became the fashion to call him 'the Irish Mussolini', maintains that

O'Higgins, in Irish politics — he was Minister of Justice in the Free State Government — was thought to stand for what was most ruthless and implacable in the party of property : the stern defence of seventy-seven executions. This was not repugnant to Yeats ; the 'right of the state to take life in its own defence' became dear to him. O'Higgins was 'their sole statesman'; Yeats did him the honour of including him, along with Grattan, Parnell and Berkeley, in a list of great Irishmen — a list in which the sole Gaelic and Catholic name is that of O'Higgins. His portrait is among 'my friends' in 'The Municipal Gallery Revisited':

> Kevin O'Higgins' countenance that wears
> A gentle questioning look that cannot hide
> A soul incapable of remorse or rest . . .

Those who — like Yeats — admired in O'Higgins a potential autocrat would not have taken it for granted that he, as his colleagues were to do in 1932, would have tamely allowed the party defeated in the Civil War to come to power through impeccably conducted free elections. But by then O'Higgins was no longer there ; he had been assassinated in 1927 :

> A great man in his pride
> Confronting murderous men

'Nobody', he had said in a phrase which impressed Yeats, 'can expect to live who has done what I have.'[1] How deeply hated he was — not only by his political opponents but by some of 'his own side' including his own police — I can remember myself. I was ten years old and returning from a drive in the country — my first drive in a motor-car — with my aunt, Mrs. Skeffington, and a friend of hers. We were

he was in fact 'an intense believer in democracy'. This may well be so ; as far as the subject of this essay is concerned, the important point is that it was as 'an Irish Mussolini' that Yeats rightly or wrongly saw him, and that he admired him for that.

[1] To Olivia Shakespear, April 1933. (*Letters*, p. 809.)

stopped at a road-block and the Sergeant, recognizing my aunt, smiled broadly and said : 'Ye'll be delighted to hear, Ma'am — Kevin's been shot !' My aunt did not smile ; she was not disposed to be amused either by murder or by policemen.

Countess Markievicz — 'Madame' as she was known among the poor of Dublin who loved her — died just after O'Higgins was murdered. She had a great following among the street-traders of Moore Street ; famed hecklers and the bane of every Free State politician, they were known at this time as 'Madame's wans'. About O'Higgins's death, one of them said : 'poor Madame's last wish'.

It was of her that Yeats had written :

> Did she in touching that lone wing
> Recall the years before her mind
> Became a bitter, an abstract thing,
> Her thought some popular enmity :
> Blind and leader of the blind
> Drinking the foul ditch where they lie ?

All Ireland was divided by the end of that week between those who mourned Countess Markievicz and those who mourned O'Higgins. The latter were probably fewer but more 'respectable'. From a window in Parnell Square I watched O'Higgins's funeral go by. I had not imagined there were so many top-hats in the world ; I was never to see so many again.[1] They were there to honour a man who had defended what they stood for, at the cost of many lives including his own. Senator Yeats must have been under one of the top-hats. The poet had stayed away from Parnell's

---

[1] I was not alone in being impressed by the top-hats. 'Rarely', noted the Dublin *Evening Mail*, 'has there been such a display of silk hats and frock coats.' The same paper recorded that 'the Fascisti in Dublin were present with their flag and black shirts and they were given a place in the procession by the police'. (*E. M.* 'Items of the Funeral', 13 July 1927.)

funeral; the Senator would not, I think, have stayed away from that of Kevin O'Higgins.[1]

VIII

In 1928, the year after O'Higgins's death, Yeats lost his Senate seat; his term had expired and the Government made no move to renew his nomination. For some time past the going had been increasingly difficult, for similar reasons to those which had applied at the turn of the century. That is to say that the specific influence of the Catholic Church in politics was growing more palpable again. It is true that the régime to which Yeats belonged had always been supported by the Church, but in the beginning it had also needed Protestant support. When it was struggling for its life, and needed money and guns from England, it had to reassure English opinion by giving places of prominence to members of the Protestant middle-class most of whom, though not Yeats, were classified as 'Southern loyalists'. When the emergency was over, and 'the Loan' negotiated, the need to placate English opinion, by showing deference to Protestants, subsided. The Government no longer needed British artillery; it still needed to have its position fully covered by the Canons of the Church. The vital principle for the party now in power was one later reduced by a member of that party to a lapidary formula — never to risk 'a sthroke of a crozier'. The fact was that the 'Sullivan gang' — Yeats's old bugbears from 1890 to 1913 — were an important component in the régime which had made Yeats a Senator. Healy was Governor-General and Yeats had called on him in that capacity; the Murphy press — which had called vociferously for the execution of the 1916 leaders — was a pillar of the Cosgrave régime; Kevin

[1] The Senate attended the funeral as a body: the press did not report the names of individual Senators attending. Senate records show that Yeats was present on the previous day at the meeting which unanimously decided that the Senate would attend the funeral as a body.

O'Higgins himself was a member of the clan, a nephew of Healy's, and a grandson of T. D. Sullivan, the first Irish parliamentarian to declare against Parnell after the divorce. Granted that Yeats's hostility to this clan — and the 'clerical bourgeoisie' for which it stood — was sincere, as it surely was, how did he become so easily reconciled to them in 1922 ? The answer is, I think, a double one. First, the Civil War had changed many things. The Protestant middle- and upper classes, which had so long regarded the social and political influence of the clergy as either a baneful or a contemptible phenomenon, had now seen its advantages as a barrier against 'anarchy'; the propertied classes had been made more conscious of a common danger and common interests, less insistent on differences and group competition. Yeats — who worked in the Senate generally in concert with the representatives of the Protestant propertied classes — could also move with them in suppressing his repugnance for what 'the Bantry band' represented. Second, the reconciliation was only partial and temporary :

> A patched-up affair if you ask my opinion.

As long as the 'clerical bourgeoisie' showed consideration for the susceptibilities of Protestants, it was possible to work with them. When the bishops began to dictate, the strain, for Yeats, became too great. The Irish bishops, crozier-happy, now extorted the legislation they wanted, forbidding divorce and the sale of contraceptives and later setting up a censorship of publications. The government party, which Yeats had supported on all major matters, carried out the wishes of the bishops.

Irish Protestants generally did not care for the new trend but most of them now made their political choices, not as Protestants but as bourgeois. The Government was obnoxiously Papist, but it was sound on the essential : the rights of property. Nor did Protestants wish to say anything to confirm their fellow-countrymen in an opinion to which they were already too prone : that the distinguishing characteristic of Protestantism is a devotion to divorce, contraceptives and dirty books. The new legislation was, in practice, not much more than a minor irritant: Belfast is not far away.

Most Irish Protestants therefore took a guarded line in the matter. But not Yeats.[1] Yeats's aristocratic feelings, and his pride as a Senator, were hurt ; the sage oligarchy to which he had felt himself to belong, the 'fairly distinguished body' which 'should get much government into its hands', was now taking its orders from a bunch of peasants in mitres.[2] The 'base' were dictating to their betters. The peroration of his speech on divorce was not a liberal one : it was the statement of the spokesman of a superior caste, denying the right of inferior castes to make laws for it : 'We against whom you have done this thing are no petty people. We are one of the great stocks of Europe. We are the people of Burke : we are the people of Grattan ; we are the people of Swift, the people of Emmet, the people of Parnell. We have created most of the modern literature of this country. We have created the best of its political intelligence.'[3]

Some have felt that Yeats's own political intelligence was not at its best on this occasion. Certainly he seemed to be committing political — or at the very least parliamentary — suicide. Yet he could not do otherwise ; to remain in politics he would have had to swallow his pride, and pride was essential to his political life. His dilemma — the dilemma which, happily for his work, pushed him away from the centre

[1] The *Irish Times*, representative of Irish Protestant opinion, editorially regretted 'the manner of Senator Yeats's intervention' on this subject (12 June 1925).

[2] Yeats's growing resentment of the Irish bishops found vent, as early as 1924, in a criticism of the style of the Pastorals : 'a style rancid, coarse and vague like that of the daily papers' (leading article in *To-morrow* quoted in Ellmann, pp. 250–1). Senator Yeats — not yet flinging prudence to the winds — did not sign this article, but got two other people to sign it.   [3] 11 June 1925.

and towards the margins of politics — was that he had become an anti-clerical conservative in a country where the clergy were an indispensable element of any practical conservative politics. Because of his conservative option in the Civil War he had cut himself off from all the forces in the country which were, in any notable degree, resistant to clerical pressure (or, for that matter, to the temptation of manipulating religious issues for their own ends). His political friends now showed themselves to be a clerical party, the direct heirs to the anti-Parnellites of the 'nineties. What was still living in the Parnellite tradition had gone on the Republican side in the Civil War and regarded Yeats with aversion and a sense of betrayal. He now, by openly defying the Church, cut himself off, for a time at least, from the modern 'anti-Parnellites'. Politically he had become for the moment completely isolated.

IX

The year 1932 was a turning point in Irish political history. In that year the party, led by Mr. Cosgrave, which had won the Civil War and ruled the country since the foundation of the State, fell from power. The party, led by de Valera, which represented the losers in the Civil War, now won a General Election and took over the Government. The respect for democratic process shown by Mr. Cosgrave's government was, in the circumstances, rather remarkable. It was, indeed, too remarkable to please many of the members of the fallen party, and some of these now set about organizing a paramilitary movement, on the Fascist model, for the intimidation of their opponents and the recovery of power. 'They have the Blackshirts in Italy,' said one of the politicians concerned, 'they have the Brownshirts in Germany, and now in Ireland we have the Blueshirts.'

Yeats took part in the launching of this movement and wrote songs for it :

What is equality? muck in the yard.

It was necessary, he explained, to break 'the reign of the mob' and 'if any Government or party undertake this work it will need force, marching men (the logic of fanaticism whether in a woman or a mob is drawn from a premise, protected by ignorance and therefore irrefutable); it will promise not this or that measure but a discipline, a way of life; that sacred drama must to all native eyes and ears become the greatest of the parables. There is no such government or party today; should either appear, I offer it these trivial songs and what remains to me of life' (April 1934).

Several months later he added this postscript:

P.S. Because a friend belonging to a political party wherewith I had once had some loose associations told me that it had, or was about to have, or might be persuaded to have, some such aim as mine, I wrote these songs. Finding that it neither would nor could, I increased their fantasy, their extravagance, their obscurity, that no party might sing them (August 1934).[1]

The picture presented in the postscript is that of a dreamy, unpractical poet hardly even on the fringes of politics, and innocent with regard to them, moved by an impulse, and misled by a friend, into a political gesture which he later regretted. On the whole this picture has been accepted.[2] Yet the evidence of the letters suggests that his involvement was considerably deeper, and more conscious than he found it convenient, in retrospect, to say.

At the moment [he wrote in April 1933 to Olivia Shakespear] I am trying in association with [an] ex-cabinet Minister, an eminent lawyer and a philosopher to work out a social theory which can be

---

[1] 'Commentary on the Three Songs', December 1934, in *The Variorum Edition*, pp. 836–7.

[2] It has even been improved upon. Mr. Arland Ussher has made the remarkable claim that Yeats's 'brief flirtation with O'Duffy's "blueshirts"' was 'something of a pro-British peacemaking gesture' (*Three Great Irishmen*, p. 92). Yeats's letters to Olivia Shakespear do not suggest that affection for England or peace had anything to do with his excitement about the Blueshirts.

used against Communism in Ireland. This country is exciting. I am told that De Valera has said in private that within three years he will be torn in pieces.[1]

A few months later to the same correspondent:

Politics are growing heroic. De Valera has forced political thought to face the most fundamental issues.[2] A Fascist opposition is forming behind the scenes to be ready should some tragic situation develop. I find myself constantly urging the despotic rule of the educated classes. ... I know half a dozen men any one of whom may be Caesar — or Catiline. It is amusing to live in a country where men will always act. Where nobody is satisfied with thought. There is so little in our stocking that we are ready at any moment to turn it inside out and how can we not feel emulous when we see Hitler juggling with his sausage of stocking. Our chosen colour is blue, and blue shirts are marching about all over the country and their organizer tells me that it was my suggestion — a suggestion I have entirely forgotten — that made them select for their flag a red St. Patrick's cross on a blue ground — all I can remember is that I have always denounced green and commended blue (the colour of my early book covers). The chance of being shot is raising everybody's spirits enormously. There is some politics for you of which your newspapers know nothing.[3]

To the same, 23 July 1933:

The great secret is out — a convention of blue shirts — National Guards — have received their new leader with the Fascist salute and the new leader announces reform of Parliament as his business.

When I wrote to you, the Fascist organizer of the blue shirts had told me that he was about to bring to see me the man he had selected for leader that I might talk my anti-democratic philosophy. I was ready, for I had just rewritten for the seventh time the part of *A Vision* that deals with the future. The leader turned out to be Gen[eral] O'Duffy, head of the Irish police for twelve years and

---

[1] *Letters*, p. 808.

[2] Earlier he had written as if he thought de Valera a Fascist. 'You are right', he wrote to Olivia Shakespear in February 1933, 'in comparing de Valera to Mussolini or Hitler. All three have exactly the same aim so far as I can judge.' (*Letters*, p. 806.) It is hard to reconcile this ambiguous and — however interpreted — untrue statement with the organization of 'a Fascist opposition' to de Valera.

[3] 13 July 1933. (*Letters*, pp. 811–12.)

a famous organizer. . . . Italy, Poland, Germany, then perhaps
Ireland. Doubtless I shall hate it (though not so much as I hate
Irish democracy) but it is September and we must not behave like
the gay young sparks of May or June. *The Observer*, the *Sunday
Times*, the only English newspapers I see, have noticed nothing
though Cosgrave's ablest ministers are with O'Duffy. O'Duffy
himself is autocratic, directing the movement from above down as
though it were an army. I did not think him a great man though a
pleasant one, but one never knows, his face and mind may harden
or clarify.[1]

To the same, 17 August 1933 :

The papers will have told you of the blue shirt excitement here.
The government is in a panic and has surrounded itself with
armoured cars. The shirts themselves are made in batches of 600
and cannot be made fast enough. The organization is for an independent Ireland within the Commonwealth. Whether it succeeds
or not in abolishing parliamentary government as we know it
today it will certainly bring into discussion all the things I care for.
Three months ago there seemed not a trace of such a movement
and when it did come into existence it had little apparent importance
until that romantic dreamer I have described to you pitched on
O'Duffy for a leader. About him the newspapers have probably
told you enough. He seemed to me a plastic man but I could not
judge whether he would prove plastic to the opinions of others,
obvious political current or his own will ('Unity of being').

To the same, 20 September 1933 :

I wonder if the English newspapers have given you any idea
of our political comedy. Act 1. Capt. Macmanus, the ex-British
officer I spoke of, his head full of vague Fascism, got probably from
me, decided that Gen[eral] O'Duffy should be made leader of a
body of young men formed to keep meetings from being broken
up. He put into O'Duffy's head — he describes him as 'a simple
peasant' — Fascist ideas and started him off to organise that body
of young men. Act II. Some journalist announced that 30,000 of
these young men were going to march through Dublin on a certain
day (the correct number was 3,000). Government panic. Would
not O'Duffy, who had once been head of the army, and more
recently head of the police, march on the Government with 30,000

[1] *Letters*, pp. 812–13.

255

plus army and police ? Result, martial law — in its Irish form — armoured cars in the streets, and new police force drawn from the I.R.A. to guard the Government, and O'Duffy's organization proclaimed. Act III. O'Duffy is made thereby so important that Cosgrave surrenders the leadership of his party to O'Duffy and all the opposition united under him. Two months ago he was unknown politically.

That was the climax : from then on the references to O'Duffy in Yeats's letters become much sparser and increasingly disparaging, and Yeats soon adopts an attitude of political disengagement, which becomes explicit in the poem 'Church and State' (November 1934) :

> Here is fresh matter, poet,
> Matter for old age meet ;
> Might of the Church and the State,
> Their mobs put under their feet.
> O but heart's wine shall run pure,
> Mind's bread grow sweet.
>
> That were a cowardly song,
> Wander in dreams no more ;
> What if the Church and the State
> Are the mob that howls at the door !
> Wine shall run thick to the end,
> Bread taste sour.

It is customary to say that, at this point, Yeats had become 'disillusioned with Fascism'. One may accept this judgment, but must also remark that the principal illusion which had been dissipated was the illusion that Fascism in Ireland stood a good chance of winning. In the spring and summer of 1933, the Fascism of the Irish Blueshirts looked to many people like a possible winner and in this phase Yeats was with the Blueshirts. By the autumn and winter of 1933–34, the Government's energetic measures — described by Yeats as 'panic measures' — made it clear that de Valera was no von Papen. O'Duffy, failing to devise anything effective in reply, revealed that he was no Hitler. The blue began to fade, and Yeats's interest in it faded proportionately.[1]

Commenting on a mildly anti-Blueshirt anecdote in a letter of Yeats, Professor Jeffares says : 'This ironic attitude to the Blueshirts reveals the true Yeats, detached and merely playing with his thoughts, except for the intervals when he wanted to achieve complete directness and accuracy'.

The date of the anecdote in question is February 1934, by which date the Blueshirts were beginning to look a little silly. The thoughts Yeats had 'played with' in the days when they had looked possibly formidable were less 'detached'. I cannot see on what grounds we are to regard the Yeats who began to sneer at the Blueshirts when they proved a flop, as being more 'real' than the Yeats who was excited about them when he thought they might win. It was the same Yeats, strongly drawn to Fascism, but no lover of hopeless causes.

In April 1934 — as we have seen (p. 253) — he was still advocating 'force, marching men' to break the reign of the mob, but professing, somewhat disingenuously, that 'no such party' as would undertake this work had yet appeared. By August 1934 — when the party for which he had in fact written the songs was on the verge of public disintegration — he has found that that party 'neither could nor would' do what he proposed for it. This, it will be noted, does *not* amount to a disavowal of the programme of 'force, marching men' to

[1] The sequence of events described by Yeats in his September letter involved, in reality, a climb down by O'Duffy who had announced a mass parade of the Blueshirts (National Guard) for 13 August, the anniversary of Collins's death. When the National Guard was proclaimed illegal the parade was called off and 'a quiet ceremony at the Cenotaph' was held instead. O'Duffy immediately became, as Yeats noted, leader of the Opposition United Party but, as a historian sympathetic to the opposition has observed : 'from the very outset the new arrangement was thoroughly unsatisfactory, it quickly became apparent that O'Duffy did not possess the special qualities that equip a man for leadership in public life'. (D. O'Sullivan, *The Irish Free State and the Senate*, p. 406.) O'Duffy resigned his chairmanship of the United Party in September 1934.

'break the reign of the mob'. The irony and detachment of the poem 'Church and State' belong to the period after the final break-up of the Blueshirt movement.

Comment on the question of Yeats's attitude to Fascism has been bedevilled by the assumption that a great poet must be, even in politics, 'a nice guy'. If this be assumed then it follows that, as Yeats obviously was a great poet, he cannot *really* have favoured Fascism, which is obviously not a nice cause. Thus the critic or biographer is led to postulate a 'true Yeats', so that Yeats's recorded words and actions of Fascist character must have been perpetrated by some bogus person with the same name and outward appearance.[1]

If one drops the assumption, about poets having always to be nice in politics, then the puzzle disappears, and we see, I believe, that Yeats the man was as near to being a Fascist as his situation and the conditions of his own country permitted. His unstinted admiration had gone to Kevin O'Higgins, the most ruthless 'strong man' of his time in Ireland, and he linked his admiration explicitly to his rejoicing at the rise of Fascism in Europe — and this at the very beginning, within a few weeks of the March on Rome. Ten years later, after Hitler had moved to the centre of the political stage in Europe, Yeats was trying to create a movement in Ireland which would be overtly Fascist in language, costume, behaviour and intent. He turned his back on this movement when it began to fail, not before. Would the irony and detachment of this phase of disillusion have lasted if a more effective Fascist leader and movement had later emerged? One may doubt it. Many in Germany who were 'disillusioned' by the failure of the Kapp *putsch* and the beer-cellar *putsch* were speedily 'reillusioned' when Hitler succeeded — and 'disillusioned' again when he lost the war.

Post-war writers, touching with embarrassment on Yeats's

---

[1] (There is a sense of course in which the poet, actually engaged in writing his poetry, is 'the true Yeats', but that is another matter.)

pro-Fascist opinions, have tended to treat these as a curious aberration of an idealistic but ill-informed poet. In fact such opinions were quite usual in the Irish Protestant middle-class to which Yeats belonged (as well as in other middle-classes), in the 'twenties and 'thirties. The *Irish Times*, spokesman of that class, aroused no protest from its readers when it hailed Hitler (4 March 1933) as 'Europe's standard bearer against Muscovite terrorism' and its references to Mussolini were as consistently admiring as those to Soviet Russia were consistently damning. But the limiting factor on the pro-Fascist tendencies of the *Irish Times* and of the Irish Protestant middle-class generally was the pull of loyalty to Britain — a factor which did not apply — or applied only with great ambivalence — in the case of Yeats. Mr. T. R. Henn is quite right when he says that Yeats was 'not alone in believing at that moment of history, that the discipline of Fascist theory might impose order upon a disintegrating world'. I cannot follow Mr. Henn, however, to his conclusion that 'nothing could be further from Yeats's mind than [Fascism's] violent and suppressive practice' (*The Lonely Tower*, p. 467). 'Force, marching men' and 'the victory [in civil war] of the skilful, riding their machines as did the feudal knights their armoured horses' (*On the Boiler*), surely belong to the domain of violent and suppressive practice.

Just as one school is led to claim that the pro-Fascist Yeats was not the 'true' Yeats, so another tries to believe that the Fascism to which Yeats was drawn was not a 'true' Fascism.

Several critics have assured us that he was drawn not really to Fascism, but to some idealized aristocracy of eighteenth-century stamp. 'In all fairness', writes Dr. Vivian Mercier, 'we should allow that his views were closer to Hamilton's or even to Jefferson's than they were to Mussolini's.'[1] As far

---

[1] 'To pierce the dark mind', *Nation* (10 December 1960). My friend Dr. Mercier, like almost all scholars from Ireland who have written on Yeats, finds his aristocratism, as an Anglo-Irish attitude, more congenial than the aboriginal writer of the present essay can find it.

as political theory is concerned this is probably correct —
although the name of Swift would seem more relevant than
that of Hamilton or of Jefferson. But it ignores one important
reality : that Yeats was interested in contemporary politics
and that he was a contemporary, not of Swift's or Jefferson's,
but of Mussolini's.[1]

He would certainly have preferred something more strictly
aristocratic than Fascism, but since he was living in the
twentieth century he was attracted to Fascism as the best available form of anti-democratic theory and practice. Mr. Frank
O'Connor, who knew him well in his last years and — politics
apart — greatly admired and liked him, has told us plainly
that 'he was a fascist and authoritarian, seeing in world crises
only the break-up of the "damned liberalism" he hated'.[2]

George Orwell, though critical, and up to a point per-
cipient, about Yeats's tendencies, thought that Yeats misunder-
stood what an authoritarian society would be like. Such a
society, Orwell pointed out, 'will not be ruled by noblemen
with Van Dyck faces, but by anonymous millionaires, shiny-
bottomed bureaucrats and murderous gangsters'. This implies
a degree of innocence in Yeats which cannot reasonably be
postulated. O'Higgins and O'Duffy were not 'Duke Ercole
and Guidobaldo', and Yeats had considerable experience of
practical politics, both in the 'nineties and in the early 'twenties.
'In the last forty years,' wrote J. M. Hone in the year of Yeats's
death, 'there was never a period in which his countrymen did
not regard him as a public figure.'[3] When he thought of rule

---

[1] He had, in any case, the assurance of his friend Ezra Pound (*Jefferson and/or Mussolini*) that the Duce was translating Jeffersonian ideas
into twentieth-century terms.

[2] 'The Old Age of a Poet', *The Bell* (February 1941). He also mentions an Abbey dispute over an attempt by Yeats to stage *Coriolanus* for
purposes of 'fascist propaganda'. Mr. Sean O'Faoláin, a more cautious
observer, who also knew Yeats at this time, speaks of his 'fascist tendencies' ('Yeats and the Younger Generation', *Horizon*, January, 1942).

[3] 'Yeats as a Political Philosopher', *London Mercury* (April, 1939).
Hone adds that, among Yeats's fellow Senators, a banker thought the

by an *élite*, it was a possible *élite*, resembling in many ways the nominated members of the Senate in which he had sat.[1] Its membership — bankers, organizers, ex-officers — would correspond roughly to what Orwell, in more emotive language, describes. Nor should it be assumed — as Orwell with his 'murderous gangsters' seems to imply — that the sensitive nature of the poet would necessarily be revolted by the methods of rule of an authoritarian state.[2] Yeats — unlike, say, his brother, or Lady Gregory — was not, in politics, a very squeamish person. Seventy-seven executions did not repel him ; on the contrary, they made him admire O'Higgins all the more. At least one of his associates of the early 'thirties might have been described as a 'murderous gangster'. And when, in 1936, Ethel Mannin appealed to him for a gesture which would have helped the German writer, Ossietzki, then in a Nazi concentration camp, Yeats refused. 'Do not', he said, 'try to make a politician of me . . .'[3]

poet would have made 'an admirable banker' and a lawyer thought that 'a great lawyer' was lost in him.

[1] 'In its early days', Yeats wrote of the Senate, 'some old banker or lawyer would dominate the House, leaning upon the back of the chair in front, always speaking with undisturbed self-possession as at some table in a board-room. My imagination sets up against him some typical elected man, emotional as a youthful chimpanzee, hot and vague, always disturbed, always hating something or other.' (*On the Boiler.*) In another mood, however, he wrote about these oligarchs in a more disparaging vein. (*A Packet for Ezra Pound.*)

[2] The late Louis MacNeice in *The Poetry of W. B. Yeats* seems to have been the first to lay much stress on Yeats's relation to Fascism, but could not quite make up his mind what that relation was. He refers to Yeats at one point as 'the man who nearly became a fascist' (p. 174), having spoken of him earlier as having arrived at 'his own elegant brand of fascism' (p. 41).

[3] To Ethel Mannin, April 1936. In fairness to Yeats it must be noted, however, that in order to help Ossietzki he would have had to recommend him to the Nobel Committee for consideration for the Nobel Prize — something which, on artistic grounds, he may well have been unwilling to do. His degree of 'toughness' on political matters, minimized as it has been by some of his admirers, should not be exaggerated either. In the Senate he supported an amendment to the Government's Public Safety Bill intended to secure independent inspection of prisons

It is true that neither Yeats nor anyone else during Yeats's lifetime knew what horrors Fascism would be capable of. But the many who, like Yeats, were drawn to Fascism at this time knew, and seemed to have little difficulty in accepting, or at least making allowances for, much of what had already been done and continued to be done. 'The Prussian police', wrote the *Irish Times* in an editorial of February 1933, 'have been authorized by Herr Hitler's Minister to shoot Communists — a term which in Germany has a wide political connotation — on sight.' The same editorial which contained this information ended with the words: 'Naturally the earlier phases of this renascence are crude, but Germany is finding her feet after a long period of political ineptitude'.[1]

Yeats read the newspapers; he also read, as Hone records, several books on Fascist Italy and Nazi Germany.[2] If, then, he was attracted to the dominant movements in these countries, and if he supported a movement in his own country whose resemblances to these Continental movements he liked to stress, it cannot be contended that he did so in ignorance of such 'crude' practices as the *Irish Times* described.[3]

(Senate Debates, I. Cols. 1440–41; 1638–9). He also sent 'warm blankets' to Maud Gonne when his government put her in jail (*Letters*, p. 696). But in all essentials he supported the Government's policy of firmness. 'Even the gentle Yeats', wrote Sean O'Casey, 'voted for the Flogging Bill' (*i.e.* the Public Safety Bill which introduced flogging as a punishment for arson and armed robbery). Yeats voted for the Second Reading (26 July 1923). This was in the aftermath of the Civil War.

[1] The *Irish Times* was in no way exceptional in this kind of comment. I cite it only because it was the journal of the class to which Yeats belonged, and he read it.

[2] Hone tells us (*W. B. Yeats*, p. 467) that Yeats had learned with 'great satisfaction' of a law of the Third Reich 'whereby ancient and impoverished families can recover their hereditary properties'. Professor T. Desmond Williams of University College, Dublin, tells me that 'to benefit from the hereditary law [of September 1933] you had to trace your ancestry back to 1760 and you had to be purely Aryan. There was provision for the return of land that had passed into "impure" hands as a result of mortgages.'

[3] It is true that the Blueshirts did not even try to go to anything like the lengths of their Continental models. It is also true that, unlike

Some writers — notably Professor Donald Torchiana in his well-documented study *W. B. Yeats, Jonathan Swift and Liberty*[1] — have insisted that, in spite of Yeats's authoritarian and Fascist leanings, he was essentially a friend of liberty. 'Both Swift and Yeats', Torchiana concludes, 'served human liberty.' The senses in which this is true for Yeats are important but clearly limited. He defended the liberty of the artist, consistently. In politics, true to his duality, he defended the liberty of Ireland against English domination, and the liberty of his own caste — and sometimes, by extension, of others — against clerical domination. Often these liberties overlapped, and the cause of artist and aristocrat became the same ; often his resistance to 'clerical' authoritarianism (his position on the Lock-out, on divorce, on censorship) makes him appear a liberal. But his objection to clerical authoritarianism is not the liberal's objection to *all* authoritarianism. On the contrary he favours 'a despotism of the educated classes' and in the search for this, is drawn towards Fascism. It is true that Fascism was not in reality a despotism of the educated classes, but it was a form of despotism which the educated classes in the 'twenties and 'thirties showed a disposition to settle for — a disposition proportionate to the apparent threat, in their country, of Communism or 'anarchy'. In assessing Yeats's pro-Fascist opinions, there is no need to regard these as so extraordinary that he must either not have been himself, or not have known what he was about.

X

Yet, in challenging the assumption that Yeats's pro-Fascism was either not 'truly Yeats' or not 'truly pro-Fascist', one must not overlook the intermittent character of his pro-Fascism and of all his political activity. If his pro-Fascism

the case of their models, the Communists whom the Blueshirts were fighting were, in Ireland, largely imaginary.

[1] *Modern Philosophy* (August 1963).

was real, his irony and caution were real too, and his phases of
detachment not less real than his phases of political commitment. The long phase of nationalist commitment (1887–1903)
was followed by a long phase (1903–16) of detachment from
almost all practical politics (except those to which the theatre
exposed him), by a critique of Irish nationalist politics, and by
the formation of an aristocratic attitude which did not find
practical political expression until after 1916 when — after a
new flare-up of nationalist feeling — he re-entered Irish
politics on the right, in the Free State Senate. After clerical
pressures had made the Senate uncongenial to him and had
extruded him from it, he withdrew again from active politics
(1928–33), only returning when a situation propitious to
Fascism seemed to present itself. When O'Duffy's Irish
Fascists failed ignominiously he turned away from politics
again, though not for ever. In the last two years of his life
politics flared up again. Always, in the long phases of withdrawal, he tended to write of all politics with a kind of
contempt, a plague-on-both-your-houses air.[1] In that same
letter in which he refused to try to help Ossietzki he wrote
'... if I did what you want I would seem to hold one form of
government more responsible than any other and that would
betray my convictions. Communist, Fascist, nationalist,
clerical, anti-clerical, are all responsible according to the
number of their victims.'[2]

[1] 'Contempt for politics' is of course a characteristic conservative
stance.
[2] *Letters*, 8 April 1936. In a similar, but significantly different,
mood he wrote to the same correspondent six months later : 'Some day
you will understand what I see in the Irish national movement and why
I can be no other sort of revolutionist — as a young man I belonged to
the I.R.B. and was in many things O'Leary's pupil. Besides why should
I trouble about communism, fascism, liberalism, radicalism, when all,
though some bow first and some stern first but all at the same pace, all are
going down stream with the artificial unity which ends every civilization.' (30 November 1938 ; *Letters*, p. 869.) But in his letters to Ethel
Mannin, who was herself of the Left, Yeats tended to understate the
specifically right-wing elements of his thought ; he more than once used

This was 'the true Yeats' — the true Yeats of a period of political inactivity when he watched, bitterly or sardonically, a game he had no chance of playing. But when he had a chance, when he saw political opportunities, as in 1891 or 1920, or thought he saw them, as in 1933 and again in 1938, he wrote differently, and with excitement. These 'manic' phases of political activity were no less real or important than the 'depressive' phases which followed them. And the options of the 'manic' phases were not haphazard or middle-of-the-road. They were either anti-English or — in Irish politics — aristocratic and, from the time Fascism had appeared, distinctly pro-Fascist. At the end, in the last two years, as we shall see, these two elements were beginning to combine.

It was Yeats's misfortune as a politician, and his good fortune as a poet, that his political opportunities or temptations were few and far between. Irish politics in their normal run have not, since the introduction of universal suffrage, been receptive to poets, aristocrats or Protestants — there have been distinguished exceptions, but that has been the general rule for many years. It is only in rare conjunctures, times of great national stress and division, that an Irish party is likely to find room for such exotics for, in such times, men welcome an ally with a name and voice. Such moments of excitement and emotion, which offered opportunities, were also the moments which most stirred the poet. Such times were the Parnell split of 1891 and the Sinn Fein split of 1920-22. The abortive Fascist movement of 1933 seemed to be, but was not, the opening of another profound fissure in Irish political life. In the first two cases, the world of Irish politics proved, when 'normalcy' had returned, no place for the poet. In the third case the poet retired from a political movement which had lost momentum. It is fairly safe to say that, if it had succeeded, it would have dropped him or forced him out ; not through any

John O'Leary to fend her off (cf. *Letters*, p. 921) ; his letters to Olivia Shakespear are in some ways more revealing.

great aversion on his part from thugs in coloured shirts, but
because an Irish Fascism, to have any chance of staying in
power, would necessarily have to become an intensely clerical
Fascism. In fact the successor movement to the Blueshirts —
the Christian Front — was a noisily Catholic clerical-Fascist
movement. This was a kind of Fascism — perhaps the only
kind — which Yeats could not accept or tolerate, since his
authoritarian view of life derived ultimately from his concept
of the caste to which he belonged, and the distinguishing mark
of that caste was its Protestantism.

In the political writings of his last two years the two
elements in his politics — the 'Irish' and the 'Protestant'
elements — entered into a new set of relations. The 'Irish'
element became more vocal than it had been since 1916 and
the 'Protestant' element was obliged to break finally with the
traditional right wing in Irish politics. Anti-English feeling,
long dormant in Yeats, became increasingly pronounced in the
period 1937–38. A series of poems, 'Roger Casement', 'The
Ghost of Roger Casement', 'The O'Rahilly', 'Come Gather
round me, Parnellites', both expressed, and did much to re-
kindle, the old pride in Irish nationalism which the cynicism
that followed the Civil War had dulled. The Casement poems
especially had a powerful anti-English charge:

> O what has made that sudden noise?
> What on the threshold stands?
> It never crossed the sea because
> John Bull and the sea are friends;
> But this is not the old sea
> Nor this the old seashore.
> What gave that roar of mockery,
> That roar in the sea's roar?
> *The ghost of Roger Casement*
> *Is beating on the door.*

No Irishman, reading these lines on the eve of the Second
World War, had forgotten that Casement had been hanged,
as well as 'morally assassinated' for trying, in 1916, to bring

help to Ireland from Germany. And some Irishmen, at least, must have reflected that if the sea was no longer the old sea, which had been friends with John Bull, the reason for this might be that the nation from which Casement had tried to bring help now possessed a powerful air-force.

Potentially, 'The Ghost of Roger Casement' was as explosive as *Cathleen ni Houlihan.*

Just at this time Yeats was writing to Ethel Mannin that, while he liked neither side in Spain, and did not want to see his old leader O'Duffy — now fighting for Franco — return to Ireland with enhanced prestige to 'the Catholic front',[1] he was attracted by the thought that a Fascist victory would weaken England.

I am an old Fenian and I think the old Fenian in me would rejoice if a Fascist nation or government controlled Spain because that would weaken the British empire, force England to be civil to India and loosen the hand of English finance in the far East of which I hear occasionally. But this is mere instinct. A thing I would never act on. Then I have a horror of modern politics — I see nothing but the manipulation of popular enthusiasm by false news — a horror that has been deepened in these last weeks by the Casement business. My ballad on that subject has had success....[2]

The success of the ballad was mainly among those who had been Yeats's political enemies and against whom he had conspired : de Valera's party. It was in de Valera's paper, the *Irish Press*, that the ballad appeared. Yeats wrote :

On Feb. 2 my wife went to Dublin shopping and was surprised at the deference everybody showed her in buses and shops. Then she found what it was — the Casement poem was in the morning paper. Next day I was publicly thanked by the Vice-President of the Executive Council (Mr. de Valera's deputy in the Government),

[1] His worries on this ground were needless.

[2] 11 February 1937. (*Letters*, p. 881.) The occasion of the ballad was the publication of Dr. W. F. Maloney's *The Forged Casement Diaries*, which claimed that British officials had forged documents in order to impute homosexuality to Casement. Controversy on this question still continues, but Casement's remains are now in Ireland.

by de Valera's political secretary, by our chief antiquarian and an old revolutionist, Count Plunkett, who called my poem 'a ballad the people much needed'. De Valera's newspaper gave me a long leader, saying that for generations to come my poem will pour scorn on the forgers and their backers.[1]

There were adequate reasons for a degree of reconciliation between Yeats and his former foes. First, from Yeats's point of view, the events of the early 'thirties had shown that, if there was a 'strong man' in Irish politics, it was not O'Duffy but de Valera.[2] Second, five years of de Valera's government had dissipated the theory — once cherished by Yeats's former political friends — that de Valera meant Communism. Third, de Valera was the main barrier against what Yeats then saw — with considerable justice — as a rising tide of clericalist power, a tide which threatened all that Yeats had built in Ireland : 'I am convinced that if the Spanish war goes on or if [it] ceases and O'Duffy's volunteers return heroes, my "pagan" institutions, the Theatre, the Academy will be fighting for their lives against combined Gaelic and Catholic bigotry. A friar or monk has already threatened us with mob violence.'[3]

In the same letter, Yeats noted how de Valera had carried in Parliament, against a pro-Franco opposition, a measure to stop Irish volunteers from going to Spain.

The fourth reason for a *rapprochement* with de Valera's party is more complex. Just as Yeats's own mind was hopelessly divided about the Spanish War — the authoritarian and Anglophobe in him desiring a Franco victory, the Irish anticlerical dreading the results — so the party of his former friends was also in confusion. But their confusion was almost the mirror-image, the inversion, of his. They wanted, or said

[1] To Dorothy Wellesley, 8 February 1937. (*Letters*, p. 880.)
[2] Even before his Blueshirt phase, Yeats had been impressed by de Valera at his first meeting with him : '... I was impressed by his simplicity and honesty though we differed throughout' (to Olivia Shakespear, 9 March 1933. *Letters*, p. 806).
[3] To Ethel Mannin, 1 March 1937. (*Letters*, p. 885.)

they wanted, a Franco victory, on Catholic grounds. But also, as the party of the Anglo-Irish treaty, the 'Commonwealth Party', they contained the most 'pro-British' elements in Irish life : the people who, in the event of Britain's going to war, would try to see to it that Ireland came in on Britain's side.

De Valera at this time was engaged, with the Chamberlain Government, in the negotiations which led to the return of the Irish ports, which the Treaty had retained under British control. Without the return of these ports Ireland's neutrality in the coming war, which it was de Valera's policy to ensure, would scarcely have been practical politics. Yeats — who, as Frank O'Connor has told us,[1] in his last years admired and defended de Valera — put his name and influence explicitly behind the recovery of the ports ; implicitly but clearly behind a policy of neutrality :

Armament comes next to education. The country must take over the entire defence of its shores. The formation of military families should be encouraged. I know enough of my countrymen to know that, once democratic plausibility has gone, their small army will be efficient and self reliant, highly trained though not highly-disciplined. Armed with modern weapons, officered by men from such schools as I have described, it could throw back from our shores the disciplined, uneducated masses of the commercial nations.

From the point of view of de Valera's party, Yeats's tentative overtures — for such, I believe, they were — would have presented some advantages. The patriotic poems undoubtedly struck a genuinely responsive note among most Irish people : their appearance in de Valera's newspaper was helpful, especially at this time, in Ireland; the prestige—by now great—of Yeats's name in England would be helpful there in relation to the ports and to neutrality. Yet, while there were reasons on both sides for some degree of *rapprochement*, it may be

[1] *The Old Age of a Poet.*

doubted whether this would ever have become close or warm. Irish political life between the wars had been too bitter for that. De Valera's memory has not the reputation of being short or inaccurate. Yeats's activities in 1922–23 and in 1933 would have been quite fresh in de Valera's mind. It is believed also that he had read, with distaste and distress, the lines :

> Had de Valera eaten Parnell's heart
> No loose-lipped demagogue had won the day,
> No civil rancour torn the land apart.

Real reconciliation had to wait for the next generation. After the war Yeats's son, Michael, joined de Valera's party and became a Senator.

XI

The two main currents in Yeats's active politics — his Anglophobe Irish nationalism and his authoritarianism — necessarily converged in the years immediately before the war, thrusting him in the direction of desiring the victory of the Fascist powers. The doctrine of John O'Leary, to whose school Yeats always claimed to belong, was Tone's doctrine : that 'England's difficulty is Ireland's opportunity'. The caution and scepticism, which were also permanent features of Yeats's personality, worked, together with his repulsion from Irish clerical Fascism, to prevent him from being carried too far by Tone and O'Leary. But an underlying wish found voice, at this time, when the prestige and authority of England were lower than they had been for centuries, in an increasingly anti-English tone, in verse and prose and in his conversation. This did not happen without a violent inner struggle.

The 'Irishry', [he wrote in *A General Introduction for my Work* (1937)] have preserved their ancient 'deposit' through wars which, during the sixteenth and seventeenth centuries, became wars of extermination ; no people, Lecky said at the opening of his *Ireland In the Eighteenth Century*, have undergone greater persecution, nor did that persecution altogether cease up to our own day.

No people hate as we do in whom that past is always alive, there are moments when hatred poisons my life and I accuse myself of effeminacy because I have not given it adequate expression. It is not enough to have put it into the mouth of a rambling peasant poet. Then I remind myself that though mine is the first English marriage I know of in the direct line, all my family names are English and that I owe my soul to Shakespeare, to Spenser and to Blake, perhaps to William Morris, and to the English language in which I think, speak and write, that everything I love has come to me through English; my hatred tortures me with love, my love with hate. I am like the Tibetan monk who dreams at his initiation that he is eaten by a wild beast and learns on waking that he himself is eater and eaten. This is Irish hatred and solitude, the hatred of human life that made Swift write *Gulliver* and the epitaph upon his tomb, that can still make us wag between extremes and doubt our sanity.

On the Boiler, written the following year, is his last political statement: a sort of political testament. 'For the first time', he wrote to Maud Gonne about this tract, in what may be his last letter to her, 'I am saying what I believe about Irish and European politics' (16 June 1938; *Letters*, p. 910). *On the Boiler* assumes — without, however, being altogether explicit about it — that the Fascist powers are winning and England is in contemptible decline. 'The Fascist countries', he writes in the section 'Tomorrow's Revolution', 'know that civilization has reached a crisis, and found their eloquence upon that knowledge.' The only fault he has to find with them is that 'perhaps from dread of attack' they encourage large families. He assumes in 'Ireland after the Revolution' that 'some tragic crisis shall so alter Europe and all opinion that the Irish government will teach the great majority of its school-children nothing but' — a list of manual and menial occupations follows.[1]

At the time when this was written, the 'tragic crisis' many

[1] ...'ploughing, harrowing, sowing, curry-combing, bicycle-cleaning, drill-driving, parcel-making, bale-pushing, tin-can-soldering, door-knob-polishing, threshold-whitening, coat-cleaning, trouser-patching, and playing upon the Squiffer'. ...

expected was that which was to lead Pétain's France to adopt somewhat similar educational policies. It is hard to resist the conclusion that Yeats, when writing this, expected, and hoped, that Ireland 'after the revolution' would be a sort of satellite of a Fascist-dominated Europe. 'The danger', he wrote in this year 1938, 'is that there will be no war, that the skilled will attempt nothing, that the European civilization, like those older civilizations that saw the triumph of their gangrel stocks, will accept decay.' The war he said he wanted was a war between the skilled and the unskilled ; as types of the skilled he took the crack German submarine commanders of the First World War, and nationally-unspecified mechanized warriors of the future, 'riding their machines as did the feudal knights their armoured horses'. As regards England his contempt, in this year of Munich, is unqualified and savage. After saying some hard things about King George V, he concludes 'Ireland after the Revolution' with the words : 'The Irish mind has still, in country rapscallion or in Bernard Shaw, an ancient cold, explosive detonating impartiality. The English mind, excited by its newspaper proprietors and its schoolmasters, has turned into a bed-hot harlot.'

Dorothy Wellesley, who was troubled by his increasingly anti-British attitude in the last years of his life, made a shrewd comment : 'Why then, in the twentieth century and when the Irish are freed from their oppressors the English, does he despise and dislike us increasingly ? Because he dislikes the stuffed lion and admires the ranting, roaring oppressors.'[1]

During Yeats's life the English government gave him a Civil List pension, and offered him a knighthood, which he refused,[2] and the Athenaeum Club gave him the honour of a special election. Since his death, the British Council has presented him to the world as one of England's glories. There

---

[1] 'Comments and Conversations', p. 195 (July 1938), in the introduction to *Letters on Poetry to Dorothy Wellesley*.
[2] Hone, *W. B. Yeats*, p. 291.

is therefore some irony in the thought that there was something in him that would have taken considerable pleasure — though not without a respectful backward glance at Shakespeare — in seeing England occupied by the Nazis, the Royal Family exiled, and the Mother of Parliaments torn down. Meanwhile in Ireland one would have expected to see him at least a cautious participant, or ornament, in a collaborationist régime.

It is probably fortunate for his future reputation, and especially his standing with the British Council, that he died in January 1939 before the political momentum of his last years could carry him any farther than *On the Boiler*.

XII

Yeats was a public figure for more than forty years ; deeply immersed in political interests, politically active whenever opportunity presented itself. His best poetry — that of his maturity and old age — had often a political theme, sometimes a political intent. The argument of this essay has been that his politics deserve to be taken more seriously than they have been, were not fundamentally inconsistent, vague or irrelevant to his 'real self' and were, in his maturity and old age, generally pro-Fascist in tendency, and Fascist in practice on the single occasion when opportunity arose.

How can those of us who loathe such politics continue not merely to admire but to love the poetry, and perhaps most of all the poems with a political bearing ?

An important part of the answer is supplied by the poet himself in a note on 'Leda and the Swan':

I wrote 'Leda and the Swan' because the editor of a political review asked me for a poem. I thought 'After the individualist, demagogic movement founded by Hobbes [*sic*] and popularized by the Encyclopaedists and the French revolution, we have a soil so exhausted that it cannot grow that crop again for centuries'. Then I thought 'Nothing is now possible but some movement from above preceded by some violent annunciation'. My fancy began to play with Leda and the Swan for metaphor, and I began this poem ; but as I wrote, bird and lady took such possession of the scene that all politics went out of it, and my friend tells me that his 'conservative readers would misunderstand the poem'.[1]

They would have been puzzled certainly :

> A sudden blow : the great wings beating still
> Above the staggering girl, her thighs caressed
> By the dark webs, her nape caught in his bill,
> He holds her helpless breast upon his breast.
>
> How can those terrified vague fingers push
> The feathered glory from her loosening thighs ?
> And how can body, laid in that white rush,
> But feel the strange heart beating where it lies ?
>
> A shudder in the loins engenders there
> The broken wall, the burning roof and tower
> And Agamemnon dead.
>   Being so caught up,
> So mastered by the brute blood of the air,
> Did she put on his knowledge with his power
> Before the indifferent beak could let her drop ?

Very little seems to be known — and perhaps little can be known — of how this process of transformation works. How can that patter of Mussolini prose 'produce' such a poem ? How can that political ugly duckling be turned into this glorious Swan ? It is in a sense like the transmutation, in 'Easter 1916', of those whom Yeats had thought of as commonplace people :

> All changed, changed utterly :
> A terrible beauty is born.

Is the connection then between the politics and the poetry only trivial and superficial ? There is, I think, a deeper connection : if the political prose and the poetry are thought of, not as 'substance' and 'metaphor', or 'content' and 'style', but as cognate expressions of a fundamental force, anterior to both politics and poetry.

That force was, I suggest, Yeats's profound and tragic

[1] June 1924 ; *The Variorum Edition*, p. 828.

intuitive — and intelligent — awareness, in his maturity and old age, of what the First World War had set loose, of what was already moving towards Hitler and the Second World War. That he is conscious of the danger a letter shows as early as 1923 : 'Unless Europe takes to war again and starts new telepathic streams of violence and cruelty'.[1] But the poetry is already responding to the telepathic streams as early as 1920, when he wrote 'The Second Coming':

> Things fall apart ; the centre cannot hold ;
> Mere anarchy is loosed upon the world,
> The blood-dimmed tide is loosed...
>
> .   .   .   .   .
>
> And what rough beast, its hour come round at last,
> Slouches towards Bethlehem to be born ?

Years afterwards, just before the Spanish War, he drew Ethel Mannin's attention to this poem : 'If you have my poems by you look up a poem called "The Second Coming". It was written more than sixteen or seventeen years ago and foretold what is happening. I have written of the same thing again and again since.'[2]

The words 'violence', 'hatred' and 'fanaticism' became keywords in Yeats's poetry. He often uses them in condemnation of the left in Irish politics — the politics of Constance Markievicz and of Maud Gonne :

> I thought my love must her own soul destroy
> So did fanaticism and hate enslave it

But he is also increasingly conscious of these same forces in himself :

> Out of Ireland have we come :
> Great hatred, little room,
> Maimed us from the start.
> I carry from my mother's womb
> A fanatic heart.

---

[1] Letter to Olivia Shakespear, 28 June 1923. (*Letters*, p. 699.)
[2] 8 April 1936. (*Letters*, pp. 850–1.) This was the same letter in which he refused to help Ossietzki.

The 'fanatic heart', an unusual capacity for hatred and an unusual experience of it, probably made him more sensitive and more responsive to the 'telepathic waves' coming from Europe than other writers in English seem to have been. The forces in him that responded to the hatred, cruelty and violence welling up in Europe produced the prophetic images of 'The Second Coming' and the last part of 'Nineteen Hundred and Nineteen':

> Violence upon the roads : violence of horses ;
> Some few have handsome riders, are garlanded
> On delicate sensitive ear or tossing mane,
> But wearied running round and round in their courses
> All break and vanish, and evil gathers head :
> Herodias' daughters have returned again,
> A sudden blast of dusty wind and after
> Thunder of feet, tumult of images,
> Their purpose in the labyrinth of the wind ; ...

It may be objected that 'Nineteen Hundred and Nineteen' and 'The Second Coming' were written not about the coming of Fascism but about the Anglo-Irish War and the Black and Tans. The distinction is less than absolute : the Black and Tans were in fact an early manifestation of an outlook and methods which the Nazis were later to perfect. The *Freikorps* on the Polish–German border were at this time trying to do exactly what the Black and Tans were doing in Ireland and the *Freikorps* were the direct and proudly acknowledged predecessors of Hitler's Nazis. There is even a direct link between the Black and Tans and the Nazis in the person of 'Lord Haw Haw' — William Joyce — who fought for the British Government in the first movement and was hanged by it for his work in the second.

Bruno Brehm, one of Hitler's novelists, made the assassination by Irish revolutionaries of Sir Henry Wilson — the principal exponent of intensified Black-and-Tan measures in Ireland — symbolic of the tragic confrontation of hero and submen. Wilson was seen in the same relation to the Irish as Hitler to Jews and Bolsheviks.

In *A General Introduction for my Work* (1937) Yeats made specific the connection between his own hatred and what was happening in Europe :

> When I stand upon O'Connell Bridge in the half-light and notice that discordant architecture, all those electric signs, where modern heterogeneity has taken physical form, a vague hatred comes up out of my own dark and I am certain that wherever in Europe there are minds strong enough to lead others the same vague hatred arises ; in four or five or in less generations this hatred will have issued in violence and imposed some kind of rule of kindred. I cannot know the nature of that rule, for its opposite fills the light ; all I can do to bring it nearer is to intensify my hatred. I am no Nationalist, except in Ireland for passing reasons ; State and Nation are the work of intellect, and when you consider what comes before and after them they are, as Victor Hugo said of something or other, not worth the blade of grass God gives for the nest of the linnet.

By the time the *General Introduction* was written, Fascist power and 'rule of kindred' were already in full swing : the length of time — 'four or five generations' — is odd and perhaps calculated : it brings to mind the retrospective 'commentaries' on the songs for O'Duffy. The paragraph itself may be taken as a kind of retrospective commentary on 'The Second Coming'.

In 'The Second Coming' the poet, perhaps from the foretaste of the Black and Tans, augured the still more terrible things that were to come. The sort of 'premonitory' intuition present in 'The Second Coming' and in other poems necessarily affected Yeats in his ordinary life as well as in his poetry. Yeats the manager, the Senator, the politician, stands in a diplomatic relation to these intimations of power. His references to Fascism, though sometimes mildly critical, are never hostile, almost always respectful, often admiring, and this especially in years of Fascist victories : 1922, 1933 and 1938.

Some reasons for this have already been suggested ; it might be added that for Yeats a band-wagon had the same high degree of attraction that it has for other political mortals :

> Processions that lack high stilts have nothing that catches
>   the eye.

If a Marxist, believing that history is going in a given direction, thinks it right to give it a good shove in the way it is going, it is natural enough that one who, like Yeats, feels that it is going in the opposite direction, should accompany it that way with, if not a shove, at least a cautious tilt.

In the poetry, however, the raw intimations of what is impending — the 'telepathic waves of violence and fear' — make themselves known, not in the form of calculated practical deductions, but in the attempt to reveal, through metaphoric insight, what is actually happening and even, in a broad sense, what is about to happen.[1] The poet, like the lady, is

> ...so caught up,
> So mastered by the brute blood of the air

that he does indeed take on the knowledge of what is happening with the power to make it known. The political man had his cautious understanding with Fascism, the diplomatic relation to a great force ; the poet conveyed the nature of the force, the dimension of the tragedy. The impurities of this long and extraordinary life went into its devious and sometimes sinister political theories and activities. The purity and integrity — including the truth about politics as Yeats apprehended it — are in the poetry concentrated in metaphors of such power that they thrust aside all calculated intent : bird and lady take possession of the scene.

[1] This continued, I believe, to the very end. Just as 'The Second Coming' contains the rise of Fascism, I think that that mysterious and beautiful poem 'Cuchulain Comforted' may contain the fall of Fascism. I hope, in a separate essay, to examine the political themes of the four last poems : the subject requires the kind of detailed — and often necessarily speculative — treatment that would be out of place in the present general review of 'Yeats's political' life.

ANARCHY

for W. B. Yeats in mid-winter

*

RANDOLPH STOW

Why should not young men be mad?
  Mad as the snow-choked sea.

Old man so coldly sane
sharp as the wind and rain,
soft as the mist and snow,
  whose iced words glow
  cold in the brain:

teach us that cold keen peace,
that dread may have release
and the cold eye and mind
  not wither, blind,
  and love not cease.

Ice clamps on heath and grass;
thin ice like warping glass
I pick up and look through
  — Horseman, to you,
  horseman, who pass.

Why should not young men be mad?
  Mad as the ice-floed sea.

YEATS'S ARABIC INTERESTS

*

S. B. BUSHRUI

Speaking the Greek's own language, just because
Your Greek eludes you, leave the least of flaws
In contracts with him ; while, since Arab lore
Holds the stars' secret — take one trouble more
And master it !

R. BROWNING, *Sordello*, Book IV

YEATS'S ARABIC INTERESTS can be traced to his more
general interests in the East. In his mind the East and
Ancient Ireland seem to have been linked, and 'it was from the
East that Yeats snatched the clue to the interpretation of
Druidic culture. . . .'[1] As early as 1885 he met the Brahmin
missionary, Mohini Chatterji, whose philosophy and approach
to life stirred his imagination and developed an already deep
interest in Indian poetry and philosophy. This early interest
in India was not with 'the India of politicians or historians or
travellers, but an India of pure romance which bears some
subtle yet obvious relation to old romantic Ireland'.[2] In the
same way the Arabia[3] which became the background of
A Vision was to be an Arabia of 'pure romance' and also
related to 'old romantic Ireland'.

I do not wish to overestimate the importance of Arabia
and the Arabs in the study of Yeats, but his interest in them
in fact stands on the same level as his interest in Indian

---

[1] J. Eglinton, 'Yeats and his Story', *The Dial* (May, 1926), p. 358.
[2] C. L. Wrenn, *W. B. Yeats : A Literary Study*, London, 1920, p. 9.
[3] Throughout this essay I have used 'Arabia' to mean the whole of
the Arabian peninsula, including Iraq and Syria.

philosophy, Japanese drama, occult practices, magic and theosophy; all these things were the background against which
Yeats's intellect worked, and helped to shape his poetic imagination. In attempting to explain or interpret them we run the
risk of stressing too much, or of reading between the lines what
may not be there, for Yeats was always independent in the
adaptation of his sources of inspiration; he took what interested him, what agreed with thoughts and ideas already in his
mind, and gave it all the stamp of his own poetic personality.
His choice was always dictated by intuition, never by logic
or scientific thinking.

I

Yeats's interest in Arabic material was stimulated and
guided by many other factors in his life and work. One of
these was his preoccupation with the occult, which naturally
led him to Eastern theosophy and to Arabic mysticism, magic
and philosophy. As early as 1896 he began to learn about
Avicenna and al-Fārābī,[1] who excited his imagination and of
whom he wrote enthusiastically in 'Rosa Alchemica'. They
moved him not as philosophers but as magicians, while Arabia
itself was the homeland of Magic, where alchemy had become
one of the greatest sciences:

There were the works of Morienus, who hid his immortal body
under a shirt of hair-cloth; of Avicenna, who was a drunkard and
yet controlled numberless legions of spirits; of Alfarabi, who put
so many spirits into his lute that he could make men laugh, or weep,
or fall in deadly trance as he would; of Lully, who transformed
himself into the likeness of a red cock; of Flamel, who with his
wife Pernella achieved the elixir many hundreds of years ago, and is
fabled to live still in Arabia among the Dervishes; and of many
of less fame.[2]

[1] Although Avicenna was of Persian and al-Fārābī of Turkish origin,
their works were written in Arabic and were very much influenced by the
dynamic force of the religion of Arabia. The force that motivated their
philosophic discoveries was Arabic, despite their non-Arab origin.

[2] W. B. Yeats, 'Rosa Alchemica', *Mythologies*, London, 1959, p. 282.

In this same essay three things are mentioned which are among the foundations of Yeats's 'fable' as he unfolds it later in *A Vision*, and which are then related to Arabia and the Arabs. These are: Robartes's sojourn outside Ireland in what is meant to be a far-off land; a book which contains 'the doctrine from which all true doctrines sprang', and which points forward to the doctrine Robartes will find later among an unknown Arab tribe; and a dance 'which wound in and out, tracking upon the floor the shapes of petals ... in the rose ... to the sound of hidden instruments ...', which again points to the dance of the Judwalis on the sand.

It was some time in 1908 that Yeats came to learn about the activities of the Arab Rosicrucian, for it was in that year that Dr. Felkin found '"real Rosicrucians" in Germany; and acquired an Arab teacher, Ara ben Shemesh, supposedly from the Mesopotamian "Temple in the Desert" of the "Sons of Fire", who told him that Christian Rosencreutz himself had come to their Temple and learned much, and that his own aim was to unite East and West',[1]

His connections with the Order of the Golden Dawn and the group known as 'Stella Matutina' brought Yeats indirectly, if not directly, under the influence of the Arab teacher Ara ben Shemesh. It is difficult to determine the precise nature of this influence, but it is certain that Ara ben Shemesh greatly influenced Dr. Felkin, the head of the revolt against Mathers within the Order, and later the leader of the splinter group which kept the Golden Dawn name and which included Yeats's group, the Stella Matutina.[2]

Certain questions immediately present themselves for

---

[1] Moore, *op. cit. infra*, p. 172.

[2] For a full account of the story of the Golden Dawn and how Yeats's connection with the 'Hermetic Students' ended amid quarrels, see V. Moore, *The Unicorn: William Butler Yeats' Search for Reality*, New York, 1954, pp. 169–79. Cf. the chapter entitled 'Stella Matutina' in the *Light-Bearers of Darkness* by 'Inquire Within', London, 1930. For Yeats's own comments on his connection with the 'Hermetic Students' see Notes in *Autobiographies*, London, 1955, pp. 575–6.

consideration. How far did Ara ben Shemesh influence Yeats? How many of his ideas were incorporated into Yeats's philosophic system? Did the fact that he came from Mesopotamia and the 'Temple in the Desert' influence Yeats in the construction of his 'fable' in *A Vision*? These questions have still to be answered.

Yeats's investigations into the fields of magic, occultist studies, Hermetism and 'psychic things' led to séances and to his consultations with different mediums.

It was at one of these séances[1] that Yeats was introduced through the American medium Mrs. E. Wreidt to an amazing Arab. A deep voice spoke through the trumpet, calling Yeats by the name 'Mr. Gates'; the voice claimed to be that of one Leo, who had been Yeats's guide for several years:

> 'I have been with you since childhood. . . . I am
> Leo the writer — writer and explorer.'[2]

When Leo continued to return through other mediums, claiming that he was a writer among the Moors (the Arabs of Spain and North-west Africa), Yeats became very interested, and tried to find out more about him. From the encyclopædia he discovered that this attendant spirit and guide of his was an Arab called al-Ḥasan ibn Muḥammad al-Wazzān al-Zayyātī (الحسن بن محمد الوزان الزياتي) or al-Ḥasan ibn Muḥammad al-Wazzāz al-Fāsī (الحسن بن محمد الوزاز الفاسي), nicknamed Yuḥanna al-Asad al-Gharnātī (يوحنا الاسد الغرناطي), who was known to the Latin West by the name of Leo Johannes Africanus.[3]

---

[1] The date of this séance is given by Moore, (*op. cit.*, p. 225), as 'the night of April 10, 1911'. In B. Bjersby (*The Interpretation of the Cuchulain Legend in the Works of W. B. Yeats*, Uppsala, 1950, p. 142), it is given as 'on the 9th of May 1912 at 6.30 in the evening'.

[2] Moore, *op. cit.*, p. 225.

[3] The information given here is based on the account given in the *Encyclopædia Britannica* (11th ed.), xvi, p. 441. Another interesting account of Leo Africanus is found in an article entitled 'Note sur les "Grans Voyages" de Léon l'Africain', by Raymond Maury, in *Hesperis*,

Yeats discovered that his 'mentor' was an Arab, born at Granada of a noble Moorish family and educated at Fez ; and that he had travelled through the Sudan, Timbuktu, the Sahara Desert, the Niger Basin, Bornu, Lake Chad, Constantinople, Egypt, Arabia, Armenia and 'Tartary'. It must have stimulated him further to find that the explorer, while returning from Egypt during one of his expeditions, was captured by pirates and taken to the court of Pope Leo X, where he was honourably received. The Pope persuaded him to accept Christianity, bestowing upon him at his baptism the names Johannes and Leo.[1] The new convert taught Arabic at the Vatican and wrote the *Descrizione dell' Affrica*, an account of the lives of Arab physicians and philosophers, a Spanish–Arabic vocabulary and some poems.

A translation of the *Descrizione dell' Affrica* was one of the books which Yeats treasured and read ; Mrs. Yeats has shown me her husband's copy of *A Geographical Historie of Africa*, a version by John Pory published in 1600.[2]

Yeats carried on an imaginary correspondence with Leo, and among his unpublished manuscripts there is a *Leo Africanus* manuscript.[3] The *Leo Africanus* papers are full of images from Leo's time, now in the desert, now in Rome. Leo is now Yeats's 'mentor', his spiritual guide, and now his opposite, or 'mask'. *Leo Africanus* was never completed and

vol. 41, 1954, pp. 379–94 ; this article has many biographical and bibliographical references. See also 'Index to the serial Publication of the Royal Irish Academy' (1912), (Transactions, vol. 15, 3rd section ; Antiquities, p. 97).

[1] Africanus's Christian names were Johannes Leo de Medici.

[2] This was reprinted later : it was published by the Hakluyt Society in 1896 (in 3 vols., edited with an introduction and notes by Robert Brown).

[3] Bjersby's note (*op. cit.*, p. 142, note 2) in connection with this manuscript is interesting : 'It is also amusing to notice how Yeats, when starting to write in Leo's name, tried to adopt a handwriting different from his own, and much more easy to read, a circumstance which renders a few lines of this otherwise almost illegible manuscript quite easy to follow'.

has received very little attention from scholars or critics, with the exception of Mrs. Bjersby,[1] whose description of it gives the impression that *A Vision* may be largely derived from the *Leo Africanus* manuscript; this is one more question that has to be answered once the manuscript is made available or published.

In the personality of Leo Africanus, Yeats found his opposite, his 'mask':

> Leo had been unscrupulous, Yeats was overcautious;
> Leo 'hard and keen like a hunting dog', Yeats soft;
> Leo 'a brooding and braggart shade', Yeats gregarious
>   yet shy.[2]

Africanus symbolized for Yeats the man of action he was always trying to become. But it should be noted that this choice of an opposite was not totally removed from Yeats's European background; the connection was established. Africanus had bridged the gap between two irreconcilable cultures and religions.

II

Yeats's Arabic researches were also stimulated by his interest in folklore; this led him to ask many questions about the nature of the Celtic race and religion, which had been a theme of controversy in Ireland ever since the publication of Toland's *Critical History* in 1726. In 1888, John Rhys[3] published his findings concerning the origin of the Celtic race; he suggested that the religion of the Celts was similar to that of the other Indo-European races and that the home of the Celts might have been in Asia. Yeats accepted this theory and repeatedly refers to it in his prose writings; in thought and feeling, at least, if not in blood and race, he found a link

---

[1] *Ibid.*, pp. 141–5.   [2] Moore, *op. cit.*, p. 236.
[3] Sir John Rhys, *Lectures on the Origin and Growth of Religion as Illustrated by Celtic Heathendom*, London, 1888.

between his 'Ancient Ireland' and Asia. In his final system he went further in defining the East that attracted him:

> I am right in thinking that my instructors imply not only the symbolical but the geographical East, Asiatic.[1]

For him the Asiatic East came to be limited to the 'Semitic East',[2] which does not include India or China, and even to what is usually referred to, in the Arab world, as the 'fertile crescent' (al-Hilal al-Khaṣīb, الهلال الخصيب) :

> The most philosophical of archaeologists Josef Strzygowski haunts my imagination. To him the East, as certainly to my instructors, is not India or China, but the East that has affected European civilization, Asia Minor, Mesopotamia, Egypt.[3]

It was the 'Semitic East', the cradle of religions and the home of the greatest of the ancient civilizations,[4] that fascinated both Yeats and his instructors.

The 'Semitic East' became geographically clearer in 1917, when he began to gather his material for *A Vision* through his wife's fantastic experience; but well before 1900 it was strongly associated in his mind with Arabia. A passage from the unpublished autobiographical novel entitled *The Speckled Bird*[5] shows that at a very early date Yeats turned his thoughts towards Arabia and linked what fascinated his imagination there with what he admired in Ancient Ireland and in the Irish poets. The hero of *The Speckled Bird* 'proposes to improve

---

[1] *A Vision*, London, 1937, p. 257.   [2] *Ibid.*   [3] *Ibid.*

[4] Yeats's belief that the Irish race had their home somewhere in the East was further strengthened by what he read in Lady Wilde's *Ancient Legends, Mystic Charms, and Superstitions of Ireland* (London, 1887, in 2 vols.), a book which he knew well; p. 340 of vol. ii: '. . . the Cradle of mankind was somewhere between the Caspian Sea and the great River Euphrates'. Cf. W. B. Yeats, Notes ('Commentary on Supernatural Songs'), *The Variorum Edition*, London, 1957.

[5] Yeats began to write this novel, on which he worked many years but never published, between 1897 and 1898. By 11 July 1898 the writing was actually begun and was going 'well but slowly' (*Letters*, ed. Allan Wade, London, 1954, p. 301).

Christianity by reconciling it with natural emotions, particularly with sexual love';[1] in other words he sets out to find a new 'doctrine', a lost book perhaps :

> He was going to the East now to Arabia and Persia, where he would find among the common people so soon as he had learnt their language some lost doctrine of reconciliation ; the philosophic poets had made sexual love their principal symbol of a divine love and he had seen somewhere in a list of untranslated Egyptian MSS. that certain of them dealt with love as a polthugic [*sic*] power. In Ireland he (found) wonderful doctrines among the poor, doctrines which would have been the foundation of the old Irish poets, and surely he would find somewhere in the East a doctrine that would reconcile religion with the natural emotions, and at the same time explain these emotions. All the arts sprang from sexual love and there they could only come again, the garb of the religion when that reconciliation had taken place.[2]

The 'lost doctrine' sought by Yeats's hero was finally found by Michael Robartes, whose Oriental adventure provided Yeats with the doctrines of a new religion. The whole story of Robartes in *A Vision* seems to have its germ in the above passage.

The link between Arabia and Ireland was seen by Yeats in more than one way and from more than one angle. He found Arabia, like Peasant Ireland, a strangely isolated country, living its own contracted life and remaining almost untouched by the influence of alien materialistic civilizations. He saw a parallel between pre-Islamic pagan Arabia and pre-Christian pagan Ireland ; in both cases it was the new religion that broke the barriers of what had previously been a wholly isolated civilization. Arabia, surrounded by an impenetrable desert which separated the central and southern parts from the rest of the world, was like Ireland surrounded by the ocean (when navigation was not yet developed), and separated from Europe and the rest of the world. Both Arabia and Ireland

---

[1] Quoted by Richard Ellmann, *The Identity of Yeats*, London, 1954, p. 52.   [2] *Ibid.*

were at one time in their history beyond the threshold of the world — each a world within the world.

Yeats must have been struck also by the fact that poetry was to the Arabs something solemn and awful, approached only with a sense of profound responsibility: it was the creation by man of something which was more than human and almost divine. This conception of poetry Yeats had already recognized in Celtic Ireland through his reading of Geoffrey Keating's bardic history of Ireland written around 1640. It is also striking that in or about the latter half of the sixth century A.D. — when the poet's voice is hardly heard throughout the rest of the world — both Arabic and Irish poetry reached an unparalleled degree of excellence. When most of the world was tongue-tied, Arabia and Ireland spoke with eloquence and beauty; during these Dark Ages the poetic imagination of Arabia and Ireland remained untouched; only in these two countries was there any imaginative life. Wilfrid Scawen Blunt, whom Yeats often met at Lady Gregory's house and whose work he admired, summarized all these ideas in a passage at the beginning of his introduction to the English translation of the Seven Golden Odes of Pagan Arabia, published in 1903:

> In Europe the nearest analogy to it [Arabic poetry] is perhaps to be found in the pre-Christian verse of Celtic Ireland, which by a strange accident was its close contemporary, and lost its wild natural impulse through the very same circumstance of the conversion of its pagan bards to an overmastering new theology.[1]

One of the reasons for Yeats's choice of Arabia as the background for the final statement of his philosophic thought was his desire to give his system a kind of authority — timeless, changeless and eternal. The anonymous author of *Among the Arabs*, published in 1875, began his introduction

---

[1] W. S. and Lady Ann Blunt (translators), *The Seven Golden Odes of Pagan Arabia*, London, published by the translators, 1903, p. ix.

with words which may very well explain the fascination which Arabia and the Arabs exerted upon Yeats :

> The Arabs are the oldest race of man in existence, having inhabited the same country, borne the same name, and observed the same customs unchanged for three or four thousand years. They are the only people that have never been wholly subdued by any foreign power. . . .[1]

Yeats's preoccupation with Arabia was naturally greatly stimulated by the interest of his contemporaries in the East in general, and Arabia in particular. At about the time when Yeats was entering upon his literary career, the interest in Eastern lore which began with the Romantics reached its height; and between 1850 and 1925 there was a flood of translations, travel books and studies all connected with Arabia, her people and language.

In 1879, a few years before Yeats published his first book, Wilfrid Scawen Blunt emphasized this new awareness of Arabia in his introduction to Lady Ann's *Bedouin Tribes of the Euphrates* :

> At the present moment, when all eyes are turned towards the East, and when Asia, long forgotten by the rest of the world, seems about to reassert itself and take its old place in history, the following sketch of what is actually going on, in one of its most famous districts, should not be without interest to the English public.[2]

Around 1843 there was a strong feeling in Christendom — especially in Ireland, Germany and America — that the return of Christ was imminent and that the 'second coming' was at

---

[1] *Among the Arabs : Adventures in the Desert and Sketches of Life and Character in Tent and Town* (with many extracts from Palgrave's 'Travels in Arabia'), London, 1875, p. 1. For a reference to the origin of the Arabs and Arabia as 'Une des pépinières du genre humain' and as 'a source of civilization', see R. F. Burton, *Personal Narrative of a Pilgrimage to Al-Madinah and Meccah* (ed. Isabel Burton), London, 1893, vol. i, p. 344, note 3.

[2] Lady Ann Blunt, *Bedouin Tribes of the Euphrates*, London, 1879, vol. i, p. vii.

hand. All eyes turned to the Holy Land and the 'fertile crescent'; missionary work was undertaken among the peoples of these lands with the greatest fervour and enthusiasm. European political interests, too, had been stimulated by Napoleon's conquest of Egypt in 1798, and cannot be dissociated from this renewed religious activity.

For the first time in history, the heart of Arabia, closed to the outside world since the beginning of time, was being discovered by European travellers, the majority of whom were English. Books in English about Arabia were written by these travellers; they included, among others, Kinglake's *Eōthen* (1844), Palgrave's *Narrative of a Year's Journey through Central and Eastern Arabia* (1865), Burton's *Personal Narrative of a Pilgrimage to Al-Madinah and Meccah* (1855) and Doughty's *Arabia Deserta* (1888). At the same time, the Arabs were once again re-forming their national personality and passing through a new Renaissance. Yeats lived at a time when it was natural for him to be aware of all this; and he moved in the literary circles to which most of those who were enthusiastically interested in Arabia belonged.

Among the books which were published during this period of intensified interest in the Arab world was Richard Francis Burton's translation of the *Arabian Nights*, which appeared (between 1885 and 1887) under the title *The Book of The Thousand Nights and a Night*.[1] Burton's work was censured on moral grounds and consequently the one thousand copies which were obtainable through private subscription became rare. Yeats must have met with it in 'the literary circles in which he moved, for instance in the group round "the Savoy" and "the Yellow Book"'.[2] One of these admirers of Burton's work was Oscar Wilde, whom Yeats came to admire and with whom he became friendly.

---

[1] Published in Benares for the Kamashastra Society for private subscribers only in ten volumes and an additional six volumes of 'Supplemental Nights'. [2] Bjersby, *op. cit.*, p. 127, note 3.

However, Yeats knew more than one edition of the *Arabian Nights*. In the dedication to 'Vestigia', with which the first version of *A Vision* (1925) was opened, he refers to a translation by Powys Mathers :

Doubtless I must someday complete what I have begun, but for the moment my imagination dwells upon a copy of Powys Mather's [*sic*] 'Arabian Nights' that awaits my return.[1]

According to Mrs. Yeats,[2] it was this version of the *Arabian Nights* with which Yeats was most familiar ; for we find him in 1935 writing to Ethel Mannin of his wish to write 'in the style of the *Arabian Nights*'[3] and in a postscript to the same letter he refers to the Powys Mathers version by name. In another letter to Ethel Mannin written in the same year, he gives the impression that the *Arabian Nights* has become one of his great favourites — equal to Balzac — and refers to it as 'serious literature'.[4] Some of the tales fascinated him greatly ; certain passages had a special significance for him. He quotes, for example, Shahrazad's words at the beginning of 'Moral Anecdotes from the Perfumed Garden' in connection with a motto which he suggests to a book written by Ethel Mannin :

I have found a quotation in the Powys Mathers translation of *The Arabian Nights* which would serve for a motto to such a book on the education of children as you may have written. Sherazada [*sic*] tells her king that she is about to tell three anecdotes which she thinks moral but others think profligate. The king suggests that

---

[1] W. B. Yeats, *A Vision* (1925), p. xiii. This translation by Mathers was from the French translation from the Arabic by Dr. J. C. Mardrus. It was published under the title *The Book of the Thousand Nights and One Night* (rendered from the literal and complete version of Dr. J. C. Mardrus ; and collated with other sources by E. Powys Mathers), Privately printed for subscribers, Casanova Society, London, 1923, in 16 volumes. All references here are to the 1937 four-volume edition of Mathers's translation, published in London by George Routledge & Sons Ltd.

[2] I am indebted to Mrs. Yeats for granting me her permission to make use of certain information which she passed on to me in conversations in 1960.　　[3] W. B. Yeats, *Letters*, p. 832.　　[4] *Ibid.*

they send away her little sister who is playing among the cushions. 'No,' says Sherazada, 'it is not shameful to talk of the things that lie beneath our belts.'[1]

Yeats regarded the frank treatment of sex in the *Arabian Nights* as healthy and natural. It is interesting to notice how he repeats, later in life, his wish to write in the 'style of the *Arabian Nights*',[2] and that his later poetry becomes less and less inhibited 'in speaking of those things which lie below our waists';[3] the sexual theme in his poetry becomes franker and more profound.

Whether in Powys Mathers's translation or Richard Burton's, there is no doubt that Yeats considered *The Arabian Nights* as one of the greatest books in the world, and that it influenced and moved him greatly. When he was asked in America which six books satisfied him most, the list he gave placed the *Arabian Nights* second only to Shakespeare :

Then somebody asked what would be my six books, and I said I wanted six authors not six books, and I named four authors, choosing not from those that I should, but from those that did most move me, and said I had forgotten the names of the other two. 'First comes Shakespeare,' I said. 'Then the *Arabian Nights* in its latest English version, then William Morris, who gives me all the great stories, Homer and the Sagas included, then Balzac, who saved me from Jacobin and Jacobite.'[4]

When Yeats disapproved of James Elroy Flecker's *Hassan*,[5] he objected especially to what he considered a

---

[1] W. B. Yeats, *Letters*, p. 832. The words of Shahrazad in Mathers (*op. cit.*, vol. iii, p. 38) are as follows : 'I think she should be allowed to stay, for "to the pure and clean all things are pure and clean", and there is nothing shameful in speaking of those things which lie below our waists'.

[2] *Ibid.*, pp. 832-3.

[3] Shahrazad's words in the Mathers version quoted in the notes above.

[4] W. B. Yeats, 'Louis Lambert' (dated July 1934), *Essays and Introductions*, London, 1961, p. 447.

[5] This play was first published by William Heinemann Ltd., London, in September 1922. It was first produced by Basil Dean on 20 September 1923, at His Majesty's Theatre, London.

misunderstanding of the spirit of the *Arabian Nights* and a complete misrepresentation of the character of Harun al-Rashid. Al-Rashid stimulated Yeats's imagination and was for him 'the mightiest of the princes of the world';[1] he becomes an important symbolic figure in Yeats's mind, though he is mentioned only once in the poetry.

Flecker's representation of Harun al-Rashid made Yeats sense in *Hassan* 'nothing but the perversity and petulance of the disease from which its author was already fading'; he found it 'more horrible than the vulgar jocularity of certain ignorant Irish dramatists'.[2] His defence of the character of Harun al-Rashid is both moving and compassionate:

We know Harun ar-Rashid [Yeats's spelling] through the *Arabian Nights* alone, and there he is the greatest of all traditional images of generosity and magnanimity. In one beautiful story he finds that a young girl of his harem loves a certain young man, and though he himself loves the girl he sets her free and arranges her marriage; and there are other stories of like import. . . .[3]

Yeats could not forgive Flecker, and he condemns the play: 'Considered as history, *Hassan* is a forgery, as literature an impertinence'.[4]

III

I have already mentioned that the story of Robartes's travels in Arabia had its origin in Yeats's unpublished novel *The Speckled Bird*; that some of the other elements which went to form the Robartes myth had already been conceived in his early essay entitled 'Rosa Alchemica'; and that similar

---

[1] W. B. Yeats, 'The Gift of Harun Al-Rashid', *The Variorum Edition*, p. 462.

[2] W. B. Yeats, 'From On the Boiler', *Explorations*, London, 1962, p. 447.

[3] *Ibid.*, p. 448. Yeats's reference here is to 'The Tale of 'Alā al-Dīn Abū Shamāt' (or the tale of Beauty-Spot found in Mathers, *op. cit.*, vol. ii, pp. 129–96), which seems to be the foundation on which Flecker built *Hassan*.   [4] *Ibid.*

ideas to those of *A Vision* had also been mentioned in *Per Amica Silentia Lunae* of 1917.

There is no need to repeat the well-known story of Robartes's discoveries. The account given in the first version of *A Vision* in 1925 was modified in the revised and corrected version of 1937: there were drastic revisions in the ideas expressed and additional parts were added, but the main elements of the narrative and the story behind the book did not change much.

The story of Robartes is very interesting here because he is created by Yeats in the image of the English traveller in Arabia. More than one of the English writers on Arabia had undertaken a journey like that of Robartes ; every one of them had travelled disguised as an Arab, sometimes spending a long time among the Bedouins of the desert.

Mrs. Yeats told me that among the works that influenced her husband most were Charles Doughty's *Arabia Deserta*[1] and T. E. Lawrence's *The Seven Pillars of Wisdom*.[2] Mrs. Bjersby very rightly points out in a short note in her book that

. . . there appear to be certain similarities between Robartes' travels in the desert and those of Doughty's. Moreover, Robartes, like Doughty, practised medicine, a circumstance which made it easier for him to get acquainted with the Judwalis sect. Likewise, Doughty through his medical knowledge won the hearts of the Bedouins. The similarities may be merely superficial, and also quite unintentional on Yeats's part, but the possibility is not quite out of the question, as, according to his wife, Yeats loved Doughty's book and read it over and over again.[3]

[1] First published by the Cambridge University Press in 1888 and then reprinted several times between 1921 and 1926.

[2] Although Lawrence's monumental account of the Arabia campaign between 1914 and 1917 was not published until 1926, a year after the first *Vision* had been published, news of his adventures was reported in the British Press during the war. Lawrence fascinated Yeats not only because he was a soldier and writer, but also because he was Anglo-Irish. Cf. Yeats's reference to Lawrence in *A Vision* (1937), p. 41.

[3] Bjersby, *op. cit.*, p. 127, note 1.

There are other similarities which Mrs. Bjersby leaves out; for example, we are told that Robartes, like Doughty, had gone to Damascus first that he might learn Arabic before his intended pilgrimage to Mecca, and that, again like Doughty, Robartes sets out on the pilgrims' trail to Mecca disguised as an Arab and spends two years among the Bedouins of the desert. Moreover, like Doughty, Robartes is a Christian and represents the European tradition.

Robartes eventually finds himself among the Judwali tribe, whose doctrines resemble those found in Giraldus's *Speculum Angelorum et Hominorum*[1] and are said to be contained in their lost book entitled *The Way of the Soul between the Sun and the Moon*.[2]

It is necessary, however, to make it clear at the start that both the Judwali tribe and their sacred lost book are fictitious. In creating this myth, Yeats was inaccurate in both his dates and names, though he was more accurate in some of his details.

There is no tribe, nor has there ever been one, known by that name. 'Judwal' (correctly 'jadwal') in Arabic means a stream or canal or a mathematical table or diagram; hence Yeats's reference to the Judwalis as 'diagrammatists'.[3] His own explanation of what their name means is interesting:

Their name means makers of measures, or as we would say, of diagrams.[4]

The derivation from Arabic 'jadwal' (جدول) is very awkward in this context. Moreover, none of the English travellers in Arabia has mentioned the name, which does not appear, for example, in Doughty. It occurs neither in the exhaustive list given in Richard Francis Burton's *Personal Narrative of a Pilgrimage to Al-Madinah and Meccah*[5] nor in Lady Ann's *Bedouin*

[1] Later corrected by Yeats to read 'Hominum'.
[2] This title is only mentioned in the first version of *A Vision* (1925). It is dropped from the 1937 version.
[3] W. B. Yeats, *Letters*, p. 644.
[4] W. B. Yeats, 'Notes to Michael Robartes and the Dancer' (1921), found in *The Variorum Edition*, p. 825.   [5] *Op. cit.*, vol. ii, pp. 119–23.

Tribes of the Euphrates.[1] Nor do Arabic genealogical sources reveal anything with regard to the Judwali tribe. The best known and most comprehensive genealogical work *Nihāyat al-arab fī Ma'rifat Ansāb al-'Arab* (نهاية الارب في معرفة انساب العرب) by Abū al-'Abbās Aḥmad b. 'Abd Allāh al-Qalqashandī[2] makes no mention of Yeats's Arab tribe, and the same is true of other sources such as Ibn Khaldūn and al-Suyuṭī.

Yeats did not know Arabic, so he could not have invented the name. It is obvious, therefore, that the name was invented by someone who knew enough Arabic to be able to derive it from the word 'jadwal' (in this sense meaning 'diagram'). At least one Orientalist helped him with his Arabic material, and in one of his letters in 1918 he reveals the name of his authority :

I am writing it all out in a series of dialogues about a supposed medieval book, the *Speculum Angelorum et Hominum* by Giraldus, and a sect of Arabs called the Judwalis (diagrammatists). [Sir Edward Denison] Ross has helped me with the Arabic.[3]

Sir Edward Denison Ross (1871–1940) was a great authority on Oriental languages ; he travelled and lived in various countries of the Middle East and in Russia. He was the founder and Director of the School of Oriental Studies at London University. But Ross was much more of a Persian scholar than an Arabist. He may have coined the word 'Judwalis'[4] without realizing the incorrectness of the form ; or he may have coined it just to please Yeats.

Mrs. Yeats told me that her husband wanted a 'fable' for his philosophical treatise and that 'he went to Denison Ross for a fable'. Mrs. Yeats added that Ross did not take Yeats seriously and they did not like each other ; that Ross thought

[1] For a list of various Arab tribes see *op. cit.*, pp. 187–97.
[2] Edited by Ibrāhīm al-Ibyārī and published in Cairo in 1959.
[3] W. B. Yeats, *Letters*, p. 644.
[4] 'In the manuscripts this word appears spelt in several ways, for instance, Judalis, Jewaylis, Jewaldes, Judwalis.' (Bjersby, *op. cit.*, p. 126, note 7.)

that Yeats was only picking his brains ; and that although the
'Judwalis' might not have existed, the 'sand diagrams' were
part of the Order to which Yeats belonged.

Although a 'Judwali' tribe does not exist, it is possible to
surmise which sect or tribe of Arabs Yeats had in mind when
he described them. Through his references to some of their
peculiarities we are able to name the one tribe in Mesopotamia
(today's Iraq) which his description fits. He describes the
Judwalis as follows :

> There are several tribes of this strange sect, who are known
> among the Arabs for the violent contrasts of character amongst
> them, for their licentiousness and their sanctity. Fanatical in
> matters of doctrine, they seem tolerant of human frailty beyond any
> believing people I have met.[1]

His reference to the 'remote Syriac origin' of their doctrines and his repeated references to their teachings and their
ancient origin, strengthen the idea that he must have had a
particular tribe in mind, although he does not use their real
name. The only tribe in Arabia (and in Mesopotamia in
particular) of which he could have been thinking, and which is
identical with his description of the Judwalis, is the tribe or
group of small tribes known as the Ṣābians (as-Ṣābi'ūn,
الصابئون).

The Ṣābians, who live in Iraq to this day, follow the most
ancient monotheistic religion known in the world ; their
religion is said to date back to the year 7000 B.C. First mentioned in the *Qu'rān* (ii, 62 and xxii, 17) together with the Jews
and Christians as 'the followers of the book of God', they were
a semi-Christian sect of Babylonia, the Elkesaites, closely
resembling the Mandaeans or the so-called 'Christians of
St. John the Baptist', but not identical with them. Islamic
theologians agree that they possessed a written revelation.
These true Ṣābians could not be very clearly distinguished
from the pseudo-Ṣābians of Ḥarrān (Carrhae), who professed

[1] *A Vision* (1925), pp. xviii–xix.

the religion of the true Ṣābians to escape the wrath of the Caliph al-Ma'mūn (A.D. 830). Ever since the time of al-Ma'mūn it has become difficult to differentiate between the Harrānians and the true Ṣābians. It is not likely that these details bothered Yeats ; the more mysterious and obscure the background, the better it served his purposes. The Harrānians, who have come to be known as Ṣābians, held a religious philosophy strongly tinged with Neoplatonic and Christian elements. Harrān, their capital, had been since the time of Alexander the Great a famous centre of pagan and Hellenistic culture ; 'its people were Syrian heathens, star-worshippers . . . versed in astrology and magic. . . . They produced a brilliant succession of eminent scholars, scientists and translators, who transmitted to the [Arabs in their Golden Age] the results of Babylonian civilization and Greek learning and became very influential in the court at Baghdad.'[1] One of the greatest translators produced by this environment was Kusta Ben Luka (Qusṭā ibn-Lūqā, قسطا بن لوقا), who was chosen by Yeats to become the founder of the Judwali doctrine. The choice of Kusta Ben Luka is explained by his association with the Ṣābians or Harrānians, who must have been at the back of Yeats's mind when he described the Judwalis.

The account of the Ṣābians given in Lady Ann's *Bedouin Tribes of the Euphrates* must have been one of the sources which Yeats used. Lady Ann writes :

There are also numerous small tribes and sections of tribes about Baghdad, but none of them deserve notice except the Sabaeans [Ṣābians], now found only in the neighbourhood of Souk esh Shiokh, a village on the Shatt el Arab below Hillah, and numbering in all about 3,000 souls.

According to the Sabaean traditions, which date from the creation of the world, their history has been as follows : Before the time of Noah, they say, all the world was Sabaean, believing in one same unseen God, and speaking the same language. . . . The Sabaeans are the descendants of Shem, and to the present day have

[1] *Encyclopædia Britannica* (11th ed.), xxiii, p. 964.

preserved the ancient tongue unchanged. In it their 'book' is written and is described as a sort of Syriac. The Sabaeans first settled in Egypt, being the same Egyptians over whom Pharaoh ruled when he oppressed the children of Israel. . . . They . . . founded a kingdom at Damascus which lasted till two hundred years after the death of their prophet, John the Baptist. . . . Then they moved to Baghdad, where they flourished until the Caliphate was overthrown by the Tartars. . . . Tamerlane (carried) away all their books to Isphahan, where it is believed they still exist. They themselves were dispersed over Irak. . . .[1]

It is clear from the passage above how much the Judwalis, as described by Yeats, have in common with the Ṣābians. The interest of the Ṣābians (or Ḥarrānians) in star-worshipping and in astrology and magic; their connections with Ancient Egypt and their final settlement in Mesopotamia — in addition to the links, established in their development as a sect and race, with Christianity, Islam, Neoplatonic, Hellenistic and pagan philosophies — all these seem to correspond with the ideas Yeats had about the Judwalis while *A Vision* was being written. Even the lost sacred book is there to strengthen what has been suggested a little earlier.

Here Yeats found the ancient authority he needed to support his system; particularly useful were the cosmopolitan and universal nature of the philosophy and teachings of this particular sect. His earlier attempts to forge links between Pagan and Christian Ireland were now revived.

Like the Ṣābians, the Judwalis were linked to Christianity in the person of Kusta Ben Luka, who was a 'Christian like the Caliph's own physician'. This is emphasized in 'The Gift of Harun Al-Rashid':

but I
Who have accepted the Byzantine faith,
That seems unnatural to Arabian minds,
Think when I choose a bride I choose for ever . . .

[1] Lady Ann Blunt, *Bedouin Tribes of the Euphrates*, vol. ii, p. 194.

Here Kusta Ben Luka is linked with Byzantium, and this is very significant when viewed in the whole context of Yeats's philosophy of history. For him Byzantium and the Baghdad of al-Rashid's time[1] seem to be complementary phases in the development of human civilization : Byzantium and Baghdad symbolized for him the reconciliation between the antinomies, while at the same time they were the two greatest centres of human civilization. Both cities became symbols of his ideal world.

In a note added to the revised *Vision* of 1937, Yeats writes :

Flinders Petrie in *The Revolutions of Civilization* says that the Eastern phase is five hundred years ahead of Europe and draws attention to the coincidence between the rise of Arabian civilization and the fall of that of Europe. My system seems to imply that the rise of Arabian civilization and that of Christianity are the same phenomena.[2]

In *A Vision*, scattered references link Baghdad with Byzantium; but Kusta Ben Luka remains the main link between these two great cities.

Although Yeats used Kusta Ben Luka in the way that suited his own poetic purposes, Kusta was a real historical figure. Arab historians know him as a great translator and a brilliant doctor, not as a philosopher; what is known about his life is very scanty. He was a translator of mathematical and philosophical works, and in addition had distinguished himself in medicine, philosophy, geometry, numbers and music. He mastered both Greek and Arabic, and the list of

[1] P. K. Hitti, *History of the Arabs*, London, 1958, pp. 301–2, writes of Baghdad during the reign of Al-Rashid as follows: 'History and legend unite in placing the most brilliant period of Baghdad during the caliphate of Hārūn al-Rashīd (786–809). Though less than half a century old, Baghdād had by that time grown from nothingness to a world centre of prodigious wealth and international significance, standing alone as the rival of Byzantium. Its splendour kept pace with the prosperity of the empire of which it was the capital. It was then that Baghdād became "a city with no peer throughout the whole world".'
[2] W. B. Yeats, *A Vision* (1937), p. 203.

his original works and translations in the *Fihrist* numbers thirty-four.[1] His works include a treatise on the division of soul and self, and two others on astronomy and numbers.

Yeats gets the dates wrong; Kusta Ben Luka could not have lived at the time of al-Rashid, for he was born eleven years after al-Rashid's death. Al-Rashid ruled Baghdad from A.D. 786 to 809; Luka was born in A.D. 820 and did most of his work in the reign of the Caliph al-Mu'tamid (A.D. 870–92). In the revised *Vision* Yeats realizes his mistake :

'The Gift of Harun Al-Rashid' seems to have the dates wrong, for according to the story Robartes told my brother, the Founder of the Judwali sect, Kusta ben Luka, was a young or youngish man when Harun Al-Rashid died. However, poetic licence may still exist.[2]

This comment reveals how anxious he was to make his 'fable' or myth credible, although this did not matter very much in the long run. Nevertheless, his choice of Kusta Ben Luka, with his Christian background, Greek learning and Arabic training, seemed to fit into the jigsaw.

The problem of the learned book called 'The Way of the Soul between the Sun and the Moon', which Yeats attributes to Kusta Ben Luka, is more complex. The literal translation of this title in Arabic would be 'Tarīq al-Nafs bain al-Shams wa al-Qamar' (طريق النفس بين الشمس والقمر). This is awkward in Arabic because the 'rhyming prose' or *saj'* (سجع) is incorrect; the word 'moon' should precede the word 'sun', in order that 'Nafs' and 'Shams' might rhyme. In any case, the title as a whole is awkward in Arabic and offends the ear. Mrs. Bjersby gives the title as 'The Way of the Souls between the Moons and the Suns',[3] which is different from that in the *Vision* of 1925. Here the word 'suns' comes last to rhyme

---

[1] See Ibn al-Nadīm, *al-Fihrist*, Cairo, al-Maktabat al-Tijāriyyat al-Kubra, 1927, pp. 410–11. This is perhaps the most important and comprehensive Arabic Bibliography of the Middle Ages.

[2] W. B. Yeats, *A Vision* (1937), p. 54.   [3] Bjersby, *op. cit.*, p. 127.

with 'souls' ('Nufūs' and 'Shumūs'). Mrs. Bjersby's foot-
note tells us that Yeats was experimenting with the title :

> In some of the manuscripts Yeats has also given the Arabic title
> in the following way : 'TARIQUAT UN-NUFUS BAYN AL-QUMUR WA'L-
> SHUMUS', the correct rendering of which would be : 'Tari-quat
> an-nufus bain al-qumur waš-šumus[1] [طريقة النفوس بين القمور والشموس].'

It has been very difficult to trace the source of this Arabic
title.[2] The first half may come from W. T. Horton's *The Way
of the Soul*,[3] since Yeats was greatly influenced by Horton,
and in 1898 had written an introduction to his *Book of Images*.[4]
The Way of the Soul not only provided Yeats with half of his
title, but also influenced his working out of some of the ideas
expressed in *A Vision*.

But the scope of *A Vision* is far wider than Horton's book ;
it is in part a theory of history, in part a study in human
psychology, and needed a title that would indicate this.
Yeats may have thought of his title in English first, and then
asked Ross for an Arabic translation ; this would account for
the titles scribbled in the margin of some of the manuscripts.

IV

The origin and source of the story of Kusta Ben Luka, as
Yeats sets it forth in his notes and commentaries, and as it is
told in 'The Gift of Harun Al-Rashid', can be safely traced to
'The Tale of 'Alā al-Dīn Abū Shamāt' in the *Arabian Nights*[5]
(this is the tale on which Flecker based his *Hassan*). Kusta's
story has also certain elements borrowed from Lord Dunsany's

[1] Bjersby, *op. cit.*, p. 127, note 2.
[2] For the last three years I have left no stone unturned in my search
for this Arabic title. My search has yielded nothing. None of the Arabic
bibliographies I have consulted, nor any of the Arabists I have approached,
could help me in tracing the title of Yeats's Arabic book to any source.
[3] *The Way of the Soul, A Legend in Line and Verse*, London, 1910.
[4] *A Book of Images*, with an Introduction by W. B. Yeats, London,
1898. The introduction was an essay of which the greater part was
reprinted as 'Symbolism in Painting'.
[5] Mathers, *op. cit.*, vol. ii, pp. 129–96.

The Tents of the Arabs,[1] a play which was first produced at the Abbey Theatre, Dublin, on 24 May 1920.[2] In Dunsany's play, Enzara, an Arab gipsy of the desert, teaches the King (or Caliph) the wisdom of the desert and its sands; eventually the King forsakes his throne to go and live with Enzara and her tribe in the desert.

Yeats admired Dunsany, and described him in 1909 as 'a man of genius', and one who possessed 'a very fine style, which he shows in wild little fantastic tales'.[3] In 1912, he introduced the Cuala Press edition of *Selections from the Writings of Lord Dunsany*, where he expresses his admiration especially for the way Dunsany wrote about the desert and its people.

'The Gift of Harun Al-Rashid' is perhaps the only work of Yeats which is entirely Arabic in its subject-matter; the material is used very skilfully to veil the autobiographical elements,[4] but the tale told here is only an extension and elaboration of the Oriental tale told in the confusing introduction to *A Vision* in 1925. *The Arabian Nights* had provided enough material for Yeats to 'construct a myth';[5] the whole atmosphere is that of the *Arabian Nights*, an effect created by careful selection of those physical objects that form the background, such as

> the fountain's marble edge,
> One hand amid the goldfish in the pool . . .[6]

---

[1] Lord Dunsany (E. J. M. D. Plunkett), *The Tents of the Arabs* (A play in Two Acts), London, 1918.

[2] L. Robinson, *Ireland's Abbey Theatre*, London, 1951, p. 131.

[3] W. B. Yeats, *Letters*, p. 529.

[4] In a note which was later suppressed, Yeats emphasizes the autobiographical aspect of the story: 'He (Kusta Ben Luka) was warned by a dream to accept the gift of the Caliph . . . his wife, a few days after the marriage, began to talk in her sleep. . . .' (Note to *The Cat and the Moon and Certain Poems* (1924) found in *The Variorum Edition*, p. 829.)

[5] W. B. Yeats, *Letters*, p. 781.

[6] W. B. Yeats, 'The Gift of Harun Al-Rashid', *The Variorum Edition*, p. 463.

and this effect is intensified by the elaborate yet controlled phraseology of the lines :

> banners of the Caliphs hang, night-coloured
> But brilliant as the night's embroidery.[1]

> Written in gold upon a purple stain.[2]

> When evening stirs the jasmin bough.[3]

> And yet the jasmin season warms our blood.[4]

> And thereupon his bounty gave what now
> Can shake more blossom from autumnal chill
> Than all my bursting springtime knew.[5]

The story could have easily come from the lips of Shahrazad.

Although 'The Tale of 'Alā al-Dīn Abū Shamāt' in the *Arabian Nights* does not correspond very precisely to the story of the poem, it may very well have been one of the sources to which Yeats turned, in search of a mythology to fit a personal experience. Jaffer is mentioned in the tale, and the story of Jaffer, 'head of the family of the Barmecides',[6] is hinted at in the poem ; perhaps Yeats thought it necessary that he should include him to complete the background. Jaffer occupies a very important place in the *Arabian Nights*, and Yeats had read the whole account of the mysterious episode of Jaffer's execution in the Powys Mathers version.[7]

One of the most outstanding Arabic features in the poem is the presence of the Djinn.[8] Here we can trace the influence of both the *Arabian Nights* and Doughty's *Arabia Deserta*, for in both we find a number of fascinating stories about the Djinn. Yeats mentions the Djinn three times :

---

[1] W. B. Yeats, 'The Gift of Harun Al-Rashid', *The Variorum Edition*, p. 461.   [2] *Ibid.*   [3] *Ibid.*, p. 463.

[4] *Ibid.*, p. 464.

[5] *Ibid.*, pp. 465–6.

[6] W. B. Yeats, *The Variorum Edition*, p. 828.

[7] Mathers, *op. cit.*, vol. iv, pp. 707–23.

[8] In spelling this word I have followed Yeats's spelling in the poem. The word is usually spelt 'Jinn'.

Or was it she that spoke or some great Djinn ?
I say that a Djinn spoke.[1]

       . . . her mouth
Murmured the wisdom of the desert Djinns.[2]

Kusta's bride is Djinn-possessed, or she is 'Daimon-possessed', as Yeats would have put it in referring to a poet. The Arabs believe that a poet's work is really the creation of his 'Daimon'; they call this in Arabic 'Shaitān al-Shi'r' (شيطان الشعر), which literally means the 'devil of poetry'. This idea of the 'Daimon' as 'devil' is echoed in the title 'Demon Est Deus Inversus' mentioned by Yeats in his first *Vision* :[3] 'Demon'[4] set over or against God certainly means 'devil'. On the other hand, for Yeats 'Daimon' could also mean that voice from within, conscience, higher self, or some divinity connected with the self.

Yeats's notion of the Daimon is not based on any profound knowledge of primitive Arabic religion. His main source was Doughty's *Arabia Deserta*, with its long and fascinating passages on the Djinn.[5] Doughty, for example, tells us that the Djinns are of two kinds; half of them are 'Kuffar' (unbelievers) or 'malicious spirits' and the other half 'Moslemin' (believers) or benevolent spirits.[6] They take the shape of animals at will, so that 'many an house cat and many a street

---

[1] W. B. Yeats, 'The Gift of Harun Al-Rashid', *The Variorum Edition*, p. 467.

[2] *Ibid.*, p. 468.

[3] W. B. Yeats, *A Vision* (1925), p. 27.

[4] 'Daimon' is Greek, 'Daemon' Latin, and 'Demon' English. The meaning of 'Demon' as given in the *Concise Oxford Dictionary* (1964) is : '. . . supernatural being, inferior deity, spirit, ghost, in-dwelling or attendant spirit, genius ; evil spirit . . . ; devil . . .'.

[5] C. M. Doughty, *Travels in Arabia Deserta*, London and Toronto, 1933 (single volume edition) ; see especially Part II, pp. 188–94.

[6] *Ibid.*, Part II, p. 188. See also Part I, pp. 258–9 : 'Mankind, after the Arabs' opinion, may be vexed in their bodies and minds by possession of the jan, of which they say "half are malignant and a half good demons, ay and Moslemin".'

dog . . . [are] jān'.¹ Yeats speaks of a similar transformation of the Daimon into animals :

[if a person] is interested in things, in places, he likes to be with many people, and that is why his Daimon has the form of a beast, but your [Robartes] Daimon would have a bird's shape because you are a solitary man.²

The Djinns Yeats speaks of here are of two kinds, one related to animals, the other to birds. But Doughty does not speak of the Djinn appearing as birds, although examples can be found in the *Arabian Nights* : Yeats must have noticed, for instance, that in 'The Tale of Kamar al Zamān and Princess Budūr', Maiumunah disguised herself as a sparrow-hawk.³

The idea of the Daimon began to take definite shape in *Per Amica Silentia Lunae* (1917) and is further developed in the *Vision* of 1925. But it is not until the *Vision* of 1937 that Yeats is perfectly sure what he really means by 'Daimon', which is now redefined to mean, among other things, man's higher self or soul ; and its knowledge is 'Spirit', once the latter has become one with the Divine ideas in their unity, otherwise called the 'Celestial Body'.

Another interesting use of Arabic desert folklore is to be found in 'The Gift of Harun Al-Rashid', in the reference to 'those emblems on the sand' ; these emblems immediately bring to mind the art of Geomancy or 'sand-divination' called by the Arabs 'Khaṭṭ al-Raml' (literally, 'the line [or lines] drawn on sand').⁴ Doughty has a few references to the art of divination and its importance in desert society. He tells us, for example, of Salih, who, 'hearing I would depart, asked me privately had I found by divination "tamyis" (تمييز), if

¹ C. M. Doughty, *Travels in Arabia Deserta*, London and Toronto, 1933 (single volume edition), Part II, p. 190.
² W. B. Yeats, *Plays and Controversies*, London, 1923, p. 459.
³ *See* 'The Tale of Kamar al-Zamān and Princess Budūr' found in Mathers, *op. cit.*, vol. ii, p. 10.
⁴ The art of 'divination' in general is called 'tamyis' (تمييز).

the chance were good for this day's journey? When I en-
quired of his art, "What! said he, you know not this?
how, but by drawing certain lines in the sand! and it is
much used here.""¹ A passage in Powys Mathers's version of
the *Arabian Nights* includes the phrase 'spreads the sands of
prophecy',² and refers to the same custom. The main source
which commends itself to me, however, is Yeats's knowledge
of Magic, which must have made him aware of all kinds of
divination and has also influenced the shape and form of 'those
emblems on the sand'.

It is also very likely that the signs traced in the desert sand
were suggested by Shelley's *Revolt of Islam* (Canto VII,
stanza xxxii):

> And on the sand I would make signs to range
> These woofs, as they were woven, of my thought;
> Clear, elemental shapes, whose smallest change
> A subtler language within language wrought:
> The key of truths which once were dimly taught
> In old Crotona; — and sweet melodies
> Of love in that lorn solitude I caught
> From mine own voice in dream, when thy dear eyes
> Shone through my sleep, and did that utterance harmonize.

The 'clear elemental shapes . . . the key of truths' become in
Yeats's poem the symbols of 'solitary truths' and 'terrible
implacable straight lines' taking the forms of 'gyres' and
'cubes':

> The signs and shapes;
> All those abstractions that you fancied were
> From the great Treatise of Parmenides;
> All, all those gyres and cubes and midnight things³
> Are but a new expression of her body
> Drunk with the bitter sweetness of her youth.⁴

¹ Doughty, *op. cit.*, Part I, p. 162.
² Mathers, *op. cit.*, vol. ii, p. 46.
³ This line originally read 'Those cones and cubes and gyres, those
midnight things'.
⁴ W. B. Yeats, 'The Gift of Harun Al-Rashid', *The Variorum Edition*,
p. 469.

The symbols of the gyres (also referred to as cones, vor-texes, spirals, perns) are from the Kabbala and the *Key of Solomon the King*.[1] Yeats's own comment on his symbols clearly points out his main source :

Then for weeks I get a symbolism like that in my Byzantium poem or in 'To D.W.' with flame for theme. All this may come from the chance that when I was a young man I was accustomed to a Kabalistic ceremony where there were two pillars, one symbolic of water and one of fire. The fire mark is △, the water mark is ▽, these are combined to make Solomon's seal. . . .[2]

Moreover, the Order had already supplied him with scores of diagrams and designs which he did not hesitate to make use of in his system.

V

'Solomon to Sheba' and 'Solomon and the Witch' (both composed in 1918)[3] are related to 'The Gift of Harun Al-Rashid' not only because they also are thinly veiled autobiographical poems about the experiences of Yeats's married life, but also because of the strong Arabic element present in them. Solomon and Sheba become symbolical figures representing wisdom and passion, mind and heart, body and soul, the negative and the positive ; but above all, the newly-married poet-philosopher and his young wife.

The two characters first appear in Yeats's poetry in 'On Woman' (1914),[4] a poem of great significance because it marks the beginning of his new frankness in the treatment of the sexual theme :

[1] Translated and edited by S. L. MacG. Mathers from Ancient MSS. in the British Museum, London, 1889.

[2] *Letters on Poetry from W. B. Yeats to Dorothy Wellesley*, London, 1940, p. 95.

[3] *See* R. Ellmann, 'A Chronology of the Composition of the Poems' in *The Identity of Yeats*, pp. 289-90.

[4] Date of composition is given by Ellmann (*ibid.*, p. 290) as 21 or 25 May 1914. It was first published in *Poetry* (Chicago), February 1916 (see W. B. Yeats, *The Variorum Edition*, p. 345).

Harshness of their desire
That made them stretch and yawn,
Pleasure that comes with sleep,
Shudder that made them one.[1]

But it was not until 1918, in such poems as the two on Solomon and Sheba, that Yeats was finally able to bring together warm affection with sexuality. It was, however, with these two poems and the earlier 'On Woman' that the sexual theme in his poetry begins to assume a new tone.

The narrative of the Queen of Sheba is a folk tradition and belongs to the story-tellers of the East, while the story of Solomon as told by Arab minstrels is entirely different from that given in the Old Testament, where in the first thirteen verses of the First Book of Kings we read of a pious, wealthy and quite human King. Anyone familiar with the figure of Sulaimān ibn Dāud (Solomon the son of David) or Sulaimān al-Ḥakim (Solomon the Wise) in Arabic folklore, notably in the *Arabian Nights*, will not be surprised to find that the Solomon of the Arabs is a totally different man from that of the Jews.

That Yeats saw Solomon more through the *Arabian Nights* than the Old Testament is clear from a reference to Solomon as a master magician, who could converse with all animals, birds and beasts, and

who understood
Whatever has been said, sighed, sung,
Howled, miau-d, barked, brayed, belled,
yelled, cried, crowed . . .[2]

Arabic tradition has it that Solomon had all birds, beasts and insects at his command ; that he understood and spoke their language ; and that he was lord and master over all the Djinn[3] who feared and obeyed him — his power was supreme both

---

[1] W. B. Yeats, 'On Woman', *The Variorum Edition*, pp. 345–6.

[2] W. B. Yeats, 'Solomon and the Witch', *ibid.*, p. 387.

[3] Solomon's power over that Djinn and birds is also mentioned in the *Qu'rān* (xxvii, 15-16 ; xxiv, 12).

in the natural and in the supernatural worlds. Solomon is a unique romantic figure in Arabic folklore; he is in a sense a more glorious Harun al-Rashid, and is represented as the wisest, richest, greatest, most virile and manly person within whom all opposites are reconciled, above all the reconciliation between the spiritual and the physical.

Sheba, who is known as Bilqīs (بلقيس), is also as fantastic a figure as Solomon in Arabic folklore. She is supposed to have belonged to one of the greatest Arab dynasties of the south-western extremity of the Arabian peninsula, the royal house of the pre-Islamic kingdom of Saba' (سبأ).[1] So Yeats's Sheba too is not the Sheba of the Old Testament, but an Arab queen of dazzling beauty who was fit match for the great Solomon. In the two poems Yeats does not hesitate to bestow upon Sheba her true nationality:

> Sang Solomon to Sheba,
> And kissed her Arab eyes.[2]
>
> And thus declared that Arab lady . . .[3]

The figures of Solomon and Sheba seem to have been suggested partly by the *Arabian Nights* and partly by Arthur Symons's dramatic poem 'The Lover of the Queen of Sheba'.[4] The parallelism between 'Solomon and the Witch', for example, and the end of Symons's dramatic poem is very close: in both poems the subject is timelessness, or the timeless

---

[1] 'Saba'' and 'Sabaeans' (despite the confusion resulting from the many ways in which the word is spelt) must be distinguished from Ṣābians, the religious sect mentioned earlier. The Sabaeans of the south derive their name from their capital city of Saba' (سبأ); the name is used loosely for the ancient dwellers in South-west Arabia, the parts now called Yemen, Aden, Hadramaut and Asir.

[2] W. B. Yeats, 'Solomon and Sheba', *The Variorum Edition*, p. 333.

[3] W. B. Yeats, 'Solomon and the Witch', *ibid.*, p. 387. It is interesting to note here that the Old Testament does not indicate the nationality of the Queen.

[4] Written on 28 May 1898 (A. Symons, *Poems*, vol. ii, London, 1924) and first published in the periodical *The Dome* (n.s., v, pp. 5–12), to which Yeats was a contributor, in January 1900.

moment of love for lovers. But in Symons's dramatic poem too there is an Arabic flavour and it is not unlikely that its source may have been a French work translated from the Arabic.

It is interesting to notice here that when Yeats chooses to write about this new phase in his life, now that he was married and proud of his achievement, and now that he had found new poetic vigour, he should express his experiences and ideas not against an Irish or Byzantine but an Arabian background dominated by an Arab queen. Perhaps Yeats's choice of this Arabian background was to release his faculties from the inhibitions of the Irish cultural background and express more freely the theme of sexual love, before he was able to express it against his own Irish background. The two poems on Solomon and Sheba and 'On Woman', therefore, point forward to the sexual imagery of the later poetry, especially to that of 'A Woman Young and Old' and the Crazy Jane poems. When he began to write more frankly about sex he was writing with Shahrazad's words in mind : 'there is nothing shameful in speaking of those things which lie below our waists'.

VI

Yeats's Arabic interests influenced his work in more ways than there is space for us to consider in this essay. Two of his plays, at least, show such an influence : *Calvary* (1920), which is his only play with a Near-Eastern background ; and *The Cat and the Moon* (1926), in which the Blind Beggar and the Lame Beggar, together with the moral of the piece, seem to have been borrowed from the *Arabian Nights*.

Calvary can be related to the interest Yeats took in Arabia, because it is built round the symbolism of desert folklore (as a matter of fact the Arabic symbolism used in it is peculiar to that play alone), and because it is related to Yeats's theory of the Daimon, to which he refers consistently throughout the play. We are constantly reminded of the desert and 'the great desert birds'[1] which are the solitary angels transformed into supernatural kites and vultures :

> Make way for Lazarus that must go search
> Among the desert places where there is nothing
> But howling wind and solitary birds.[2]

Here Yeats is writing under the influence of Doughty, who had suggested in *Arabia Deserta* the supernatural nature of the great scavengers of the desert.

The Cat and the Moon seems to have been based on the tale of 'The Blind Man and the Cripple' in the *Arabian Nights* ;[3] the two strange and peculiar characters symbolize in the play what they symbolize in the Arabian tale. Despite the remark that he had found these two symbolic figures in some 'mediaeval Irish sermon', Yeats echoes the same words as used by Burton when he comes to explain the moral behind the story of the two figures :

. . . and chose for theme the lame man, the blind man, and the well. It seemed that I could be true to the associations of such places if I kept in mind, while only putting the vaguest suggestion of it into the play, that the blind man was the body, the lame man was the soul. When I had finished I found them in some mediaeval Irish sermon as a simile of soul and body. . . .[4]

Burton's words are as follows :

Now the Blind [Man] is the similitude of the body which seeth not save by the spirit, and the Cripple that of the soul, for that it hath no power of motion but by the body ; the garden is the works,

[1] W. B. Yeats, *Collected Plays*, London, 1952, p. 450.
[2] *Ibid.*, p. 452.
[3] For this tale see the tales of 'King Jali'ad of Hind and His Wazir Shimas : Followed by the History of King Wird Khan, Son of King Jali'ad, with His Women and Wazirs' in Burton's *The Book of the Thousand Nights and a Night*, vol. ix, pp. 67–9.
[4] W. B. Yeats, 'Introduction to the Cat and the Moon', *Explorations*, London, 1962, p. 402.

for which the creature is rewarded or punished, and the Overseer is the reason which biddeth to good and forbiddeth from evil. Thus the body and the soul are partners in reward and retribution.[1]

Moreover, Yeats's predilection for strange and deformed figures in his poetry and drama, using these as special types of human personality in his philosophic system, was partly influenced by the fantastic characters he found in the *Arabian Nights*. The Hunchback, the Saint, the Fool, the Lame (Cripple) Man, the Blind Man — all are in one way or another related to their counterparts in the *Arabian Nights*, although some of these figures he had already come across in Irish folklore and Irish mythology.

The Arabic material he came to know was the source of his philosophy of the Daimon, and of his desert imagery and his symbolic use of desert birds — such as hawk, kite, falcon and vulture — and desert beasts, which is most evident in one of his greatest poems, namely, 'The Second Coming'.

The most outstanding influence, however, was the change in his attitude towards the use of the sexual theme and sexual imagery in his poetry. Expressions such as the 'devil between my thighs'[2] are echoes of what Yeats had read in the tales of the *Arabian Nights*. The influence of the Oriental tales on this aspect of his poetry is one that should be fully explored in a separate essay.

We also notice how many fascinating Arabs populate the world of Yeats's imagination. The earliest is the heroine of one of his first plays, *Mosada* (June 1886). From Mosada, the Moorish girl, we move to the Arab geographer, explorer, writer, poet and adventurer Leo Africanus; to the 'Arab Rosicrucian' Ara ben Shemesh, who for many years influenced Yeats's group of the 'Stella Matutina' through Dr. Felkin; to the Arab Queen who becomes Solomon's young bride; to Kusta Ben Luka and his Arab wife; to Harun al-Rashid and

[1] Burton, *The Book of the Thousand Nights and a Night*, vol. ix, p. 68.   [2] *The Variorum Edition*, p. 300.

his Arab court; and finally to the mysterious and unknown Arab tribe of the Judwalis.

In collecting such material Yeats was helped by Arabists whom he met or who were his friends, such as Sir E. Denison Ross and Wilfrid Scawen Blunt; while his interest was stimulated by creative artists such as Oscar Wilde[1] and Edmund Dulac[2] and by contemporary men of action such as T. E. Lawrence.

Above all, two books stand singularly as the most important sources of his inspiration and the most powerful factors in influencing his imagination so far as his Arabic researches are concerned — these are the *Arabian Nights* and Doughty's *Arabia Deserta*.

[1] Mrs. Yeats told me that her husband was enchanted by Wilde's fairy tale 'The Happy Prince'; and that when it was translated into Arabic and widely read in Arabia he considered that the climax of Wilde's success.

[2] *Essays and Introductions*, p. 221 : 'I am writing with my imagination stirred by a visit to the studio of Mr. Dulac, the distinguished illustrator of the *Arabian Nights*' (April, 1916).

THE FASCINATION OF WHAT'S DIFFICULT:
A SURVEY OF YEATS CRITICISM AND
RESEARCH

*

K. G. W. CROSS

A N ACCOUNT OF YEATS CRITICISM from the reception of his earliest verse to, say, 1950 would make an interesting and rewarding study. *The Wanderings of Oisin* was well received by those who, like Oscar Wilde, were quick to note the emergence of a poet of distinction, while subsequent volumes commanded the respectful attention of three generations of critics. Even so, his reputation was by no means securely established at the time of his death. In 1939 he was still regarded primarily as the poet of Ireland, the dominant influence behind the Abbey Theatre and the Irish Literary Movement. As Nobel Prize winner and former Senator of the Irish Free State he was as much public figure as poet. The qualities of the later poetry were not widely recognized ; the plays were felt to be no more than interesting experiments in an uncongenial medium ; much of the prose writings were dismissed as the aberration of genius. The popular image was still that of the Pre-Raphaelite young man of the early portraits, or of the stern old man whose strange, lilting tones had sometimes been heard over the B.B.C.

It was when Yeats came to be considered in relationship to some of his more extravagantly praised contemporaries that his critics took refuge in a certain evasiveness. He was not felt to be a 'modern' poet in the sense in which Pound or Eliot were fashionably considered modern : his preoccupations were thought to be not peculiarly twentieth-century concerns.

When Yeats died, many of those who proclaimed him the fore-most poet of the century would have been hard put to it to explain why. Among the countless moving tributes to his many-sided genius none was more generous in its praise of the poet than the Memorial Lecture delivered to the Friends of the Irish Academy by T. S. Eliot, yet to re-read it today is to be struck more by Eliot's uneasiness with Yeats than by his con-viction that Yeats is, as he declared, 'the greatest poet of our time — certainly the greatest in this language, and so far as I am able to judge, in any language'. Eliot admitted to being out of sympathy with certain aspects of Yeats's thought and feeling, while similar difficulties had been encountered by F. R. Leavis and other critics of the *Scrutiny* persuasion in their efforts to 'place' Yeats. These uncertainties reappear in the essays contributed to the Yeats Memorial Issue of *The Southern Review* (Winter, 1942), by R. P. Blackmur, Allen Tate, and other 'New Critics'. Attempts to apply their critical method to Yeats's poetry underlines the inadequacy of 'an immediate response to the words on the page', as G. S. Fraser demonstrates in the chapter on Yeats and the 'New Criticism' in his *Vision and Rhetoric* (1959). The poetry clearly calls for something more than a close and attentive reading of the text.

The difficulties of Yeats's poetry are of an altogether differ-ent order from the deliberate ambiguities, allusiveness and calculated obscurities of much modern verse. With Eliot, often, to track an allusion to its source is to dispose of a difficulty for all time, whereas the difficulties of Yeats's poetry refer back to the complex and contradictory character of the poet himself. His ideas and beliefs, his absorption with the arcane and the occult, his love for Maud Gonne, his involve-ment with Irish politics and the literary movement, his relationship with his friends, and his lofty conception of the poet's rôle colour all his writings like a deep dye. In the quarter of a century since his death much has been done to set the record straight, as each year's harvest of scholarly and critical writing brings a deeper understanding and keener appreciation of Yeats's work. The shadow of his reputation now falls longer and darker across our century, obscuring much that was once thought to be of comparable significance and as enduring. The man who by a deliberate effort of will and imagination made himself a great poet is by common consent one of the truly heroic figures of our time : in the receding perspective of history Yeats comes more and more to dominate the scene.

The definitive text of Yeats's poems is the two-volume limited edition published by Macmillan (London) in 1949, in which were incorporated the poet's final revisions. This forms the basis of *The Variorum Edition of the Poems of W. B. Yeats* (New York, 1957), superbly edited by the late Peter Allt and Russell K. Alspach, which takes cognizance of all published versions and includes works not printed in the definitive edition. Stephen Maxfield Parrish's *Concordance to the Poems of W. B. Yeats* (Ithaca, 1963), based on *The Variorum Edition*, lists the 10,450 'significant' words that make up Yeats's poetic vocabulary, and is an invaluable adjunct to the study of the poetry. The eagerly awaited *Variorum Edition of the Plays*, on which Brigadier-General and Mrs. Alspach have worked long and devotedly, is happily already with the publishers.

The making available of Yeats's prose writings is a publishing achievement of the past decade that has been questioned for its seeming lack of editorial method. *Autobiographies* (London, 1955) brings together Yeats's autobiographical writings, including *Estrangement, The Death of Synge*, and *The Bounty of Sweden*, which includes the lecture on *The Irish Dramatic Movement* that was not printed in *The Autobiography of William Butler Yeats* (New York, 1953). The 1937 version of *A Vision* was reissued 'with the author's final revisions' by The Macmillan Company, New York, in 1956, and 'with corrections' by Macmillan, London, in 1962 : the texts are nearly identical. The vastly different version of *A Vision* first published in 1925 in an extremely limited edition remains unobtainable. *Mythologies* (1959) contains Yeats's short stories (with the exception of *John Sherman* and *Dhoya*, neither of which has been reprinted since 1908), and *Per Amica Silentia Lunae*. Much of what Yeats called his 'critical prose' is collected in *Essays and Introductions* (1961), which contains *Ideas of Good and Evil*, *The Cutting of an Agate*, and the less familiar *Essays : 1931 to 1936*. It includes the 'Modern Poetry' broadcast of 1936, and prints for the first time *A General Introduction for My Work* and *An Introduction for My Plays*, which were written for a complete edition of Yeats's works which was never produced. *Explorations* (1962), a further selection from his prose works made by Mrs. Yeats, reprints *The Irish Dramatic Movement, 1901–1919*, and the important *Pages From a Diary Written in 1930*. It also includes Yeats's last prose work, *On the Boiler* (with some minor yet puzzling omissions), and a number of his previously uncollected introductions. Donald R. Pearce has usefully edited *The Senate Speeches of W. B. Yeats* (Bloomington, 1960 ; London, 1961), but users of this book will do well to see also W. B. Stanford's 'Yeats in the Irish Senate', in *A Review of English Literature* (July, 1963).

Clearly a good deal remains to be done if, in defiance of the poet's curse, all that he wrote and cast away is to be made available. From the considerable body of Yeats's unpublished manuscript Curtis Bradford has recently transcribed and edited two significant prose works, 'Modern Ireland', an address Yeats delivered to American audiences during 1932–3, and 'Discoveries : Second Series', comprising essays on 'The Doctor in Spite of Himself', 'The Return of the Stars', '[Pantheism]', and '[Changing Canons of Form]', brief reflections on Hugh Lane's impressionist pictures and on Castiglione's *The Courtier*. Both pieces appear in *The Massachusetts Review* (Winter, 1964). Marion Witt's collection of Yeats's fugitive prose awaits permission for publication. Allan

318

Wade's excellent edition of *The Letters of W. B. Yeats* (1954)
is unfortunately far from complete ; although Yeats's letters
to George Moore, A. E., Lionel Johnson and Maud Gonne are
known to have been lost or destroyed, those to Synge, Shaw,
Joyce, Pound, Gordon Craig and Mrs. Yeats would, if released
for publication, swell the volume to more than three times its
original size. Yeats's important correspondence with T. Sturge
Moore has been ably edited by Ursula Bridge (1953), while the
Letters on Poetry to Dorothy Wellesley (1940), significant for
the light it sheds on the later poems, has been reissued as an
Oxford Paperback (1964). A few more letters are to be found
in current periodicals, the most important being twenty-three
letters to Lady Gregory, edited by Donald T. Torchiana and
Glenn O'Malley, in *A Review of English Literature* (July,
1963). O'Malley and Torchiana have also edited letters
written by John Butler Yeats to Lady Gregory between 1898
and 1907, several of which refer to Yeats. They are printed
in *The Massachusetts Review* (Winter, 1964). In the same
issue of *The Massachusetts Review* John Unterecker prints
letters Yeats wrote in 1918 to Mrs. James Duncan, the curator
of Dublin's Municipal Gallery of Modern Art. They concern
Yeats's proposed visit to Dublin in order to deliver a lecture
on Blake and to report on his investigations of psychic mani-
festations, but their reflection of the troubled times in which
they were written is conveyed by the editor's title, 'A Fair
Chance of a Disturbed Ireland'. H. W. Häusermann prints
some Yeats letters to W. J. Turner in *English Studies* (August,
1959; August, 1960), and there are two letters to John
O'Leary in *The Irish Book* (Autumn, 1963). Hazard Adams
awaits permission to publish his edition of Yeats's twenty-one
letters to Mabel Beardsley. Two sections of Yeats's unfinished
novel, *The Speckled Bird*, have been published, in *The Bell*
(March, 1941), and *Irish Writing* (Summer, 1955). An excerpt
from his unfinished play, *The Country of the Young*, a variation
upon Lady Gregory's *The Travelling Man*, is given, with a

discussion of the text, by Hazard Adams in *P.M.L.A.* (June, 1957). In his *Yeats's Iconography* (1960) F. A. C. Wilson gives a synopsis of an unfinished and untitled play which he calls *The Bridegroom*.

Yeats's numerous note-books and manuscripts have been extensively drawn upon by Joseph Hone, A. N. Jeffares, Richard Ellmann and Virginia Moore in their studies of the poet's life and work, and by Thomas Parkinson, Curtis Bradford, Jon Stallworthy, and others in their attempts to follow the evolution of his poetry. There are important collections of manuscripts and letters by Yeats in the Library of the University of Texas, the Lilly Library of Indiana University (the Wade Collection), and the National Library of Ireland. Trinity College, Dublin, has the MS. of *Mosada*, and there is more material in the New York Public Library, the Huntington Library, Harvard University Library, Mills College Library at Oakland, Calif., the University of California Library at Berkeley, the Deering Library of Northwestern University and the British Museum, but much still remains in private hands. Until these papers have been properly sifted and edited our picture of the poet will remain less sharply focused than one would wish.

Before concluding this brief survey of currently available editions of Yeats's works — and their limitations — mention should perhaps be made of some recent publications in paperback format. The central position occupied by Yeats in the undergraduate study of literature in American universities is no doubt reflected in M. L. Rosenthal's *Selected Poems and Two Plays of William Butler Yeats* (New York, 1962), which includes *Calvary* and *Purgatory*, and is furnished with a useful introductory essay, explanatory notes and glossary. *A Vision* — an unlikely choice, one would have thought, not so long ago — was also issued as a Macmillan Paperback (New York) in 1962. Doubleday Anchor Books brought out *The Autobiography of William Butler Yeats* in 1958, while *The Celtic*

Twilight, together with a selection of early poems, edited and introduced by Walter Starkie, was published as a Signet Classic in 1962. George Brandon Saul's *The Age of Yeats* (New York, 1964) is an admirable anthology of poems, plays and stories by Yeats and his countrymen — A. E., Gogarty, Synge, Joyce, James Stephens and others. In England the growing demand for Yeats's works in schools and universities has been met by the inclusion of A. Norman Jeffares's *Poems of W. B. Yeats*, with its seventy pages of valuable annotation, in Macmillan's Scholar's Library series (1962). Professor Jeffares has also edited *Selected Poetry* (1962), *Selected Plays* (1964), *Selected Prose* (1964) and *Selected Criticism* (1964) of Yeats for Macmillan's St. Martin's Library series. Designed to bring Yeats's writings within reach of a wider audience, the annotated selections of Rosenthal and Jeffares deserve to be considered as contributions to Yeats scholarship for their balance of learning and good sense. They point towards the volume of *Commentary* that one would like one day to see on the shelf beside the *Variorum Poems* and *Plays*.

Allan Wade's *A Bibliography of the Writings of W. B. Yeats* (1951, rev. ed. 1958), a work of meticulous scholarship, is the indispensable work of reference. It lists Yeats's many publications, including books edited or with an introduction by him, his contributions to periodicals (the bibliographical information here is a little sketchy) and translations. The revised edition lists books published by the Cuala Press, and contains an appendix on 'Yeats and Broadcasting' by George Whalley. Russell K. Alspach contributed some additions to Allan Wade's *Bibliography* in *The Irish Book* (Autumn, 1963). George Brandon Saul's two volumes, *Prolegomena to the Study of Yeats's Poems* and *Prolegomena to the Study of Yeats's Plays* (Philadelphia, 1957 and 1958), contain much bibliographical and other information in elucidation of particular poems and plays, and form a useful compendium of scholarly and critical opinion. *The Permanence of Yeats* (New York, 1950, 1961), a collection of critical essays edited by James Hall and Martin Steinmann, gives what is to date the fullest select bibliography of Yeats criticism published before 1950, while the more important critical works since then are listed in the bibliography appended to J. I. M. Stewart's volume of *The Oxford History of English Literature, Eight Modern Writers* (1963). My own *Bibliography of Yeats Criticism* (in collaboration with R. T. Dunlop), listing reviews of books by Yeats as well as books, articles and theses wholly or in part concerned with him, is now with the publishers. Useful surveys of trends in Yeats scholarship are those by A. Norman Jeffares, 'An Account of Recent Yeatsiana', *Hermathena*, lxxii (1948), George Brandon Saul, 'Thread to a Labyrinth : A Selective Bibliography in Yeats', *Bulletin of the New York Public Library*, lviii (1954), and Hazard Adams, 'Yeats Scholarship and Criticism : A Review of Research', *Texas Studies in Literature and Language*, iii (1962). An indication of the increasing attention being given to Yeats's plays is to be found in Donna Gerstenberger's 'Yeats and Theatre : A Selected Bibliography', *Modern Drama*, vi (May, 1963). The Catalogues of the exhibitions held in the Library of Trinity College, Dublin, *W. B. Yeats : Manuscripts and Printed Books* (1956), and in the University of Kansas Library (1958) are important, while that of the exhibition of paintings, drawings, photographs and letters bearing on Yeats's life and work, held at the Whitworth Art Gallery, Manchester, and at Dublin, *W. B. Yeats : Images of a Poet* (Manchester, 1961), has permanent significance as an introduction to the poet.

A full-scale critical biography of the kind Yeats merits has yet to be written. For all its virtues, Joseph Hone's *W. B. Yeats, 1865–1939* (London, 1942, rev. ed. 1962) suffers from the limitations of an authorized biography. Hone's personal acquaintance with the poet, and his own Anglo-Irish background, enabled him to write of Yeats as the Irish man of letters, and his freedom of access to private papers makes his biography still an invaluable source book, but it leaves out much that we should like to know while documenting a good deal that is of only peripheral interest. *W. B. Yeats : Man and Poet* (London, 1949, rev. ed. 1962) by A. Norman Jeffares, another Anglo-Irishman, goes far deeper, containing much information not to be found elsewhere, as well as lengthy quotations from Yeats's unpublished diaries, notebooks, letters and manuscripts. Jeffares is as much concerned with Yeats's shaping of his imaginative life as with the external facts of his biography, and his book is still the best guide to the poet's reading and source material. Richard Ellmann's *Yeats : The Man and the Masks* (1948, rev. ed. 1961) also relies heavily on Yeats's unpublished papers, but it is more directly concerned with the development of his art, which is related to an examination of the poet's various personae. Ellmann seeks to minimize the importance of Ireland in Yeats's life and work, while emphasizing the influence of Yeats's father upon the poet's thought. He also attempts to show the relevance of Yeats's experiments with magic and the occult to his poetic achievement. Hone's record of Yeats's lifelong involvement with Irish affairs, Jeffares's account of his intellectual background and philosophical development, and Ellmann's study of his artistic evolution have not been surpassed : despite many specialized studies of more recent date it is to these three books that the student must turn for the facts about Yeats. Monk Gibbon's *The Masterpiece and the Man : Yeats as I Knew Him* (1959), which purports to show Yeats as he was in later life, is more a work of self-advertisement than of biography.

Yeats's varied activities brought him into close contact with many of the most important figures of his time, and he is to be glimpsed in countless volumes of reminiscences, autobiography or literary biography. In addition to John Masefield's *Some Memories of W. B. Yeats* (1940), the personal tributes by Maud Gonne, Lennox Robinson, W. G. Fay,

Edmund Dulac, C. Day Lewis and others, collected by Stephen Gwynn in *Scattering Branches* (1940), and the autobiographical writings of George Moore, Katharine Tynan and Lady Gregory, there is a good deal about Yeats in Sir William Rothenstein's *Men and Memories* (2 vols., 1931–2), and *Since Fifty* (1939), A. E.'s *Song and Its Fountains* (1932), Oliver St. John Gogarty's *As I Was Going Down Sackville Street* (1937), Maud Gonne MacBride's *A Servant of the Queen* (1938), Lennox Robinson's *Curtain Up* (1942), Mary Colum's *Life and the Dream* (1947), and Max Beerbohm's *Mainly on the Air* (rev. ed. 1957). Joseph Hone's *J. B. Yeats : Letters to his Son W. B. Yeats and Others* (1944) is of particular importance, as is Lennox Robinson's edition of *Lady Gregory's Journals* (1946). Among works of critical biography devoted to his contemporaries and associates Yeats figures prominently in Mark Longaker's *Ernest Dowson* (Philadelphia, 1945), Frederick L. Gwynn's *Sturge Moore and the Life of Art* (Lawrence, Kansas, 1951), David H. Greene's and Edward M. Stephens's *J. M. Synge, 1871–1909* (New York, 1959), David Krause's *Sean O'Casey : The Man and His Work* (1960), Alan Price's *Synge and Anglo-Irish Drama* (1961), and Elizabeth Coxhead's *Lady Gregory : A Literary Portrait* (1961). The Yeats who features in the books on O'Casey and Lady Gregory does not appear in a very favourable light. Highly personal portraits of the poet are to be found in L. A. G. Strong's *Green Memory* (1961), and Gogarty's posthumously published *William Butler Yeats: A Memoir* (1963), the latter being predictably unreliable but entertaining.

Many of the authors listed above view Yeats through Irish eyes, or from an Irish standpoint, and it is significant that the first book solely about Yeats, Horatio Sheafe Krans's *William Butler Yeats and the Irish Literary Revival* (1904), set the poet in his national context. So did Joseph Hone in his preliminary study, *William Butler Yeats : The Poet in Contemporary Ireland* (1916), and Yeats necessarily occupies a large place in such general surveys as A. E. Boyd's *Ireland's Literary Renaissance* (1916), A. E. Malone's *The Irish Drama* (1929), Una Ellis-Fermor's *The Irish Dramatic Movement* (1939, 1954), and Robert Farren's *The Course of Irish Verse in English* (1947), which considers Yeats in relation to such forbears as Callanan, Ferguson and Mangan. Most recently, Estella Ruth Taylor, in *The Modern Irish Writers : Cross Currents of Criticism* (Lawrence, Kansas, 1954), and Herbert Howarth, in *The Irish Writers : Literature and Nationalism, 1880–1940* (New York, 1959), have sought to place the poet against the wider perspective of the Irish literary and political scene. The relationship between Yeats's work and his local environment has been illuminatingly pointed to by Richard M. Kain in his *Dublin in the Age of William Butler Yeats and James Joyce* (Norman, Oklahoma, 1962), while Sheelah Kirby's *The Yeats Country* (Dublin, 1962) is a useful little guidebook to the country around Sligo. None of these books, however, goes far enough in its exploration of Yeats's Irish background. Arland Ussher's provocative essay on Yeats in his *Three Great Irishmen* (1951) is perhaps the best account of the poet's Irishness, but it does not pretend to examine in any detail the influence on his work of Yeats's changing attitudes towards Irish politics, and takes little account of the Irish literary and theatrical movements. A more serious defect of this and other studies of Yeats and Ireland is the failure to do more than hint at the nature and strength of the Anglo-Irish tradition that was a major source of his inspiration. For some indication of this, one must still refer to the opening chapter of T. R. Henn's *The Lonely Tower : Studies in the Poetry of W. B. Yeats* (1950). In *The Irish Comic Tradition* (1962) Vivian Mercier convincingly demonstrates the continuity between Gaelic and Anglo-Irish comedy, and has some good things to say about Yeats's Irish humour, but what is badly needed is a full-length study of Yeats and Ireland, with particular reference to the nationalist movement, the literary revival, and the

Anglo-Irish tradition — a work comparable in scope to Thomas Flanagan's excellent account of *The Irish Novelists, 1800–1850* (New York, 1959).

Of earlier studies not mainly biographical a general introduction to Yeats's poetry that has not outlasted its usefulness is the chapter in David Daiches's *Poetry and the Modern World* (1940). If Louis MacNeice's *The Poetry of W. B. Yeats* (1941) seems today rather thin and outmoded it can still be read for its perceptive comments on particular poems. Like W. H. Auden's essay 'Yeats as an Example' (in *The Permanence of Yeats*), its main interest lies in its reflection of what poets of the nineteen-thirties found to praise in Yeats. V. K. Narayana Menon's *The Development of W. B. Yeats* (1940, rev. ed. 1960), a rather superficial book, has not worn well. Writing in the early years of the war, Dr. Menon felt constrained to quarrel with Yeats's distrust of democracy and his authoritarian views. By way of contrast, G. S. Fraser's *W. B. Yeats* (Writers and Their Work: No. 50, 1954, rev. ed. 1960), perhaps the best brief introductory essay on the poet, emphasizes 'the broad and deep humanity that provides the substance of his art'. Donald Stauffer's *The Golden Nightingale* (1949), subtitled 'Essays on Some Principles of Poetry in the Lyrics of William Butler Yeats', attempted more than could be successfully accomplished within its brief compass, yet it was the first study to profit from Yeats's hint about the way in which one poem lights up another, and its insistence that the lyrics cannot be read in isolation was a valuable corrective to the attempts of the New Critics to approach a Yeats poem as if it were by Donne or Eliot. Hugh Kenner, in 'The Sacred Book of the Arts', reprinted in his *Gnomon: Essays on Contemporary Literature* (1958), argued even more strenuously that the unit in which to discuss Yeats is 'not the poem or sequence of poems but the volume'. This view is developed by John Unterecker in *A Reader's Guide to W. B. Yeats* (1959), where he claims that 'the total effect of the lyrics has an epic quality'. Unterecker's commentary on the poems is often helpful, but his chapters on Yeats's doctrine of the mask, his 'system' and his symbolism are less than adequate; the book hovers uneasily between general and specialist studies of Yeats.

The best recent book for the general reader is A. G. Stock's *W. B. Yeats : His Poetry and Thought* (1961, paperback 1964), which does much to redress the balance of earlier studies. In place of the starry-eyed participant in the mumbo-jumbo of the Magical Order of the Golden Dawn, the Yeats who emerges from Miss Stock's book is an Anglo-Irishman not so very different from his own imagined ideal reader — the 'wise and simple' fisherman in grey Connemara clothes. The book begins rightly by emphasizing the differences between Ireland and England, and is particularly enlightening on the development of the mature Yeats, which Miss Stock relates to the two events which changed his life and his poetry — the Easter Rebellion and the writing of *A Vision*. The chapters devoted to an examination of that difficult book tend to oversimplify Yeats's thought, yet they do substantiate the claim that it is 'a great achievement in its own right'. Few books about Yeats communicate a more sensitive appreciation of his poetry. A. N. Jeffares's *W. B. Yeats : The Poems* (1961), a short introduction to the range of Yeats's poetry, finds space for useful analyses of some of the major poems, and comments thoughtfully on Yeats's use of rhetoric. The survey of the lyric poetry in Bhabatosh Chatterjee's *The Poetry of W. B. Yeats* (Bombay, 1962) throws some light on the continuity of image and idea that runs from the earlier to the later work, but the book disappointingly fails to take cognizance of the critical work of the past decade, the manuscript having been completed in 1952 and not revised for publication. Peter Ure's *Yeats* (Writers and Critics, 1963), and the Yeats chapter in J. I. M. Stewart's *Eight Modern Writers* (1963) are two well-informed, up-to-date accounts that will satisfy all but the specialist.

Hazard Adams, in the survey of Yeats criticism referred to above, shows that 1950 marked a turning point in Yeats studies. In that year Hall and Steinmann's *The Permanence of Yeats* brought together the best critical essays of the past two decades, which, despite the brilliant performance of critics like Cleanth Brooks, Blackmur, Tate, and others, revealed something of the equivocal position Yeats held at that time. His greatness was conceded almost with reluctance by some contributors, many of whom confessed to some embarrassment that a poet of Yeats's gifts could take such 'nonsense' seriously, as Auden put it. In the same year, however, T. R. Henn's *The Lonely Tower* attempted to make sense of Yeats's doctrines, anticipating the course of much subsequent enquiry in its chapters on 'The Phases of the Moon', '*A Vision* and The Interpretation of History', and the connection between Yeats's poetry and the visual arts. Henn's book has suffered the fate of other pioneer studies in being partially eclipsed by its successors, yet as I have said it remains the best account of Yeats's Anglo-Irish inheritance, and deserves its place beside the first major studies of Yeats by Hone, Jeffares and Ellmann. The attempt to understand Yeats without recourse to sources beyond the particular poem came virtually to an end with Vivienne Koch's rather crotchety book, *W. B. Yeats : The Tragic Phase* (1951), in which a dozen of the *Last Poems* are submitted to close analysis. Despite some valuable insights the book suffers from the same limitations as earlier attempts to read the poems in isolation. Thomas Parkinson's *W. B. Yeats, Self-Critic : A Study of his Early Verse* (1951) put Yeats scholarship on a new footing by turning to the poet's revisions and criticisms of his early poems. Taking his cue from Peter Allt's long essay, 'Yeats and the Revision of his Early Verse', *Hermathena*, lxiv (1944), Parkinson reveals an interaction between the development of Yeats's technical skill and the growth of the poet's mind, and the influence on his art of his work for the Abbey Theatre.

Richard Ellmann's second book, *The Identity of Yeats* (1954), a critical biography of the poetry rather than of the poet, traces the evolution of theme, symbol, style and pattern from the early to the late verse, and argues for a consistency of thought and constancy of attitude underlying the changes of diction and imagery. Ellmann perhaps overstates his case, but in directing attention to elements in the early poetry that foreshadow the later achievement his book affords a necessary corrective to the view that only the late Yeats matters. Yeats's doctrine and the Yeatsian aesthetic have since been the subject of more exhaustive examination than Ellmann permits himself, but the book remains of the utmost importance for its insistence that the identity of Yeats is stamped everywhere on his verse. In 1954 Virginia Moore's long, ill-arranged book, *The Unicorn : William Butler Yeats's Search for Reality*, undertook the first detailed study of Yeats's doctrinal sources — Hermetism, Druidism, Cabalism, Neoplatonism, Gnosticism, Rosicrucianism, etc. Useful for its citation of passages from Yeats's unpublished papers not previously drawn upon by Hone or Jeffares, *The Unicorn* irritates by its failure to come to terms with the poetry and the sentimentality of the author's approach.

A survey of the poetry that seems not to have received the notice it deserves is B. L. Reid's *William Butler Yeats : The Lyric of Tragedy* (1961). 'We begin to live when we have conceived of life as a tragedy', Yeats wrote in 1922, and taking this as his text Reid reconstructs from Yeats's prose writings what the poet understood by tragedy, and tries to discover how far tragic emotion strengthens his poetry. Reid is an excellent critic of Yeats's verse, and his book is not the mechanical exercise it may seem from this bald summary, but a sensitive response to the tragic experience as Yeats embodied it in his poetry. It is his tragic vision that lends the poetry the 'unifying moral subject' that Stephen Spender and other poet-critics of the nineteen-thirties failed to find in Yeats. The latest — and largest — of these works of a more or less general nature is Morton Irving Seiden's *William Butler Yeats : The Poet as a Mythmaker, 1865–1939* (1962). It covers in more scholarly fashion territory already familiar to readers of *The Unicorn*, but affords a much more systematic guide to *A Vision* and what went into it, the poems being treated as fragments of the great myth that lay behind that work. Part One, dealing with 'The Quest for a Faith', is the fullest account to date of Yeats's numerous sources, and is more successful than Part Two, 'Artifacts of Eternity', which attempts to show how the poems arose from the mythology. One is not always convinced by Dr. Seiden's identification of the symbolic patterns underlying the poems, but one is grateful for the industry that has assembled so much information.

The first of the specialized studies of Yeats was Dorothy M. Hoare's *The Works of Morris and Yeats in Relation to Early Saga Literature* (1937), a comparative study which explains why Morris told Yeats, 'You are my kind of poet'. J. P. O'Donnell's pioneer essay on Yeats's symbolism, *Sailing to Byzantium* (1939), seems tentative compared with what has since been written on the subject, but Peter Ure's *Towards a Mythology : Studies in the Poetry of W. B. Yeats* (1946) puts forward within its brief limits a stimulating and provocative view of the relationship between poetry and myth. Professor Ure's account of Yeats's dramatization of the Cuchulain story prepared the way for Birgit Bjersby's careful study, *The Cuchulain Legend in the Works of W. B. Yeats* (1950), which shows what personal meaning that heroic figure held for the poet. Although the subject has been frequently touched upon there is as yet, strangely, no complete study of Yeats's use of Irish mythology. Of the many possible comparative studies only Blake has so far been treated, by Margaret Rudd in *Divided Image : A Study of William Blake and W. B. Yeats* (1953), which discusses the influence on Yeats of Blake's mystical thought, and by Hazard Adams, in *Blake and Yeats : The Contrary Vision* (1955), a much more rigorous examination of the symbolic systems underlying their poetry. Some remarks about the relationship of Blake and Shelley to Yeats in Harold Bloom's *Shelley's Mythmaking* (1959) suggest a line for further research, and there is clearly room for more studies of the relationship between Yeats and his distinguished contemporaries in England and abroad. The title of Priscilla Shaw's *Rilke, Valéry, and Yeats: The Domain of the Self* (1964) is a hint of things to come, as is the chapter on Eliot and Yeats in A. Alvarez's *The Shaping Spirit* (1958).

Also in need of detailed and unprejudiced re-evaluation is the literary *milieu* in which Yeats served his literary apprenticeship, and the effect on his thinking of his association with the poets of the eighteen-eighties and -nineties. In *Autobiographies* Yeats tells us that he 'learned to think in the midst of the last phase of Pre-Raphaelitism', and was 'in all things Pre-Raphaelite'. F. R. Leavis, in *New Bearings in English Poetry* (1932), indicated the weaknesses of late nineteenth-century English verse, and showed how Yeats outgrew them, but Parkinson's *W. B. Yeats, Self-Critic* reveals that no-one was more conscious of these weaknesses than the poet himself. Yeats's fellow-Rhymers are still in disgrace, but what he learned from them about the nature and forms of art calls for careful reconsideration. Graham Hough's *The Last Romantics* (1949), one of the few books to consider Yeats in this context, is better on Ruskin and the development of English aestheticism than it is on the poet. *A Study in Yellow : The 'Yellow Book' and Its Contributors* (1960), by Katherine Lyon Mix, is an interesting background study that says little specifically about Yeats. One great merit of Frank Kermode's brilliant and controversial essay, *Romantic Image* (1957), is its recognition of the significance of the poets of Yeats's 'tragic generation'.

Kermode's book is really concerned with Yeats's involvement in the Symbolist Movement, a subject which has given rise to much debate ever since Edmund Wilson grouped

Yeats — none too happily — with Valéry, Proust, Joyce and
Eliot, in *Axel's Castle* (1931).   C. M. Bowra's *The Heritage of
Symbolism* (1943), Enid Starkie's *From Gautier to Eliot : The
Influence of France on English Literature, 1851–1939* and
E. Davis's monograph, *Yeats's Early Contacts with French
Poetry* (1961), all claim a greater direct influence of the French
Symbolists on Yeats than his imperfect command of the
language would have permitted.   Kermode, however, in his
chapter on the iconography of the dancer in late nineteenth-
century art, convincingly relates Yeats to a contemporary
European tradition.   It is when he goes on to claim that the
poetic theories of Pater and Symons furnished Yeats with all
he needed that one must insist that Yeats's formulation of a
poetic theory in the 1890s, and his subsequent elaboration of it,
was a much more considerable — and original — achievement
than Kermode allows.   This is brought out in one of the most
important books on Yeats in recent years, Edward Engelberg's
The Vast Design : Patterns in W. B. Yeats's Aesthetic (1964),
which reconstructs from the poet's scattered observations on
art and artists the successive stages in his evolution of a co-
herent theory of art.   The Yeatsian aesthetic, Engelberg shows,
was founded upon the poet's philosophy of history, which in
turn grew out of the historical reassessments of Greek and
Renaissance art and culture given currency by Walter Pater,
Yeats's indebtedness to whom is here explored fully for the
first time.   The philosophical context of Engelberg's examination of Yeats's ideas is not English aestheticism, nor French
Symbolism, but the wider pattern of European thought from
Hegel to Nietzsche and Balzac — a background which lends
authority to the conclusion towards which the book moves,
that Yeats was 'the last of the great European poets'.

Engelberg's detailed discussion of the part played by
painting and sculpture in the shaping of Yeats's aesthetic links
his book with another major work of scholarship, Giorgio
Melchiori's *The Whole Mystery of Art : Pattern into Poetry*

in the Work of W. B. Yeats (1960), which follows Henn's lead in exploring the influence of the visual arts upon Yeats's poetry. Melchiori charts Yeats's complex world of images with considerable subtlety and skill, tracing not only the visual sources of such symbols as the unicorn, swan, tower and dome, but also the mental processes that went to the making of such poems as 'Leda and the Swan' and 'The Second Coming'. His argument that visual imagery had priority for Yeats received unexpected support when Charles Madge published in *The Times Literary Supplement* (20 July 1962) a reproduction of a Greek bas-relief undoubtedly seen by Yeats in the British Museum, which exactly fits the description of the rape of Leda in Yeats's poem. Also concerned with Yeats's sources, but from a different point of view, are two excellent books by F. A. C. Wilson, *W. B. Yeats and Tradition* (1958) and *Yeats's Iconography* (1960), about which the opinion of Yeats scholars is sharply divided. Wilson has greatly increased our knowledge of Yeats's gnostic, Neoplatonic, and esoteric sources, but his insistence that the occult symbolism and the tradition from which it derives be taken seriously has found little favour. In his first volume, a study of Yeats's last five plays, Wilson's understanding of Hermetic lore enables him to discover the allegorical significance of such difficult works as *The Herne's Egg, Purgatory* and *The Death of Cuchulain*, while in his second book he uses the same method to interpret *Four Plays For Dancers, The Cat and The Moon*, and some related lyrics. Together they form an extreme statement of the view that Yeats's poetry requires 'for its full resolution an ulterior body of knowledge'.

Symbolism and the Symbolist Movement continue to interest scholars and critics, for books like William York Tindall's *The Literary Symbol* (1955) merely hint at how much remains to be done. *The Way Down and Out : The Occult in Symbolist Literature* (1959), by John Senior, argues for a direct connection between occult movements and literary symbolism, but in the author's terms Yeats turns out not to be a symbolist at all — his poems are not 'koans' or 'yantras'. Barbara Seward's *The Symbolic Rose* (1960) has an interesting chapter on Yeats's enrichment of personal feeling through association with a traditional symbol. A positivist approach to the problem of symbolical method in the arts is suggested by Susanne K. Langer in her *Philosophy in a New Key* (1942) and *Feeling and Form : A Theory of Art* (1953), but more fruitful, perhaps, is the approach of Northrop Frye in *Anatomy of Criticism* (1957) and in his essay, 'Yeats and the Language of Symbolism', reprinted in *Fables of Identity : Studies in Poetic Mythology* (1963).

A general account of Yeats's work for the theatre is given in most of the books I have mentioned, but the plays themselves received little critical attention until quite recently, despite a spirited defence of them by Ronald Peacock, in *The Poet in the Theatre* (1946), and Eric Bentley's essay, 'Yeats as a Playwright' (1948), reprinted in *The Permanence of Yeats*. The chapter called 'A Poet's Stagecraft: 1899–1911', in Thomas Parkinson's *W. B. Yeats, Self-Critic*, a study of *The Shadowy Waters*, shows how Yeats's poetry profited from his experience with the Abbey Theatre. Donald Pearce's 'Yeats's Last Plays', *E.L.H.*, xviii (March, 1951), is an important article, and among recent evaluations of particular plays mention must be made of Haskell M. Block's 'Yeats's *The King's Threshold* : The Poet and Society', *Philological Quarterly*, xxxiv (April, 1955), Norman Newton's 'Yeats as Dramatist: *The Player Queen*', *Essays in Criticism*, viii (July, 1958), and Elliott B. Gose, Jr.'s 'The Lyric and Philosophic in Yeats's *Calvary*', *Modern Drama*, ii (February, 1960). Denis Donoghue's study of *The Shadowy Waters*, 'Yeats and the Clean Outline', forms a chapter in his excellent account of modern British and American verse drama, *The Third Voice* (1959). F. A. C. Wilson was the first to base a full-length study of Yeats on the plays, but his concern was primarily with their symbolism rather than their dramatic qualities. A fresh and stimulating interpretation of the relationship between the symbolism of *A Vision* and twelve of the late plays is contained in Helen Hennessy Vendler's *Yeats's 'Vision' and the Later Plays* (1963). The language of the plays rather than Yeats's stagecraft is the main focus of attention, but Miss Vendler's intelligent and sympathetic reading of the late plays should do much to gain them a wider hearing. The dramatic structure, characterization and dominant themes of the plays are discussed in Peter Ure's *Yeats the Playwright : A Commentary on Character and Design in the Major Plays* (1963). Ure examines three important early plays, *The Countess Cathleen*, *The King's Threshold* and *Deirdre*, in considerable detail, then proceeds to group the later plays according to theme and subject-matter in order to illustrate the variety of Yeats's dramatic techniques, but the argument is conducted in terms remote from the actuality of the theatre, and the book remains disappointingly slight. Two books on the plays were announced for publication in 1964 : David R. Clark's *W. B. Yeats and the Theatre of Desolate Reality* is an assessment of Yeats's achievement in relation to contemporary society and realistic drama ; S. B. Bushrui's *Yeats's Verse-Plays : The Revisions, 1900–1910*, studies the evolution of Yeats's dramatic skill in his revisions of the early plays.

Yeats's practice of constantly revising and rewriting his poems has given rise to a number of valuable studies, among them Parkinson's *W. B. Yeats, Self-Critic*, Curtis Bradford's 'Yeats's Byzantium Poems : A Study of Their Development', *P.M.L.A.*, lxxv (March, 1960), and, most recently, Jon Stallworthy's transcriptions and translations of manuscript drafts of poems, *Between the Lines : Yeats's Poetry in the Making* (1963), and 'Two of Yeats's Last Poems', in *A Review of English Literature* (July, 1963). Stallworthy brings scholarly caution and critical insight to the difficult task of deciphering Yeats's shorthand scrawl, and his book throws new light on the poet's methods of thinking and writing. Thomas Parkinson, in his second book, *W. B. Yeats : The Later Poetry* (1964), is also concerned with Yeats's methods of composition. This important work draws extensively on the early drafts, note-books and prose writings in an attempt to arrive at the principles that motivated the poet, and it provides us with the first full-length study of the poetics behind the later poetry. Parkinson's opening chapter on Yeats's attitude to modern art and his concept of personality should be read in conjunction with George T. Wright's *The Poet in the Poem : The Personae of Eliot, Yeats, and Pound* (1960), which it supplements. Parkinson shows that Yeats's poetry was largely determined by his dramatic sense, the operation of which is revealed in his detailed readings of some major poems. A final chapter suggesting the relevance of Yeats's poetics to current poetic problems indicates a course of enquiry that needs to be pursued. I have not seen Thomas R. Whitaker's *Swan and Shadow : Yeats's Dialogue with History* (1964), but Whitaker's previously published papers on 'The Dialectic of Yeats's Vision of History', *Modern Philology*, lvii (November, 1959), and 'The Early Yeats and the Pattern of History', *P.M.L.A.*, lxxv (June, 1960), leave no doubt as to the significance of its contents.

The achievement of the past two decades of Yeats criticism can be assessed if one compares the essays in *The Permanence of Yeats*, with their air of brilliant amateurism, with the contributions to *Yeats : A Collection of Critical Essays* (1963), edited by John Unterecker, or the Yeats issue of *A Review of English Literature* (July, 1963), or with the lectures broadcast from Radio Eireann and collected by Denis Donoghue in *The Integrity of Yeats* (1964). The uncertainty of the earlier volume has been replaced by a confidence in Yeats's enduring qualities. Of the 'New Critics' only Yvor Winters, in *The Poetry of W. B. Yeats* (1960), remains unconvinced; his polemical pamphlet travesties Yeats's opinions, but it is enough to set against the ridicule he heaps on the poet's aristocratic ideal Cleanth Brooks's contention, in *The Hidden God* (1963), that Yeats's poetry 'asserts the dignity and power of the human spirit against the spiritual and intellectual corruption of our time'. Much recent criticism has shown that Eliot was right when he recognized Yeats as 'one of those few whose history is the history of their own time, who are a part of the consciousness of an age which cannot be understood without them'. Scholarship has told us much since then of Yeats and the history of his age, but with increasing understanding of his life and work has come a greater assurance of his worth and a growing conviction that he was, like the poet and dramatist born three centuries before him, not of an age but for all time.

NOTES ON THE CONTRIBUTORS

HAZARD ADAMS, Professor and Chairman of the Department of English at the University of California, Irvine, has taught in Cornell, Texas and Michigan State Universities. He has been a Fulbright Lecturer at Trinity College, Dublin. His published work includes *Blake and Yeats : The Contrary Vision* (1955), *The Contents of Poetry* (1963) and *William Blake : A Reading of the Shorter Poems* (1963) as well as several articles in learned journals.

RUSSELL K. ALSPACH, Brigadier-General, U.S. Army Retired, was formerly Professor of English and Head of the Department of English in the United States Military Academy, West Point, New York. In 1962–3 he was Visiting Professor in the Graduate School of the University of Pennsylvania. He is the author of *Poetry of the Celtic Renaissance, Irish Poetry from the English Invasion to* 1798, co-editor of *The Variorum Edition of the Poems of W. B. Yeats,* and has contributed numerous articles on Yeats to scholarly magazines. He is the editor of *The Variorum Edition of the Plays of W. B. Yeats* to be published in 1965.

SUHEIL BADI BUSHRUI is a Senior Lecturer in English at the University of Ibadan. He is a Jordanian and a graduate of Alexandria and Southampton Universities. He has lectured for some time at the Khartoum Technical Institute and has been at Ibadan since 1962. He has published a number of critical articles in Arabic and English, and is the first to have begun translating Yeats into Arabic. His book *Yeats's Verse-Plays : The Revisions, 1900–1910* was published in 1965, and he has also edited, with Professor D. E. S. Maxwell, *The Art of Yeats* (a collection of essays for the Yeats centenary).

K. G. W. CROSS is a graduate of Trinity College, Dublin. He has lectured in Rhodes University and the University of Adelaide and was a Senior Lecturer in the University of Sydney until his appointment in 1964 to the Chair of English at the new University of Newcastle, New South Wales. He is co-editor of *A Bibliography of Yeats Criticism* and has published articles in scholarly journals. At present he is engaged on an edition of the plays of John Marston. His study of *Scott Fitzgerald* has recently been published in the Writers and Critics series.

DAVID DAICHES, Professor of English and Dean of the School of English and American Studies at the University of Sussex, was educated at the University of Edinburgh and Balliol College, Oxford. He has taught at the Universities of Edinburgh, Oxford, Chicago, Cornell and Cambridge, and has been Visiting Professor at several American universities, the Sorbonne and other European universities. He has published over twenty books of which perhaps the most important are *The Novel and the Modern World* (1939; 1960), *Robert Burns* (1950), *Critical Approaches to Literature* (1956), and *A Critical History of English Literature* (1960).

EDWARD ENGELBERG is Associate Professor of English in the University of Michigan, Ann Arbor. He was educated at Brooklyn College, and the Universities of Oregon and Wisconsin. He has been a Fulbright Research Scholar at St. Catharine's College, Cambridge (1955–6). His publications include *The Vast Design; Patterns in W. B. Yeats's Aesthetic* (1964), and he has written articles in various scholarly journals. He is at present working on a study of the hero of sensibility in French, German and English literature from 1800 to the present day.

T. R. HENN, Fellow of St. Catharine's College, Cambridge, since 1926, was Senior Tutor (1945–57) and President of the College (1957–61); he is an Honorary Fellow of Trumbull College, Yale University. He was educated at the University of Cambridge, where he was later Chairman, Faculty Board of Fine Arts (1952–63), Chairman, Faculty Board of English (1947–51 and 1961–5), and Judith E. Wilson Lecturer in Poetry and Drama. He served as Brigadier, General Staff, and was awarded C.B.E. (Mil.) and the U.S. Legion of Merit and was twice mentioned in Dispatches. He has been Director of the Yeats Summer School, Sligo, for the past four years. His published work includes: *Longinus and English Criticism* (1934); *Field Sports in Shakespeare* (1934); *The Lonely Tower* (1950; 1965); *The Apple and the Spectroscope* (1951; 1963); *The Harvest of Tragedy* (1956); *Science in Writing* (1960); *The Plays and Poems of John Millington Synge* (editor, 1963); *Passages for Divine Reading* (1963) and *Poems* (1964).

A. D. HOPE was born in 1907 at Cooma, New South Wales. He went to school in Hobart, Tasmania, and attended the Universities of Sydney and Oxford. He is now Professor of English at the Australian National University, Canberra. *Poems* appeared in 1961; another collection, *The Wandering Island*, was published in Australia in 1955.

In Excited Reverie

A. Norman Jeffares is Professor of English Literature at the University of Leeds. Educated at Trinity College, Dublin, and Oriel College, Oxford, he has taught at the Universities of Dublin, Groningen and Edinburgh, and was Jury Professor of English at the University of Adelaide from 1951 to 1957. He has lectured in various Indian, African, Canadian and American universities and has written on Commonwealth and American literature as well as on Anglo-Irish literature, his main interest. He edits the quarterly *A Review of English Literature*, the New Oxford English Series, and is chief editor of *Writers and Critics* and joint editor of *Biography and Criticism*. He has written a biography *W. B. Yeats : Man and Poet* (1949; 1962) and edited Yeats's plays, poems, prose and criticism in St. Martin's Library as well as his poetry in The Scholar's Library.

Brendan Kennelly is a Lecturer in English at Trinity College, Dublin ; he was educated there and at the University of Leeds. He has published several volumes of verse : some of these — *Cast a Cold Eye* (1959); *The Rain, the Moon* (1961); *Poems* (1963) — jointly with Rudi Holzapfel ; and *Let Fall no Burning Leaf* (1963); *My Dark Fathers* (1964). His novel, *The Crooked Cross*, was published in 1964, and he is writing a book on the Gaelic sources of Anglo-Irish writings.

Hugh MacDiarmid (the pen-name of C. M. Grieve) now lives near Biggar in Lanarkshire. He was educated at Langholm Academy and at Broughton Junior Student Centre, Edinburgh. He became a journalist, carried out research for the Fabian Society and joined the R.A.M.C. in 1915. He worked on the *Montrose Review* (1920–9), lived in London in 1929, in Liverpool in 1930. He lived in Whalsay in the Shetland Islands (1933–41) ; worked in Glasgow as a manual labourer and entered the Merchant Service until 1945. He was awarded a Civil List pension in 1950, and is an honorary graduate of the University of Edinburgh (1957). His published works include *A Drunk Man Looks at the Thistle* (1926); *Stony Limits and Other Poems* (1934); *Selected Poems* (1934); *The Islands of Scotland* (1939); *Lucky Poet* (1943); and *Collected Poems* (1962).

Conor Cruise O'Brien, Irish writer and diplomat, was educated at Trinity College, Dublin, and entered the Irish Civil Service in 1942, moving to the Department of External Affairs of Ireland in 1944. After a short spell as Counsellor at the Irish Embassy in Paris, he became, in 1956, Head of the United Nations Section of the Department, and a member of Ireland's U.N. Delegation. In 1960 he was made Assistant Secretary-

340

General of the Department of External Affairs, and the following year achieved recognition throughout the world as representative of the U.N. Secretary-General in Katanga. He resigned from this post and from the Irish Service in December 1961, and shortly afterwards took the post of Vice-Chancellor of the University of Ghana.

His publications include a study of Catholic novelists, *Maria Cross*, written in 1952 under the pseudonym 'Donat O'Donnell', *Parnell and his Party* (1957), the editing of *The Shaping of Modern Ireland* (1959), *To Katanga and Back* (1962), and *Conflicting Concepts of the United Nations* (1964). He is at present engaged on a collection of essays, to be entitled *Writers and Politics*.

LENNOX ROBINSON, playwright, poet and story-teller, died in 1958. He was Manager of the Abbey Theatre from 1910 to 1914 and from 1919 to 1923. His first play, *The Clancy Name*, was produced at the Abbey in 1908, but perhaps the best known of his many plays are *The Far-Off Hills* (1931) and *Killycreggs in Twilight* (1937). He edited *The Golden Treasury of Irish Verse* (1925) and co-edited *The Oxford Book of Irish Verse* (1958).

W. R. RODGERS was elected to the Irish Academy of Letters in 1951 to fill the vacancy caused by the death of Bernard Shaw. After taking his degree at Queen's University, Belfast, he studied for the Ministry and was, from 1934 to 1946, Minister of Loughgall Presbyterian Church, Co. Armagh. From 1946 to 1952 he was a producer and script-writer for the British Broadcasting Corporation, London. His publications include *Awake, and Other Poems* (1941), *Europa and the Bull* (1952) and *Ireland in Colour* (1956). At present he is working on *Poems* and *The Character of Ireland*.

JON STALLWORTHY works as an editor with the Oxford University Press. He was educated at Magdalen College, Oxford, and won the Newdigate Prize in 1958. He is the author of *Between the Lines : W. B. Yeats's Poetry in the Making* (1963) and he has also published two collections of poetry, *The Astronomy of Love* (1961) and *Out of Bounds* (1963), as well as various articles in critical journals.

A. G. STOCK, University Professor and Head of the Department of English in Rajasthan University, India, since 1961, was previously Professor and Head of the Department of English in the University of Dacca, East Pakistan (1947–51), Reader in English, University of the Punjab, India (1951–6) and Jivindas Professor and Head of the Department of English at the University of

Calcutta, India (1956–61). Previously she was a lecturer in the W.E.A. and in training colleges in England. She is the author of *W. B. Yeats : His Poetry and Thought* (1961 ; paperback edition, 1964).

JULIAN RANDOLPH STOW was born in 1935 at Geraldton, Western Australia. He was educated at Geraldton schools, Guildford, and the University of Western Australia. His first two novels and first collection of poems were written as an undergraduate. He has been at various times a mission worker among aborigines in north-western Australia, a cadet patrol officer in New Guinea, Lecturer in English Literature at the Universities of Adelaide, Leeds and Western Australia. He has also lived in East Anglia, the Highlands of Scotland, Malta and New Mexico. He is now travelling and writing in the United States as a Harkness Fellow. His publications include the novels *To The Islands* (1958) and *Tourmaline* (1963), and a verse collection *Outrider* (1962), illustrated with paintings by Sidney Nolan. His new novel *The Merry-go-round in the Sea* will be published in 1965.

DONALD T. TORCHIANA, an Associate Professor of English at Northwestern University, Illinois, was educated at De Pauw University and the State University of Iowa. He taught for three years at the State University of Iowa before reading at Northwestern University. He held a Fulbright Lectureship at University College, Galway (1960–2). He has written *W. B. Yeats and Georgian Ireland* (1965) as well as articles in various journals. He is editing a volume of J. B. Yeats's letters to his American friends.

INDEX

Note : Passing references to any item in this index on several consecutive pages are indicated by the first and last page-number only. Pages where an item is discussed more fully are shown in **bold type.**

343

Z

Index

349

Skeffington, Frank, 207, 230
Skeffington, Mrs. Hanna Sheehy, 207-8, 247-8
Skeffington, Dr. Sheehy, 246
Sligo, 20-22, 25, 29, 71, 158, 212, 325
Southern Review, The, 316
Spectator, The, 187-8
Spender, Stephen, 168, 186, 329
Spenser, Edmund, 93-95, **97-101**, 103-4, 106, 122, 271 ; *View of the Present State of Ireland*, 97
Stallworthy, Jon, 335 ; *Between the Lines*, 109, 335
Stanford, W. B., 318
Starkie, Enid, *From Gautier to Eliot*, 332
Stauffer, Donald, *The Golden Nightingale*, 326
Steinmann, M., *see* Hall, J. and Steinmann, M.
Stella Matutina, 282, 313
Stendhal, 41
Stephens, Edward, *see* Greene, David H. and Stephens, E.
Stephens, James, 19, 243-4, 321
Sterne, Laurence, 103
Stevens, Wallace, 87
Stevenson, R. L., 179
Stewart, J. I. M., *Eight Modern Writers*, 322, 327
Stock, A. G., *W. B. Yeats*, 327
Strong, L. A. G., 179 ; *Green Memory*, 324 ; *A Letter to W. B. Yeats*, 111
Strzygowski, Josef, 286
Stuart, Iseult (*née* Iseult Gonne), 6, 8, 138
Studies in Bibliography, 204
' Sullivan gang ', the, 217, 234-6, 238, 249
Sullivan, T. D., 250
Swift, Jonathan, 63, 106, 251, 260, 263 ; *Gulliver's Travels*, 124, 271
Swinburne, A. C., 36, 94, 185
Symons, Arthur, *Poems*, 310-11 ; *The Symbolist Movement in Literature*, **72-73**, 79, 332

Synge, J. M., 33, 35, 39, 87, 112, 114, 120, 319, 321 ; *Playboy of the Western World*, 33, 227, 239

Tate Gallery, 22
Tate, Allen, 90, 316, 328
Taylor, Estelle Ruth, *The Modern Irish Writers*, 325
Tennyson, Lord, 94, 106 ; *Idylls of the King, The*, 95
Texas Studies in Literature and Language, 322
Thomas, Dylan, 173
Thomas, Edward, 178
Thurber, James, 159, 161
Times, The, 187
Times Literary Supplement, The, 188, 333
Tindall, William York, *The Literary Symbol*, 333
Todhunter, John, 106
Toland, John, *Critical History*, 285
Tomorrow, 251
Tone, Wolfe, 212, 270
Torchiana, Donald, 210, 263, 319
Trench, Herbert, 179
Trinity College, Dublin, 19, 26, 29, 149
Tullylish, 24
Turner, W. J., 178-9, 184, 191, 319
Tuve, Rosamund, *Elizabethan and Metaphysical Imagery*, 102, 104, 122
Tynan, Katharine (Mrs. Hinkson), 94, 106, 215, 324

United Ireland, 219
Unterecker, John, 319 ; *A Reader's Guide to W. B. Yeats*, 326 ; (ed.) *Yeats: a Collection of Critical Essays*, 336
Ure, Peter, *Towards a Mythology*, 330 ; *Yeats*, 327 ; *Yeats the Playwright*, 335
Ussher, Arland, *Three Great Irishmen*, 245, 253, 325

Index

'General Introduction for my Work' (printed in *Essays and Introductions*), 214, 270, 277, 316; 'Ghost of Roger Casement, The', 266-7; 'Gift of Harun Al-Rashid, The', 113, 293, 299, 301, **302-6**; *Green Helmet, The*, 67, 168, **202-3**; 'Gyres, The', 110;

Happiest of the Poets, The, 119; 'He Remembers Forgotten Beauty', 65; *Herne's Egg, The*, 108, 194, 333; *Hour-Glass, The*, 202;

'In Memory of Major Robert Gregory', 42; 'Irish Airman Foresees his Death, An', 42; *Island of Statues, The*, 70-71, 74, **79-85**, 88-89, 94-95, 97;

King of the Great Clock Tower, The, 194, 202; *King's Threshold, The*, 335;

'Lake Isle of Innisfree, The', 17, 71; *Land of Heart's Desire, The*, 69-70, 197; 'Lapis Lazuli', 63, 154, 168; 'Last Confession, A', 113; *Last Poems*, 328; 'Leda and the Swan', 109, **273-4**, 333; *Letters on Poetry to Dorothy Wellesley*, 171, 176-8, 186, 190-1, 272, 308, 318; *Letters of W. B. Yeats* (ed. A. Wade), 94-95, 98, 140, 187, 191, 214-15, 217-19, 225, 228, 244-5, 247, 254-5, 262, 264-5, 268, 271, 275, 286, 291-2, 295-6, 303, 318; 'Long-legged Fly', 120;

'Mad as the Mist and Snow', 103; 'Madness of King Goll, The', **51-54**, 55-56; 'Man Who Dreamed of Faeryland, The', **57-60**; 'Michael Robartes and the Dancer', 295; 'Miserrimus', *see* 'Sad Shepherd, The'; *Mosada*, 313;

'Mountain Tomb, The', 111; 'Mourn and then Onward', 217, 219; 'Municipal Gallery Revisited, The', 39, 247; 'My House', 41; *Mythologies*, 280-281, 318;

'New Faces, The', 116; *Nine One-Act Plays*, 195; 'Nineteen Hundred and Nineteen', 276; 'No Second Troy', 61, 66, 120;

On Baile's Strand, 202; *On the Boiler*, 117, 211, 259, 261, **271-3**, 318; 'On a Picture of a Black Centaur', 109; 'On a Political Prisoner', 238; 'On Woman', 309, 311; *Only Jealousy of Emer, The*, 202; 'O'Rahilly, The', 266; *Oxford Book of Modern Verse*, 106, 116, **171-92**;

Packet for Ezra Pound, A, 261; *Pages from a Diary Written in 1930*, 41, 77, 79, 106, 108, 318; 'Parnell's Funeral', 216; 'People, The', 225; *Per Amica Silentia Lunae*, 106, 294, 306, 318; 'Phases of the Moon, The', 106, 328; *Plays and Controversies*, 197; *Poems*, 196-197, 199, 202; *Poems and Ballads of Young Ireland*, 48; *Poetical Works*, 196, 199, 204; 'Prayer for My Daughter, A', 101; 'Prayer for My Son, A', 114; *Purgatory*, 121-2, 194, 333;

'Reprisals', 119, 239; *Responsibilities*, 67, 86; *Resurrection, The*, 202; 'Roger Casement', 266; 'Rose of Battle, The', 64; 'Rose of the World, The', 60, 63-64, 109; 'Rose Tree, The', 118, 238-9;

'Sad Shepherd, The' ('Miserrimus'), **48-50**, **60**, 86; 'Second

PRINTED BY R. & R. CLARK, LTD., EDINBURGH